Multiculturalism in the New Japan

Asian Anthropologies
General Editors:
Shinji Yamashita, The University of Tokyo
J. S. Eades, Ritsumeikan Asia Pacific University

Volume 1
Globalization in Southeast Asia: Local, National, and Transnational Perspectives
Edited by Shinji Yamashita and J. S. Eades

Volume 2
Bali and Beyond: Case Studies in the Anthropology of Tourism
Shinji Yamashita

Volume 3
The Making of Anthropology in East and Southeast Asia
Edited by Shinji Yamashita, Joseph Bosco, and J. S. Eades

Volume 4
Centering the Margin: Agency and Narrative in Southeast Asian Borderlands
Edited by Alexander Horstmann and Reed L. Wadley

Volume 6
Multiculturalism in New Japan: Crossing the Boundaries Within
Edited by Nelson H. H. Graburn, John Ertl, and R. Kenji Tierney

First published in 2008 by
Berghahn Books
www.berghahnbooks.com

©2008 Nelson H. H. Graburn, John Ertl, and R. Kenji Tierney

Library of Congress Cataloging-in-Publication Data

Multiculturalism in the new Japan : crossing the boundaries within / edited by
Nelson Graburn, John Ertl, R. Kenji Tierney.
    p. cm. — (Asian anthropologies ; vol. 6)
    Includes bibliographical references and index.
    ISBN 978-1-84545-226-1 (hardcover : alk. paper)
    1. Multiculturalism—Japan. 2. Japan—Ethnic relations. I. Graburn,
Nelson H. H. II. Ertl, John. III. Tierney, R. Kenji.

HM1271.M8433 2007
306.44'60952—dc22   2006100544

British Library Cataloguing in Publication Data

A catalogue record for this book is available from the British Library

Front cover photograph: The editors wish to thank Professor Shoji Hiroshi for
permission to use the photograph of entrance panel showing a collage of faces
illustrating the exhibition "Taminzoku Nihon/Multiethnic Japan" at the
National Museum of Ethnology, Suita, March-June 2004.

Printed in the United States on acid-free paper

ISBN 978-1-84545-226-1   hardback

MULTICULTURALISM IN THE NEW JAPAN

Crossing the Boundaries Within

Edited by
Nelson H. H. Graburn
John Ertl
R. Kenji Tierney

Berghahn Books
New York • Oxford

CONTENTS

PREFACE

THIS VOLUME STEMS FROM A CONFERENCE titled "Japan: Crossing the Boundaries Within" held at the University of California, Berkeley in March 2002. Current and former Berkeley students are responsible for a large part of both the conference and this book. The project also owes much to the support of other faculty and units at the university.

The idea for the conference stemmed from the convergence of my own research on the internal internationalization of Japanese domestic tourism and Kenji Tierney's extensive work on Sumo, which was becoming dominated by "foreign" wrestlers. The experiences of Berkeley students conducting doctoral research in the 1980s and 1990s showed that the monolithic stereotype of the xenophobic Japanese was full of exceptions. Jeff Hester's work with *Zainichi* Koreans in Osaka and John Nelson's work on contemporary religions in Nagasaki and Kyoto were illustrative of these new trends. Yuko Okubo's work among Osaka schoolteachers and immigrant families and Keiko Yamanaka's work among immigrants showed considerable ambivalence towards minorities, but all contained accounts of some Japanese welcoming or even supporting the visible foreigners. John Ertl's Master's research in a small town in Tochigi Prefecture showed a very positive attitude towards foreigners, and undergraduate Aina Hunter reported on the very positive reception she and other African Americans had received in Japan.

Among Japanese social scientists, Takezawa brought to our attention the publicity about the positive relations between minority and majority residents of Kobe following the Hanshin earthquake of 1995, and the emergence of the concept of *tabunka kyôsei* (many cultures living together). Sociologist Komai Hiroshi's activism towards immigrants became famous and was exemplary of a growing band of Japanese professionals working to form a "new Japan." My own experiences in Japan since 1974 found marked changes in attitudes about both foreigners and immigrants and the possibilities of non-Japanese, even Korean, ancestry being discussed openly with humor and some pride. We wanted to write a book that would make clear to people unfamiliar with Japan that there are great changes taking place in many ways and levels and in many positive directions leading, we hope, to a nation more fully aware and proud of its cultural mosaic.

We approached our colleagues in order to provide funding for the conference and to underwrite the transportation, accommodation, and catering for participants. We would particularly like to thank Professor Andrew Barshay, Director of the Center for Japanese Studies, and Professor Bonnie Wade, Director of the Asian Studies Program, for their quick and generous offers to finance the conference. The Department of Anthropology, through chair Professor William Hanks, designated the event as one of a series celebrating the Department's Centennial (1901–2001) and gave us generous support. The conference finally took place with an opening welcome from Professor Barshay followed by four papers on the Friday, followed by a dinner, and on the Saturday another eleven papers (by twelve participants) with commentary throughout by Emeritus Professor George DeVos.

In the years since the conference, we again have to thank the Center for Japanese Studies at Berkeley for generously supporting further research included in this book. I should like to thank Professor Shinji Yamashita for his support and advice and Professor Matsubara Takatoshi, Director of the Research Institute on Korean Studies at Kyushu National University, Fukuoka, whose invitation to spend three months in Kyushu in the spring of 2005 allowed me to carry out intensive library research and pull together the last intellectual threads of the volume.

In 2003, graduate student John Ertl joined as co-editor and continued to provide editorial support while conducting his doctoral research in Japan. Graduate student Yuko Okubo helped me with many translation and bibliographic matters, as well as serving along with Mitzi Carter as my teaching assistant in 2004. During the 2003–2004 academic year, graduate student Maki Tanaka helped me examine some more works on Japanese immigration. I also thank University of California, Berkeley Inter-Library Services for their efforts in securing several texts that were hard to acquire.

In March 2004 John Ertl traveled with me in Osaka where, coincidentally, we were able to attend the opening day of a daring new temporary exhibition, "Taminzoku Nihon—Zainichi Gaikokujin no Kurashi" ("Multiethnic Japan—Life and History of Immigrants"), curated by Minpaku Professor, Shôji Hiroshi. During the spring of 2005 we returned to Minpaku to interview Professor Shôji about this path-breaking exhibition, its reception in the community, and its lingering influence. We also extend our gratitude to Minpaku graduate student Kotani Sachiko, who had been carrying out her doctoral dissertation research on the Korean immigrant community in the San Francisco Bay, for help and guidance while in Osaka.

I must end by expressing my gratitude to the participants and contributors themselves who have patiently stuck with us over the years, following our advice and our peregrinations. To my two co-editors, to generations of Berkeley students, as well as to my Berkeley colleagues who encour-

aged and underwrote our efforts, and to Jerry Eades and Marion Berghahn, I thank you.

Nelson Graburn
Porto Alegre, Brazil
September 2007

INTRODUCTION:
INTERNAL BOUNDARIES AND MODELS OF MULTICULTURALISM IN CONTEMPORARY JAPAN

Nelson Graburn and John Ertl

Introduction: Multiculturalism in the New Japan

THIS VOLUME ILLUMINATES THE COMPLEX social processes resulting from the activism of native and immigrant minority communities in
Japan and shows that their influence is prevalent throughout the localities,
the margins, and the grassroots, and extends into central institutions as
well. It also reveals and highlights some of the more positive directions
among these processes.[1] The sociopolitical goal of these directions is to
transform Japan from an asserted homogeneity into a multicultural society
that not only admits its cultural diversity but also upholds and celebrates
this complex political situation. There are no perfectly construed models
for a multicultural society in the world, as the concept of multiculturalism
is a value-laden prescription rather than a descriptive condition. Furthermore, each nation has its own history and its own mix of "minorities" and
non-native immigrants and historically the two are necessarily connected,
and at some points indistinguishable. Japan is now a nation with 1.91 million officially registered foreigners, constituting nearly 2 percent of the
total population (Nakamura 2005), with an additional unknown number
of non-registered immigrants and ethnically unclear Japanese nationals.
Our title phrase, "the new Japan," is again both prescriptive as well as
descriptive in usage. Following Sugita (2001), we perceive a third era of renewal taking place today, along the lines of Japan's previous ages of transformation after 1868 and 1945.

Endnotes for this chapter begin on page 24.

After the Meiji restoration Japan's elite judged both their country and the Japanese people as physical bodies that were dangerously weak. The new government, committed to the twin policies of *fukoku kyôhei* (wealthy country, strong military), took up the challenge of renegotiating its treaties with the Western powers. Japan underwent self-strengthening both by acquiring industries, institutions, and military forces, and by disciplining the people with new forms of mental and physical education in a national school system. Within three decades Japan tested out these new strengths with resounding success: against China in 1895 and against Russia in contention for control of the Korea-Chinese border regions in 1904–1905. These successes in turn encouraged those directing the nation to further military adventures into Manchuria, China, Southeast Asia, the Aleutian islands, and on to Pearl Harbor. Such ventures eventually led the nation to a series of resounding defeats and tragedies, resulting in near physical destruction of many of Japan's cities and industries, and the abandonment of militarism.

Spurred on by both the instruction and the example of the Allied Occupation, the new postwar government set off to catch up and compete with the world again,[2] this time in respect to industrial production. Starting small and gaining market shares in industry after industry, Japan signaled her new "coming out" with the 1964 Tokyo Olympic Games and the 1970 Osaka World's Fair. Much of the competing world in time came to fear "Japan as Number One" (Vogel 1979) and reacted with economic and legal measures to stymie that success by imposing import restrictions that included banning whaling and forcing Japan to import beef, and by accusing Japan of almost inhuman proclivities such as "clannishness" in work and leisure" or working so hard as to provoke sudden death. Nevertheless, Japan's newfound international self-confidence led to ever-widening export markets and to increasing numbers of affluent tourists exploring the world. The end of this cycle came rather suddenly[3] at the end of the 1980s, following crippling economic consequences stemming largely from property speculation at home and abroad.

Entering the contemporary era that we are primarily concerned with in this book, Japan remains a significant economic and political power, but no one expects Japan to conquer the world in the same way again. One arena in which Japan may take the lead would be in sustaining a high standard of living while safeguarding the environment. In many respects Japan has given the world leads to follow in respect to energy conservation, recycling, and tax incentives for fuel-efficient vehicles. On the other hand the numbers of large-engine cars and the proliferation of suburban tract housing and shopping centers are indicators that Japanese consumption patterns are not always aligned with political goals. As Japan has increasingly opened its borders and economic markets to the international community over the past few decades, it has also faced similar challenges relating to immigration and intercultural diversity. The many chapters in this volume extend a growing number of analyses on the changing international demographics and increasing intercultural contact in this nation that has long been described as one of the most homogeneous nations in the world. It would be a disservice to praise Japan as a model multicultural nation, as many forms of discrimination and structural inequalities continue to persist. However, changes in both the national policies and popular imagination regarding multiculturalism in Japan have lent an overall positive tone to the chapters in this volume. We find that multiculturalism has become a key concept used to describe areas where old hegemonies are giving way to new social forms, while simultaneously providing a model and a method for achieving a new Japanese state.

Multiculturalism in the Anthropology of Japan

For many readers the notion of "Japanese multiculturalism" may ring as an oxymoron. Even despite increasing globalization and international migration, Japan still maintains one of the lowest figures of foreign national residents and a considerable share of these resident aliens, such as second- and third-generation Chinese and Koreans, are not always noticeably foreign.

Regardless of the numbers, the visibility of foreign residents has increased substantially, as politicians, academics, and the mass media have brought a spotlight upon the contributions and consequences foreigners have brought to Japan (e.g., Douglass and Roberts 2000; Komai 2001; Lie 2001; Oguma 2002; Weiner 1997). Complementing immigration there has been a concerted internationalization effort set out by the government to ease the transition to life in Japan for foreigners, increase interpersonal exchanges between Japanese and foreign nationals at home and abroad, and to improve the image of Japan overseas. This has included the adoption of multiculturalism as an ideal for public policy, aimed towards reversing previous policies that erased cultural distinctions and worked to keep minorities at the bottom of the social chain (cf. Hale 2002; Turner 1993).

Multiculturalism is by no means a comprehensive effort made by the central administration, for as much as it may be lauded for slowly changing its stance towards minority and foreign national residents, it has been the activism and volunteerism of concerned citizens (Kingston 2004) and vocal scholars (Shôji 2004) that has brought multiculturalism to its current prominence. Furthermore, multiculturalism is inherently an international issue that has been brought about through debates on the nature of Japanese national character. It is well documented that the postwar literature called *Nihonjinron* (Japanese character studies), which included English language translations financed by the government, was one of the avenues through which the "myth" of Japanese homogeneity was formed and disseminated (Befu 1983). The origins of this discourse in the postwar period are often traced to the publication of Ruth Benedict's *Chrysanthemum and the Sword* (1946) (Aoki 1999), which stimulated interest in how Japan is perceived by outsiders (especially Americans) and went on to sell over 2.3 million copies in Japanese (Fukui 1999: 173). This text was representative of the national character studies developed by anthropologists working during the Second World War, which feature advanced "nations" as the primary unit of analysis, comparable with other nations in terms of similarities and differences (Neiburg and Goldman 1998). The national character approach set the framework for future studies that continued to explain Japan in holistic terms, often using the United States as its convenient cultural opposite (e.g., Doi 1973; Nakane 1973). The prominence of Japanese national character studies perpetuated the most basic of assumptions that the study of Japan was the study of "the Japanese people." This bias reinforced the illusion of homogeneity as studies largely ignored the legacy of Japan's recent colonial endeavors, expansion to its frontier territories, and historical interactions with the outside world, favoring analyses that stressed enduring and native cultural traits (Ryang 2004).

Complementary to national character studies has been considerable research on Japan's minority and indigenous groups during the postwar era. Minorities are generally divided into three categories: Japan's "indigenous" peoples, the Ainu, Okinawan, and Buraku; Koreans and Chinese brought to Japan during the Pacific War and their descendents; and recent migrant workers from Latin America and Asia. While studies of Japan's minorities are admirably aimed at illuminating the racial and ethnic diversity of the Japanese islands, commonplace categorizations such as "outcaste" and "minority" have often been found inappropriate, especially as individuals and their representative organizations reject such classifications themselves, as they may allow for the imposition of sanctioned inequalities (Weiner 1997). Much of the early research on minorities inadvertently reinforced the image of Japanese homogeneity, as representations of "Japan's minorities" tended to isolate difference in specific geographic peripheries (Hokkaido, Okinawa, inner-city neighborhoods) or treat these groups as "invisible" (DeVos and Wagatsuma 1967; Yoshino R. and Murakoshi 1977) and "vanishing" (Etter 1949; Hilger 1971) and thus of little influence on mainstream society. By representing their subjects as "minority groups," each with their own specific culture in danger of eradication or assimilation, the category of "the Japanese" is presumed to be an equally uniform majority. Even the routine practice of counting minorities trivializes their influence on the mystique of Japanese homogeneity, regardless of whether the numbers were shown to be increasing or declining, as it compartmentalizes individuals into categories that are either Japanese or non-Japanese.

Sparked by the new wave of immigrants to Japan from the early 1990s, the study of Japanese multiculturalism came to prominence based upon a changing stance to the study of diversity. Instead of arguing that notions of Japanese homogeneity are falsified by the presence of ethnic "others," the study of Japanese multiculturalism begins by complicating the category of "the Japanese" by examining how it has been formed through particular historical engagements within Japan and between Japan and the outside world (Morris-Suzuki 1998). This research emerged from the lengthy retort, mostly by Western trained scholars, to Japanese attempts to form a postwar nationalism through *Nihonjinron* that built up notions of Japanese uniqueness and superiority during a period of sharp economic growth (Befu 2001; K. Yoshino 1992). The most straightforward texts of this genre are the many new ethnographic and historical studies of specific immigrant and "minority" groups (Ryang 1997; Sered 1999; Sjoberg 1993; Tsuda 2003a). These are companioned with broad edited volumes on ethnic minorities and immigrant groups, their interrelations to each other and the Japanese state, and on the condition of migration to and from Japan (Douglass and Roberts 2000; Weiner 1997). Responding to deficiencies in earlier studies that defined these groups as the marginal "other" in contrast to the dominant Japanese "self," these texts have showcased the historical interactions and political motivations that led to their seclusion. To oppose the so-called myth of Japanese homogeneity many authors have written their own counter narratives that detail a long history of ethnic, national, and linguistic diversity (Denoon et al. 1996; Lie 2001; Murphy-Shigematsu 1993). Some narratives extend into the archaeological record to explain the origins of the Japanese ethnicity from the earliest prehistoric evidence through the formation of the early Yamato State, arguing that archaeological, linguistic, and biological evidence shows a great deal of repeated exchange and mixture with the Asian continent (Hudson 1999; Kaner 1996).

Research on Japanese multiculturalism has great potential for altering the belief in Japanese homogeneity, and we hope that our text will add to the increasing narratives on the multifaceted nature of culture and identity in Japan. The following chapters show that global issues such as immigration, business practices, and cultural exchanges are best understood in the dynamics of particular localities. Where previous studies focused on larger processes of international migrations or indigenous minority movements, this book with its emphasis on ethnography allows for critical examinations of categories such as nation, ethnicity, race, and culture, by showing how their immediate articulations always manipulate and subvert universal classifications. Through a broad range of silhouettes and anecdotes on the contemporary conditions of minorities and immigrants, Japanese citizens' engagements with diversity, and the local manifestations of national policies and global processes, this volume demonstrates that multiculturalism has become a pervasive ideology in Japan that varies widely in terms of its form, content, and manifestations.

Models of Multiculturalism

Japan is a nation best understood or defined by its relation to powerful others (Ohnuki-Tierney 1990). From the Japanese point of view, Nakane (1978) claimed that Japanese people are always conscious of belonging within or outside a group or frame. The *"uchi-soto"* (inside outside) and *"omote-ura"* (front or back) distinctions are highlighted. Since the early modern period, membership at the national level has usually been posed as *Nihonjin* versus *gaikokujin* (Japanese versus foreigner). Since the opening to the West it is usually non-Asians, particularly Caucasians, who have typified foreigners. Chinese, Koreans, and others may be *Ajiajin* (Asians)—significantly this categorization from time to time specifically excludes Japanese, especially when they have wanted to identify with the "advanced" industrialized Western world. There is also an intermediate category of those who are not truly outside, but are different or exotic, expressed in Japanese as *imin, ikoku*. For instance this term is used in Japanese guidebooks about Okinawa (see Komai 2003; Nugaido 1997: 16; Oguma 2002).

By the early twentieth century many Japanese leaders had traveled abroad and learned Western ideas of democracy and socialism. A few members of the two "internal" minorities, the Ainu and the Burakumin, fomented resistance movements under the rubric of what we would now call human rights. The Suiheisha (Levelers Association) was established in 1922 as the first stable Buraku rights organization, informed by increasing activity of tenants' groups and labor unions and backed by socialist ideology out of Russia (Neary 1997: 57). From 1945 until the 1980s, the cultural divisions internal to Japan were not granted recognition: the "internal others," Ainu, Okinawans, and Buraku, were denied ethnic difference, and other non-Japanese, such as *Zainichi* (Japan-dwelling) Chinese and Koreans were ignored, though 90,000 were sent to North Korea (Morris-Suzuki 2005). However, the Burakumin Liberation Movement reformed, aided by homegrown communists, and attracted media attention by protesting continued discrimination. Whether directly sparked by the Civil Rights movement in the United States or by anticolonialism generally, Burakumin social and educational history has shown remarkable parallels with that of African Americans in terms of residential discrimination, education, and affirmative action.

Japan was then engaged in its second great encounter with the Western world, mainly through the economic sphere of trade. After the Occupation had left, contacts with foreigners increasingly took place not at home ground but in foreigners' home countries. Efforts were made to familiarize traveling Japanese with foreign language and cultures, so that they could communicate more effectively and feel more self-confident. Thus informal and later governmental initiatives of internationalization (*kokusaika*) were implemented in many forms. This term can be very flexible, embracing both positive intercultural relations and the reification of ethno-national boundaries. When *kokusaika* was imposed, many ordinary Japanese balked at the idea of having to engage with foreigners in their homeland (Lebra, 1993: 13), much as Japanese tourists may return from overseas thankful that they live in Japan.

One way of advancing internationalization and bringing trade to participating localities was the establishment of social, business, and educational exchange programs. Sister-city relations were set up, at first with the United States, and began to recreate their distinctiveness and identity through such programs (Ertl, chapter 4). These "international cultural exchanges" became generally known as *kokusai kôryû*, a term that has another meaning for ethnic education, referring to the interactions and exchanges between immigrant groups, such as Vietnamese and Koreans, without mainstream Japanese taking part (Okubo 2005). Though international exchange programs are still going strong, they have been massively supplemented by outbound and inbound international tourism, especially by commercial homestay programs for young people in which the outgoing Japanese outnumber the foreigners coming in.

However, in the past twenty-five years Japanese have not only looked outward for trade and tourism, accompanied by *kokusaika* policies, but parts of the nation have been "internationalized" through immigration. The immediate cause for this shift was not only the global engagements of the successful Japanese nation (Eades et al. 2000) but increasing numbers of foreign workers brought in or entering illegally (Douglass and Roberts 2000; Komai 1999, 2001) to work at jobs Japanese consider *kitanai, kitsui, kiken* (dirty, demanding, dangerous). Awareness of these minorities arose only when visibly non-Japanese arrived in numbers, such as Vietnamese refugees, and immigrant workers, especially Filipinos, South East Asians, and South Asians including Singhalese and Nepalis, and Middle Easterners. The new workers and refugees came to be called *nyûkama* (newcomers) and by back formation the long-standing minorities became known as *ôrudokama* (oldcomers). According to Morris-Suzuki (1998: 194) Hatsuse Ryûhei of Kobe University coined the phrase *uchinaru kokusaika*, which can be glossed as internal or domestic internationalization (Hatsuse 1985) to point to a change in the internationalization goals and processes. This has generally been termed *kokunai kokusaika*, or "domestic internationalization."

It became increasingly difficult to uphold a model of homogenous Japan from the 1980s, although the belief that Japan is, always has been, and should be homogenous directs right-wing public policy makers. New terms emerged to describe and explain Japan's new social body. Many of them, like *kokusai kôryû* changed meaning over time, and most expressed an ambiguity felt by different parts of Japanese society or even ambivalence within one individual. These words cannot have exactly the same connotations as their English equivalents and their use is very much situational. For instance the vague word *esunikku* (ethnic) has been imported to describe exotic, different, even primitive, applied to imported arts, clothing, and cuisines; more recently *daibâshiti* (diversity) has emerged with a generally positive ring, especially for tourist consumption. Both these "borrowed" terms are used in commercial situations for commodities, not people, and they strike a rather lightweight liberal chord. However, it could be that borrowed words are used to cover up or soften the implications of their Japanese equivalents, and being from the West makes them seem more acceptable if they express sociocultural realities that the West might expect.

One key term is *tabunka kyôsei*, "many cultures living together," which closely resembles the concept "multiculturalism." One key example of *tabunka kyôsei* emerged following the great Kobe earthquake of January 1995 (Takezawa, chapter 1) when Japanese, Koreans, Chinese, and other foreigners living in the same devastated neighborhoods began to help each other; this positive development was lauded by the press, print, and television and held up as an example of something new in Japan. In other instances the clash of cultural differences within Japan has not been uniformly positive. There is confusion over the nature of a society that includes foreign residents and workers, as shown in these remarks about *tabunka kyôsei* by Toshio Iyotani (1995: 5, quoted in Pang 2000: 114–115):

> "My ... point concerns the co-existence of cultures, or multiculturalism.... Yet discussions about the coexistence and symbiosis of cultures often are tinged with the tacit conviction that the differences between cultures make mutual understanding between them impossible. Accordingly, arguments supporting 'respect for other cultures' may help avoid cross-cultural friction, but they also risk premature closure of any possibility for mutual understanding. In effect, arguments for cultural coexistence and those for cultural exclusion boil down to the same thing."

Seeing the negative side of *tabunka kyôsei*, some sociologists prefer to use the phrase *tabunka-shugi*, which might also be translated as multiculturalism but could engender a more neutral "hands off" connotation of the fact of, or the study of multiculturalism (Ishii and Yamauchi 1999; Sekine 2003). Yet *tabunka-shugi* could also be interpreted as the policy of, and in favor of, multiculturalism.

Kyôsei, literally meaning "symbiosis," generally means "living together" side-by-side in a relationship, positively as in commensality. Taking *kyôsei* to mean "solidarity," we can see the parallel with Emile Durkheim's two classic models[4] of solidarity from *Division of Labour* (Durkheim 1893). John Lie (2001: 50, 163) writes about the Japanese monoethnic identity of *Nihonjinron* as being based on a model of mechanical solidarity (between groups of equals, who may also be rivals) as opposed to Durkheim's original intent of showing that the solidarity of complex societies is always based on organic solidarity (interdependence amongst diverse people, closer to "symbiosis"). At one end of this continuum lies the dangerous situation pointed out by Iyotani, that of separate but equal (which allows separation, segregation, or ghettoization), and at the other, the mutual dependence shown by Takezawa (chapter 1) in describing the interethnic cooperation after the Kobe earthquake. One central theme of this volume illustrates how cultural pluralism is situational and articulated differentially throughout Japan. For example, Burgess (chapter 3) shows the necessary cooperation of foreign wives in rural communities; Yamanaka (chapter 4) and Tsuda (chapter 6) show the interdependence between Japanese employers' need for cheap labor and migrant workers' need for comparatively good wages; and Ertl (chapter 4) shows the need for internationalization to stimulate local industry and identity.

Komai Hiroshi, an Advocate for Immigrants in Japan

"The most admirable thinkers within the scholarly community ... do not split their work from their lives. They seem to take both too seriously to allow such dissociation, and they want to use each for the enrichment of the other." (Mills 1959: 195)

Japanese multiculturalism would be little more than a fanciful flight of intellectual reflection were it not for the grassroots activism of concerned individuals working to construct this ideal society in their local communities. The most evident figures in the struggle to form a harmonious multicultural Japan are perhaps the civil servants and public educators that are required by central government directives and community needs to form outreach programs, moderate conflicts, and conduct language and cultural training for immigrants and local citizens. In other cases it is religious, industrial, and other leaders that instruct or impose upon others their ideals about how to think about and act in "international" situations. Involved citizens are prevalent in neighborhoods throughout Japan, who choose for various reasons to reach out to their foreign neighbors, host international students, visit a foreign country, and form interpersonal "multicultural" relationships. The actions of such individuals, of many different nationalities and ethnicities, are featured by the authors of every chapter of this volume. In addition, most of the contributors function as activists in their own right, as their writing is not only a description of the conditions of multiculturalism but an offshoot of their efforts to embrace and enact change in the communities where they lived. The following is dedicated to outlining the life and work of Komai Hiroshi, the most noteworthy and ubiquitous scholarly figure on immigration and Japanese multicultural society. This examination of his activism provides an introduction to the social conditions and motivation that infuse the multiculturalism movement in Japan today.

Komai Hiroshi was born in Dalian, China during World War II. Like most Japanese colonizers, he was repatriated to Japan in 1945 and he remembers the discrimination he faced in elementary school (personal communication 2005). Until recently a professor of sociology at Tsukuba University, Komai is Japan's most active scholar of immigration and multiculturalism; he is a true "public intellectual," leading demonstrations, organizing activist symposia, and writing briefs to Japanese courts and ministries. Trained at the University of Tokyo as a sociologist of Southeast Asia working on the modernization of Thailand (Tominaga et al. 1969), he also carried out research on the revival of Buddhism since the Communist rule in Cambodia (Komai 1997). He became interested in the lives of migrant workers who left to work in industrialized countries. Working in North America he published on both immigrant workers (Komai 1978) and on "immigrant employers" (Komai 1979). He is best known for his research, publications, and public activism with foreign workers in Japan, changing his focus from the condition of temporary guest workers (Komai 1990) to a realization that many of them might stay in Japan (Komai 1994, 2001; Shipper 2003). Komai is well known overseas for his widely recommended *Foreign Migrants in Contemporary Japan* (2001) (Abe 2002). He belongs to overseas research groups from Monterey's "Human Flows Project" to Bangkok's Chulalongkorn University "Intellectual Exchange" and has a strong relationship with Melbourne's LaTrobe University, whose Transpacific Press published his 2001 work.

He was the lead author and editor of the six-volume *Kôza: Gurobaru suru Nihon to Imin Mondai* (Japan and the Immigration Issue in Globalization Series) (Komai 2002) with thirty-nine co-authors, some members of minority populations. He points out there are many different kinds of immigration into Japanese society; for comparisons the authors examine immigration in the United States, France, Germany, England, the European Union, and South America. The recession of the 1990s slowed demand or halted labor immigration, but it later re-emerged. Komai proposed that rather than trying to control immigration (*shutsu nyûkoku kanri*) the Japanese agenda should be to construct an ideal multicultural society. In "How to Build a Multicultural Society," which introduces the final volume, he defines multiculturalism as the attempt to create a national culture through respecting the various cultures of ethnic minorities and short-term and long-term immigrants, both those who have adopted the host nationality and "foreigners" who have not. He asserts that multiculturalism is the local manifestation of the developing "global culture" (Komai 2002: 20–21; see also Komai and Watado 1997).

Within Japan he points to three critical sites: corporations in intensive international competition, universities facing the crisis of survival due to falling birth rates, and the Catholic Church (and other churches) overrun with dependent immigrant followers. He contrasts Chinese immigrants as widely dispersed and highly qualified, with a strong tendency to settle in Japan and participate in fields related to China or Chinese culture, with Filipinos who play a large role in "reproductive work," and "the revitalization of energy in others" (as nurses and household workers) and procreation (2002: 30). Factors inhibiting multiculturalism include the public school culture for immigrant children (see Okubo, chapter 9), corporations' indifference to foreign workers' demands, and discrimination against Chinese. He notes the dependency of third-world immigrants (except the Chinese) on their overburdened Muslim, Catholic, and Protestant churches, for emotional, social, and practical support.

In 1999 Komai helped organize a mass public appeal to the Ministry of Justice on behalf of about-to-be-deported "visa overstayers," and spoke about "The Settlement of Foreigners" at a related symposium. In 2000 he led a group of scholars in rebuttal of Tokyo Governor Ishihara's statement that illegal *sankokujin* (third-country people) would riot after national disasters (Komai et al. 2000), asserting that the word *sankokujin* was derogatory and that Ishihara described them as *fuhô-taizai* (illegal overstayers) as though they were violent criminals. Komai claims that the press and politicians are wrong in blaming Japan's rising crime rate on foreigners: although foreigners are more likely to be picked up for crimes, police figures show they are responsible for less than 2 percent of violent crime and there has been no disproportionate increase in the numbers committed by foreigners.

In March 2000 the second Basic Plan for Immigration Control took effect, aiming to reduce the numbers of undocumented immigrants in light of the reduction of the labor demands. Komai's research contended that hardworking, long-resident immigrants were unlikely to be involved in crime because detection would lead to deportation. In spite of this, Prime Minister Koizumi increased the 2004 budget for cracking down on illegals. Governor Ishihara and Justice Minister Nozawa accompanied police on night patrols to pick up "illegals." Katsu Yoshinari, head of the pro-immigrant NPO Asian People's Friendship Society, agreed with Komai, blaming the xenophobic politicians for the crackdown which worsened relations between foreigners and Japanese (Matsubara 2003).

In 2003, Komai joined the Asian People's Friendship Society march for human rights in Shibuya. Taking a long-term view (Yamaguchi 2003), he reiterated warnings that the Japanese workforce will drop by half by 2050, with only two workers for each elder. Japan needs 600,000 foreign migrants annually to maintain the labor force ratio. The 2000 reform of the Basic Immigration Law, primarily a crackdown on overstayers, was also a victory for NGOs because it promised the acceptance of certain needed kinds of immigrants, and better training, internships, and treatment of foreigners and refugees. Hammar (1999) advocated that settled residents should have most of the rights and protections of citizenship regardless of nationality. In 2000 illegal migrants dropped to about 200,000 and the reformed Basic

Immigration Law accepted NGO demands that treatment of immigrants should make "special dispensations" proportionate to their integration into the Japanese community. In the end Komai concludes that high demand for cheap or lower-skilled labor is over and that admitting such people legally would "only make an underclass stratum in Japanese society" (2003: 5).

Chapter Summaries

Yasuko Takezawa's opening chapter focuses on the 1995 "breakthrough" after the Hanshin earthquake in Kobe that made the public aware of the living situations of poor and foreign communities, and that gave rise to the now common phrase *tabunka kyôsei*. Kobe has long prided itself on being one of Japan's most international cities. *Gaijin*, the prototypical "White" foreigners, were visible and their former quarters in Kobe's Kitanocho area are now a source of historical Meiji-era tourism. Other foreigners, such as the early twentieth-century Koreans and Chinese, and recent newcomers including more Chinese, Vietnamese, and South American *Nikkeijin*, were not so visible to most Kobe residents. Kobe was de facto multicultural before the 1995 earthquake, but not in public discourse nor as an ideal model. These minorities, even though subject to the instruments of the modern state, were out of sight and out of mind before 1995 (e.g., Anderson 1983; Taylor 1994). The Kobe case brings together a number of critical elements: the concept *tabunka kyôsei* in its positive sense of interdependent, symbiotic, living together (the Durkheimian "organic"), as a description of the freely given mutual aid between "foreigners" and "Japanese;" secondly we see a range of local peoples and initiatives working and becoming permanent NGOs, especially churches and neighborhoods, alongside local municipal departments. Local Japanese fought to have "illegal" immigrants get their medical bills paid. One lasting effect of this increased exchange has resulted in the creation of an "Asia town" in Nagata ward.

Business partnerships and joint ventures were early forms of post-World War II internationalization. Tomoko Hamada "started" as a translator for international business negotiations and was also one of the first to demonstrate the long-term insupportability of the "Japanese employment system" (1980). Japanese businessmen's model of *kokusaika* was not one of multiculturalism. The business structure and dynamics were innovative but Japanese business culture prevailed. For decades Westerners railed against the rigidity of these business practices and exerted different kinds of *gaiatsu*, foreign pressure, to foster change. Hamada (chapter 2) shows that it was the collapse of the bubble, the reverse flow of foreign capital buying up ownership of car companies, and the failures of Japanese companies that finally brought about change. She focuses on Renault's purchase of a controlling interest in Nissan, and the imposition of a foreign executive Ghosn who performed a miracle turnaround, and at the same time dramatically changed the business culture. English was imposed as language of administrative meetings and foreign-national executives have become more common since then. Business culture has become more multicultural (but not necessarily female-friendly); the form of multiculturalism embraced here is more accurately globalized neoliberal capitalism. This chapter joins John Nelson's on religion and Kenji Tierney's on sumo, which show change taking place in the central institutions of Japanese society.

Chris Burgess's portrayal of a polyglot hinterland community bears out a number of claims. Counter-intuitively, this case of foreign wives promoting intercultural and international appreciation takes place in one of the most remote, conservative hinterland areas in Japan, reinforcing the point that "cosmopolitanism" is not restricted to the wealthy or college educated. The second point is the agency and initiative of the immigrants who know realistically what they are up against and take a long-term strategy in winning over the local people. As Yamashita (chapter 5) also points out, it is the women who are the activists in this transformation. But we must realize that these women willingly came to Japan, they have close allies in their husbands, they come from fairly educated backgrounds and got employment in Yamagata and, above all, they are all in the country legally. These women's legal immigrant status allows them to act without local NGOs, NPOs, or municipal offices helping them. One might look suspect that in the long run these women will adapt and their children will assimilate so to become "homogeneous" all over again. But these smart women see how Japanese pay attention to American culture, and how the World Cup raised Korea in esteem. They have found positive reception and have been able to introduce personally crucial elements of their native cultures to their new families and community.

John Ertl focuses on the interrelated national policies of internationalization (*kokusaika*) and decentralization (*chihô-bunken*) within the context of local government and civil action in Ishikawa Prefecture. Examining a broad range of internationalization strategies, Ertl claims that many projects are aimed towards the creation of unique municipal identities that may allow them to compete for central government and foreign capital investment. For example, Kanazawa City has been promoted as a "world city" and has built a strong network of sister-city relationships, business ventures, and training exchange programs with cities in several different countries. In contrast the remote town of Rokusei, which has only a few foreign residents, is introduced to show how ubiquitous and essential internationalization has become in Japan. Relating his personal experiences working for Rokusei Town, Ertl examines the impact education initiatives to "internationalize" the nation, including the Japan Exchange Teaching (JET) program (McConnell 2000). While its immediate goals are to improve foreign language and culture education and form a cosmopolitan coun-tryside, the program may be more effective in stimulating local pride and knowledge of both Japan and the community through the "dialectic" ex-changes that take place. Furthermore, many of these guests, filled with positive experiences, return to their home countries to become informal spokespeople for Japan.

Shinji Yamashita's wide-ranging field experiences provide a macro-per-spective to the topic of international marriages by Japanese women abroad and of Japanese men in Japan. These marriages eventually create new "hy-brid" cultural forms as in-marrying spouses do not simply assimilate and become "mono-cultural" locals. Alliance by marriage is one of the world's oldest politico-cultural links between nations and ethnic groups. The di-rection of these links is subject to a particular power-logic that men of a more powerful group will have relations with and marry women of com-plementary and lower status groups (Graburn 1983b; Kelsky 2001). This recalls Levi-Strauss's (1949) work on the circulation of women between groups of men, which Leach (1951) proved later to be incomplete by bring-ing in social hierarchy as a power gradient, resulting in an excess of women "at the bottom" and an excess of powerful men "at the top." But in Yamashita's case, Japanese women who marry Balinese men provide a counter example to this "ero-power" logic. MacCannell's (1976) concept of alienation from home and the search elsewhere for "authenticity" may ex-plain middle-class Japanese attraction to ideal communities overseas as *fu-rusato* (native place) tourism. Rea (2000) found such tourists in England's Lake District and in Prince Edward Island, Canada, and more recently we see Japanese *hanryû* (Korean boom) tourists at the sites of the nostalgic Ko-rean television drama *Winter Sonata* (*Fuyu no Sonata*).

Gaku Tsuda's background as a Japanese American and his work among Brazilian *Nikkeijin* migrants position him well to conduct research on "both sides of the immigrant fence." The *Nikkeijin* are a special legal im-migrant category created by the revised 1990 Basic Immigration Law in the hope of replacing the inflow of Asian blue-collar workers with more ac-ceptable descendants of emigrant Japanese. By 2000 there were 275,000 Brazilian and 54,000 Peruvian *Nikkei* in Japan. It surprised the officials, the Japanese population, and the migrants themselves that their identity as admired, mainly middle-class "*japonês*" in financially distressed Brazil, also positioned them as loud, South American lower-class foreigners in Japan. Tsuda gives evidence of many kinds, including television portrayals, of their "outsider," bad neighbor, and lazy worker image (Tsuda 2003b). Tsuda mentions that there are exceptions to this stereotype, including flu-ently bilingual *Nikkeijin*, Japanese who enjoy the flexible and expressive lifestyle of *Nikkei*, and others who feel sentimental attachments because of their essential (bodily, ancestral) similarities. Because *Nikkei* are "legal" workers, after the bubble burst and the excess of good blue-collar jobs dried up, employers tended to hire or keep them and relegate the hard-working, more visible, and often illegal immigrants to lower-paying and unstable jobs. In many cases, illness and layoffs led to poverty, threats of deportation, or desperate measures, which the disadvantaged now blame on the "cheap Brazilian labor." The *Nikkeijin,* in spite of their marginalization, have built communities where they can enjoy, express, and consume their Brazilianness, as well as obtain services from local governments and NGOs. While most of Tsuda's informants preferred *Nikkeijin* to more visible kinds of immigrants, Tsuda concludes that multiculturalism—in the sense of incorporating people of different cultures and languages as ethnic equals—is unlikely to take hold in Japan.

Jeff Hester's chapter examines the contemporary identity politics of *Zainichi* Koreans, who are the families and descendants of forced laborers brought to Japan during the Second World War. In spite of cultural and linguistic assimilation, separatist nationalism identifying with either South Korean *Mindan* or North Korean *Chôsen* maintained an oppositional separateness until recently. Resident Koreans have recently experienced social and economic advancement and decreasing marital and employment discrimination, and by legal standards their population has been falling for fifteen years as they have relinquished Korean nationality and intermarried with Japanese nationals. Koreans' ability to voluntarily change their names and become "hyphenated Japanese" without a specific cultural change demonstrates the fragilely constructed nature of nationality or foreignness. Out of Koreans' decisions to naturalize are emerging new types of "Japanese," such as *Kankoku-kei Nihonjin, Chôsen-kei Nihonjin, Korian-kei Nihonjin* (all kinds of "Japanese with Korean ancestry"), *Nihonseki Chôsenjin* (Korean with Japanese nationality), or *Korian-Japanîzu* (Korean-Japanese). This parallels the emergence of Asian Americans, Chinese Americans, and other hyphenated Americans in the past thirty to forty years. It threatens the dominant essentialist equation that "race equals culture equals citizenship," in which the boundaries of racial groups are supposed to coincide with cultural and linguistic communities and hence with citizenship. When things do not coincide, such as foreigners speaking perfect Japanese or Japanese citizens of European descent, they become the building blocks of new kinds of Japaneseness.

Keiko Yamanaka focuses on a group of immigrant Nepalis, many of whom are illegal visa overstayers, phenotypically visible, and low paid blue-collar workers. Yamanaka originally met these individuals through her research in Nepal, and tells us that they represent many ethnic groups who share historical experiences of temporary overseas labor and sending remittances home. Unlike the numerous "legal" South American *Nikkei* immigrants that have many official avenues of support, this small group of Nepali immigrants has formed an active and broad network of Japanese friends and fellow immigrants to assist in daily living and difficult crisis situations. They are able to manage their situation, despite a certain degree of poverty, discrimination, and threat of deportation, by exercising agency over their status. By empowering themselves and being reliable workers, they gain employers' support and admiration from other Japanese. Though they are sometimes hunted by the police and blamed for rising crime, their employers want to retain them, and through their own community organizations and friends in NGOs they fight for pay and benefits and for humane justice. Yamanaka asserts that a passive tolerance of foreigners and growing grassroots activism are forming the basis of an admirable "civil society" in Japan.

Yuko Okubo studies the education for newcomer minority children, either immigrants or children of immigrants, some foreigners and some naturalized, in an Osaka school district. This case illuminates the historical sequence of indigenous "old" and "new" minority educational politics. This Buraku community, with relatively good housing, schools, and services, is no longer dominated by Buraku as they have moved into and assimilated with the general community. *Zainichi* Koreans moved in, worked with them politically and took advantage of *Dôwa* self-awareness education and afternoon "ethnic club" classes where city-paid special teachers helped raise their identity awareness by using their proper Korean names, speaking Korean, using Korean clothing and toys, and celebrating Korean festivals. Similar classes were started for recent Chinese and refugee Vietnamese who moved into the subsidized housing, plus extra "Japanese language" classes and teachers so they would not fall behind in their regular studies. Soon, the Korean classes stopped because students preferred afternoon sports, leaving only Chinese and Vietnamese children with special "ethnic" club-classes. This school is specially designated for receiving immigrant students and teachers direct the clubs to help the children retain and nurture their ethnic identities. Okubo views the program as a form of segregation, as it forces these children to act publicly as visible subjects, under the rubric of "international exchange," according to the teachers' stereotypes of their nationality. She suspects most parents will reject this special distinction and the ethnic clubs will collapse and the minority children will rejoin their Japanese peers.

Mitzi Carter and Aina Hunter bring to the fore central features such as stereotyping, race, visibility, hybridity, class, and gender. They did not personally experience the stereotype of Japanese as anti-Black racists, but their Blackness brought up the mostly unmentioned ethnicity, the Whiteness of most European American tourists and social scientists. Their welcome matched that of White students, both in the cities and the countryside. They confront Black sociologist John Russell (of Gifu University) for extending his analysis of male Blackness in Japan to females. They agree that the stereotype of Blacks is conflated with and narrowed to the very visible Black males in the military, but they want to construct a separate model for Black women. They also point out that racism in Japan is exercised differently from the United States. Though it appeared fashionable to "consume blackness" in niche roles at the high fashion end and in *ganguro*[5] counterculture, the authors and their friends suspected the stability of these positive relations. Carter's childhood memory of intercultural relationships brought up the volatile topic of Black *konketsuji* (children of mixed race): her mother trying to save her from becoming dark "like her father" reminiscent of the shame parents felt in the 1950s and 1960s, when most *konketsuji* babies were sent to a private orphanage whose philanthropic Madame won national praise for exporting almost all of them to America and Europe (Strong 1978). Carter observes, following Valentine (1990) that such "hybrids," like Brazilian *Nikkei*, are more "out" than complete outsiders, yet sometime more "in" than other foreigners.

John Nelson emphasizes the regional nature of internationalism and multiculturalism in Japan (see also Takezawa, Ertl, Okubo, and Graburn). Cities such as Kagoshima, Nagasaki, Kobe, and prefectures such as Kagoshima and Fukuoka are "imagined" as having special relationships with different foreign cultures at various times in history. These popular narratives form the fabric by which Japan is both woven together and regionalized. Some of these regions are associated with 16th century or modern Christianity. While Christianity was originally thought to be a kind of Buddhism, it has remained a markedly foreign-associated religion. Nagasaki's contemporary "distinctive regional culture" embraces: the coming of the Portuguese, mass conversion and then banishment of Christians, trade with the Dutch, and above all, memorializing the atomic bomb. Nelson shows how church leaders are multireligious without losing their identity by working together and positioning themselves as anti-establishment. In Nagasaki, much is made of the added element of the instant death of over 15,000 Korean forced laborers in 1945; for Koreans Christianity is not so "foreign-affiliated." With 30 percent of the Korean nation, it was a main source of organized resistance and fervor against the Japanese colonizers. Nelson (1996, 2002) demonstrates that the Nagasaki humanistic ecumenism is rare in Japan, but Christian actions against prostitution (Graburn 1983b) and remilitarization, continue to have far-reaching effects.

Kenji Tierney's study of sumo centers upon a key topic for understanding ethnicity and nationhood, as sports are an almost universal metonym for cultural and political bodies, and stand at the heart of debates about identity and belonging. Tierney shows that Sumo was cultivated as a nationalist and imperialist entity, which spread along with the demographic and colonial diaspora, and then was "cut off" at the end of the Second World War. Since then Pacific Islanders and more recently Asian mainland, Middle Eastern, and European wrestlers have participated in sumo. The Sumo association has reacted with restrictive rules concerning belonging to a *heya* (house, team), the ownership of a *heya*, or being a visitor or becoming "visibly" Japanese, or becoming Japanese national. Caught between chauvinistic feelings and a dearth of recruits, the "Asian," and in particular Mongolian, proportion has grown to the point that five of six recent second level champions are "foreign," one is Bulgarian and another Georgian. Tierney straightforwardly asserts that this case throws into question who is a foreigner and therefore who is Japanese. The constructed nature of "nationality" is also reflected in other sports, for instance different high school sports leagues have different rules (within the same sport); in baseball *Zainichi* Koreans "are Japanese" hence not statistically visible, whereas in soccer they "are foreigners" (Manzenreiter and Horne 2004).

Tourism can be an indicator of self-other and national-international relationships. Nelson Graburn (1983a) initially studied domestic travel with historical continuities from the Edo period. Although the structure of travel arrangements was similar for domestic and overseas travel, the destinations were separable. The nature of attractions in Japan has now weakened this distinction. While overseas tourism is an expression of internationalization (*kokusaika*), domestic tourism has become a form of "internal internationalization" (*kokunai kokusaika*). There has been a massive construction of "foreignness" in theme parks, as well as the enhancement of touristic and regional identity of many formerly downplayed aspects of foreignness, particularly concerning Korean cultural heritage, Christianity both hidden and active, Meiji and Taisho foreigners' houses, and all things Dutch, as well as cuisines, clothing styles, and entertainment. More than that, the search for humane social qualities that used to be thought of as especially Japanese, such as *furusato* (native place) (Graburn 1995; Ivy 1995) are now eagerly sought abroad, in Prince Edward Island and the Lake District (Rea 2000), and perhaps Bali and the United States (Yamashita, chapter 5) or even in Korea-bound (*hanryû*) tourism. MacCannell (1976) asserts that modern tourism stems from alienation at home, so we can learn from today's tourism what are positive and negative attitudes about the self and others.

Conclusion

Communities of Acceptance

All over Japan there are individuals who choose to welcome foreigners and to celebrate difference. A group has formed in Tokyo for "multicultural exploration" to search out cultural difference and celebrate it (Yuginuma 2000). Many visible and even illegal foreigners are defended by neighbors, not just by exploitative employers, and often the police do not want to take action against them (Yamanaka, chapter 8; Kaneko 1998). Despite financial barriers (Yamaguchi 2003), NGOs and volunteers are celebrating cultural difference and helping foreign nationals to remain in

Japan. In non-metropolitan areas organizations such as "Japan Tent" in Ishikawa Prefecture invite foreigners to enjoy homestays, and present them proudly at local events (Ertl, chapter 4). Resident and visiting foreigners are often invited to play public roles in *matsuri* (Shinto community rituals) and municipal festivals. There are many Japanese who enjoy meeting foreigners abroad and who try to entertain international visitors at home. Some do criticize "boutique internationalism," which is restricted to food, fashion, and short home visits or to interaction between middle classes, leaving working class immigrants ignored or discriminated against.

There are no clear answers about Japanese attitudes towards foreigners in their country and there are a few dramatic cases of overt, sometimes violent discrimination, not all of which are directed against lower-class people. One case described by Arudou (2004) occurred at Otaru Hot Springs where a Caucasian Japanese citizen and his racially mixed family were refused entry. When asked why, they were told that the business decided to bar all Caucasians because some Russians had behaved inappropriately, upsetting Japanese customers, and it would be unfair to discriminate just against Russians. Arudou asked if the members of his family could enter, and was told that only the darker, more Japanese-looking one of his two daughters would be admitted, showing again how problematic Japanese identity is becoming.

Throughout Japan there are still people who conflate the problems of immigrant labor and foreign tourists with crime. For instance, in 2003 one-third of respondents to a nationwide survey wanted no increase in foreign tourists because they committed crimes (Mainichi 2003). Police reported that "foreign crime" was up and sixteen thousand foreigners were prosecuted, but the irony is that 40 percent of their crimes resulted from cases of "being foreign," that include illegal entry or visa overstay. Discrimination against foreigners, as well as against the disabled, frequently emerges on the Internet as a source and measure of anonymous hostile feelings. Yet there are counter-indications, such as the thirty-seven thousand petition signatures against deporting Burmese refugee Khin Maung Latt in 2003 (Austin 2004).

Marriages

One major factor aiding the multicultural trend is intermarriage. One of Burgess's informants (chapter 3) said, "That's real *uchinaru kokusaika*—inside the family internationalism." Not only are mainstream Japanese marrying formerly avoided Burakumin and Koreans, but increasingly they are marrying foreigners. Yamashita (chapter 5) shows that in parts of Tokyo 10 percent of the marriages are "mixed," when foreign women marry Japanese men and Japanese women marry foreigners in Japan or increasingly in Bali and California. Burgess explores how these multicultural nuclear families have settled in Northeast Japan and negotiated a stable multicultural identity and societal transformation.

Japanese international marriages grew from a trickle to very visible trend in the 1980s. The rural exodus to take less onerous jobs in towns and cities drained farming areas of young unmarried women; in some villages there were only three unmarried women for every ten unmarried men. Though men were stoic and maintained their local livelihoods, advancing age (40s and 50s) made them think seriously about the need for heirs and getting wives from outside Japan. For instance, the local government in Tozawa, in rural Tohoku, helped send local men to visit nearby countries looking for spouses. A series of marriages ensued with mainly Korean but also Chinese and Filipina wives. The village celebrated their international friends and it became a mild tourist attraction, much as the place Burgess studied. Before the Korea-boom spawned by *Winter Sonata*, the in-marrying Korean wives said that Korean men were stiff and arrogant and Japanese men were gentler. Similar trends, at first mainly with Filipina wives (Faier 2003; Suzuki 2000), then Koreans, and more recently a majority Chinese resulted from the efforts of over two hundred travel agencies, as well as personal visits and online computer searches.[6] Many Japanese considered the flow benign or amusing and thought that Japanese and other East Asian matches are compatible because the children do not stand out, even though Tokyo's right-wing Governor Ishihara declared that this was "genetic pollution of the nation" (Komai 2003).

In order to assess the impacts on multiculturalism, we must carefully separate out the different kinds of "international" marriages. Probably the largest single portion comprises the marriages between highly assimilated *Zainichi* Korean nationals and non-Korean Japanese of the same class. These have the least impact because such a couple is hardly "multicultural," even if they continue to have more positive feelings about Korean culture than others around them, which may continue even when the Korean national becomes Japanese (Hester, chapter 7). However, the children of such couples may completely assimilate to Japanese ethno-nationality. The children of the common second kind of international marriage, between East Asian immigrants and Japanese, could go either way (Okubo, chapter 9). Because most are physically similar to Japanese, their children could easily assimilate so long as they leave behind their language, their native names, and some of their cultural habits of food and child rearing. They may however maintain a lingering, positive cultural interest in their overseas ethno-nationality. Okubo implies that Chinese-Japanese marriages are less likely to produce children who want to assimilate because of their strong orientation as Chinese, as opposed to Vietnamese who came to Japan as refugees and never expect to return to Vietnam.

More striking if less common are other kinds of international marriages, those of Japanese with non-Mongoloid Asians and those with Caucasians.

Marriages of Japanese women to South Asian men, like marriages to American Blacks, are rather uncommon and may be looked down on by their families. Children of these marriages would always be conscious of their biracialism and biculturalism (Carter and Hunter, chapter 10) and may have difficulty adjusting to life in Japanese communities. Those advocating against hybridity frowned upon marriage with Caucasian men in the past too, although it has become fairly prevalent among middle-class women today. The personal account published as a *manga* (illustrated) book *Dârin wa Gaikokujin* (My Darling is a Foreigner) (Oguri 2002) has been followed a number of *kokusai kekkon* (international marriage) manuals, and among this class of people, children of dual nationality are considered prestigious. The common word for mixed children *hâfu* (a half) is being replaced by *daburu* (double), expressing an advantage rather than a deficiency. Such children could undoubtedly become bicultural in a positive way and would circulate easily among the middle classes of both parental cultures, furthering the multiculturalism of both. Additional multicultural and bilingual children emerge from the experience of *kikokushijo,* those children that return to Japan after long periods of life and education abroad (Goodman 1990). These children have gone from being considered severely disadvantaged because of their poor Japanese language and cultural skills to being eagerly endeared as future global leaders.

Though international marriages form about 5 percent of all marriages in Japan and 10 percent in Tokyo, their effects on the next generation are going to be much higher because international marriages (however defined) have a 2.9 fertility rate[7] (Curtin 2002), more than twice the overall Japanese fertility rate of 1.3. In Tokyo, for instance, the next generation of schoolchildren[8] should be about 25 percent non- or half-Japanese, a dramatic change from anything in the recent history of Japan.

Construction of National Identity

A nation constructs its identity in contrast to opposing nations. Regions on the other hand construct their identity in comparison with surrounding locales. The poles of self-other are not opposites but are relational, as the other becomes the self in changing circumstances (see Bachnik 1998; Kondo 1990). While Japan has long made claims to an ideal of homogeneity, Japanese people are well aware of their internal differences. It is only in contrast to other nationalities that Japan becomes an essential homogeneous category. Japan may appear to be "one nation, one race" in an international context, but within the nation, and particularly between localities, individuals maintain multiple categories that distinguish themselves from one other. The unique contribution of this volume is that its authors approach the theme of Japanese multiculturalism through an examination of how distinctions between self-other are worked out between people of national and ethnic differences in specific local settings.

At the national level Japan has begun to change its stance regarding its ethnic makeup. When Japan signed the United Nations Charter of Human Rights in 1979, it followed with a declaration that there were no unrecognized minorities in Japan. This stance was officially reversed with the acceptance of the ethnic difference and special status of the long-assimilated Ainu people in 1996. During this period the increase in foreign immigrants has been generally greeted as a welcome addition to the state. This changes the tune of Japanese national solidarity from mechanical to organic, in that Japan has become a functional nation of many ethnically and nationally different people. But this distinction may not change the category of "Japanese" as far as race-ethnicity-culture is concerned, as Japan is now a place where Koreans, Chinese, Ainu, Burakumin, and Brazilians live alongside native Japanese.

There is a danger in treating these categories in the singular—as for example when Chinese or Filipino immigrants are perceived to be of a certain language and culture, and more importantly seen as coming to Japan for similar purposes. Okubo's analysis of school practices and Tsuda's interviews with Japanese and Brazilian *Nikkeijin* immigrants highlight the stereotyping of other groups' attitudes and behavior. The Japanese state welcomes its minority populations but in the process keeps them at a distance through the distinction that they are awarded. It is an awkward position for the national government as its old policies of either assimilation or disregard for minorities have given way to a new discrimination, mostly positive in intent, through its fervent recognition and classification of minorities. Thus this allows Japan to protect the category of Japanese ethnicity from rupture while garnering international respect for its recognition of minority rights (see Hale 2002).

This book illustrates that there are very important differences in how Japanese municipalities and local citizens categorize and interact with foreign residents. Non-Japanese are not simply set aside as separate from everyone else, but are participants in many spheres of activity that constitute the community. While there are obstacles for foreigners in acclimating to Japanese society, this is a two-way process in which local residents are forced to learn about their new international neighbors. This is particularly evident in Burgess's contribution in which the immigrant wives work to gain acceptance on their own terms from their neighbors. Old boundaries created by Japan's policy of segregating foreigners through political districting are being broken down, as Takezawa relates in the case of the Hanshin earthquake when neighbors came together to help one another ignoring the political boundaries that separated Korean and Japanese residents. At the grassroots level, Japanese and international residents are joined in solidarity based on residency rather than citizenship or nationality. As members of a community, foreigners are often welcomed and included, bound together by a singularity, not by race, but by common goals for the good life. Solidarity is a unity of purpose and direction, in which residence and participation are the only prerequisites for membership. This is particularly evident in rural municipalities struggling to develop new forms of community based not on old ties to land—as with the old *jichitai* (self-governing structures) divisions—but on a sense of common humanity and equality (Ertl, chapter 4).

Our contributors span the range of hopefulness. Burgess is most optimistic that Japan has reached a critical point at which acceptance of the multicultural ideal is already underway. His work, along with the Yamanaka and Nelson chapters and other works (Douglass and Roberts 2000; Komai 2001, 2003) show that the seeds can be planted by a small minority of economic or marital immigrants aware of the ideal and of the human rights discourse behind it, who not only defend themselves but engage the local population to fuel a new atmosphere of positive curiosity and acceptance. If Komai's (2001) claim that the Japanese hatred of foreigners is partly retribution for having been defeated by them in World War II, that memory should be diminishing. At the other side, the conclusions of Tsuda and Okubo are more dubious (see also McCarty 1997; McCormack 1996). Tsuda says his Japanese informants were somewhat tolerant of Brazilian *Nikkeijin* but verbally less welcoming of other immigrants, and Okubo demonstrates that teachers' efforts to avoid assimilation of Asian children forces the children to remain foreign subjects and thereby reinforce the visible cultural boundaries.

Japan has changed over the past twenty years and it will never again be able to hold on to an unchallenged model of homogeneity. Like many industrial countries Japan needs a constant stream of immigrants just to keep the labor force from plummeting. The fertility rate is far below replacement[9] and will not rise much, any more than the numbers of elderly who need to be supported will diminish. Japan needs a steady increase of new workers annually to maintain its economy and national population, and it will not be able to do so with immigrants that are all physically and culturally similar. As Japan's population declines, it will appear visibly increasingly hybrid, especially as it is the ethnically "homogeneous" Japanese who are decreasing fastest. In this era of changing demographics and increasing cultural diversity, the character of Japanese identity will undergo further transformation. With multiculturalism as the ideological backbone of Japanese public policy, diversity and intercultural exchange will continue to be promoted over practices of assimilation and homogenization. While multiculturalism holds great promise for forming positive affection towards ethnic and national minority groups, it brings with it the potential to proscribe status upon individuals that may be inappropriate or unwelcome. However, the many chapters in this volume illustrate that national-ethnic distinctions are not the only markers of identity, and are possibly becoming increasingly less deterministic, as the specific exchanges and encounters that take place in local settings are leading to new pluralized communities in Japan that are inclined to incorporate diversity rather than ignore or remove it.

Notes

1. Of course, what is judged a positive direction depends upon the reader. The authors of this book, both Japanese and non-Japanese, share a culturally and politically liberal outlook and promote the appreciation of cultural diversity within Japan and the alleviation of discrimination and cultural or racial hierarchy, especially the feelings of degradation, anger, and despair that often result from the latter. In part this work is an antidote to "Japan bashing" and does not even wish to castigate Japanese for believing the "myth of homogeneity," as we prefer to emphasize the models that replace the myth.
2. Van Wolferen (1989) and others claim that the "new" governments consisted of the same old people in new clothing, owing, in part, to the collusion of the occupying forces—strengthening the argument about self-redefinition in relation to and in competition with the geopolitical "other."
3. Actually some had predicted the "bubble burst" at least a decade before (Hamada 1980) and in hindsight we may say that the signs were there as the system "hollowed" by cronyism, inexorable demographics, and blind optimism, much as Yurchak has shown for the late Soviet Union (Yurchak 2005).
4. Durkheim's analysis was framed as a guide to reforms in France, which was at the time fraught with labor strikes and emerging anti-Semitism. His analysis, while correct in focusing on the complex division of labor, failed to note that "superior" societies were also held together in part by the "mechanical solidarity" of manufacturers' associations, political parties, and labor unions, and, conversely, all "primitive" societies were also bound together by that prototypical form of organic solidarity, the marriage alliance, a fact on which his heir Claude Levi-Strauss based his work.
5. *Ganguro*, literally "black face," is the Japanese name for teenagers and young women who darken their skin, wear very light colored mouth and eye make-up and often wear outlandish clothes (Miller 2000).
6. Though South Korea also has as strong set of values about homogeneity and keeping the blood "pure," Korean men are also seeking and finding overseas brides, in China and Vietnam, and 8 percent of Korean marriages were to foreigners in 2003. Though this was said to have started with farmers in Japan, in Korea it is a more urban phenomenon of the non-affluent. Yamashita writes about the flight of Japanese women overseas (see also Kelsky 2001), and there are now reports that middle-class Japanese women are employing matchmaking agencies to meet with well-to-do men in European cities.
7. Unfortunately "international" marriages have a higher breakup rate than monoethnic ones. This is particularly true of those who marry American GIs and there are thought to be about four thousand children of dual nationality whose fathers abandoned them in Okinawa.
8. Exactly the same phenomenon is beginning to be seen in the classrooms of major European cities whether the differential birth rate is the same, but there are fewer mixed marriages, so most children are direct offspring of the immigrants and refugees.
9. Replacement rate is 2.1 total fertility rate (number of live births per woman in her lifetime). Japan at less than 1.3 is similar to the countries of Eastern, South-

ern, and Iberian Europe. Many Northern and Western European countries have even lower fertility rates (Galicia, Spain recently recorded the record low for peacetime humans, at 0.89), but those countries, like it or not, all have continuing legal or illegal labor migration. Even Canada has a policy of recruiting at least sixty thousand a year to keep up its workforce.

References

Abe, Atsuko. 2002. "Japan's New Challenge: Becoming a Multi-ethnic Society?" Review of *Foreign Migrants in Contemporary Japan* by Hiroshi Komai. *Electronic Journal of Contemporary Japanese Studies*, 10 February, Review 3. http://www.japanesestudies.org.uk/reviews/Abe.html

Anderson, Benedict. 1983. *Imagined Communities: Reflections on the Origin and Spread of Nationalism*. London: Verso.

Aoki, Tamotsu. 1999. *"Nihonbunkaron" no Henyo: Sengo Nihon no Bunka to Aidentitii* [The Transformation of "Nihonbunkaron": Postwar Japanese Culture and Identity]. Tokyo: Chûkôbunronshinsha.

Arudou, Debito. 2004. *Japanese Only: The Otaru Hot Springs Case and Racial Discrimination in Japan*. Tokyo: Akashi Shoten.

Austin, Mark. 2004. "Are Visa Overstayers Criminals?" *Daily Yomiuri*, 16 February.

Bachnik, Jane. 1998. "Time, Space and Person in Japanese Relationships." In *Interpreting Japanese Society: Anthropological Approaches*, 2nd edition, ed. Joy Hendry, 91–116. London: Routledge.

Befu, Harumi. 1993. "Internationalization of Japan and Nihon Bunkaron." In *The Challenge of Japan's Internationalization: Organization and Culture*, ed. Hiroshi Mannari and Harumi Befu, 232–65. Nishinomiya: Kwansei Gakuin University.

———. 2001. *Hegemony of Homogeneity: An Anthropological Analysis of "Nihonjinron."* Melbourne: Trans Pacific Press.

Benedict, Ruth. 1946. *Chrysanthemum and the Sword*. Boston: Houghton Mifflin.

Curtin, J. Sean. 2002. "On International Marriages in Japan." *Japan Forum* 13 March. http://lists.nbr.org/japanforum

Denoon, Donald, Mark Hudson, Gavan McCormack, and Tessa Morris-Suzuki, eds. 1996. *Multicultural Japan: Paleolithic to Postmodern*. Cambridge: Cambridge University Press.

DeVos, George, and Hiroshi Wagatsuma. 1967. *Japan's Invisible Race: Caste in Culture and Personality*. Berkeley: University of California Press.

Doi, Takeo. 1973. *The Anatomy of Dependence*. Tokyo: Kondansha International.

Douglass, Mike, and Glenda S. Roberts, eds. 2000. *Japan and Global Migration: Foreign Workers and the Advent of a Multicultural Society*. London: Routledge.

Durkheim, Emile. 1893. *La division du travail social. Etude sur l'organisation des sociétés superieurs.* Paris: Alcan. [Trans. 1947. *The Division of Labour in Society.* Glencoe, IL: Free Press.]

Eades, Jerry, Tom Gill, and Harumi Befu, eds. 2000. *Globalization and Social Change in Contemporary Japan.* New York: International Specialized Book Service Inc.

Etter, Carl. 1949. *Ainu Folklore: Traditions and Culture of the Vanishing Aborigines of Japan.* Chicago: Wilcox and Follett Co.

Faier, Lieba. 2003. "On Being Oyomesan: Filipina Migrants and their Japanese Families in Central Kiso." Ph.D. diss., University of California, Santa Cruz.

Fukui, Nanako. 1999. "Background Research for *The Chrysanthemum and the Sword.*" *Dialectical Anthropology* 24 (2): 173–180.

Goodman, Roger. 1990. *Japan's "International Youth:" The Emergence of a New Class of Schoolchildren.* Oxford: Clarendon Press.

Graburn, Nelson H. H. 1983a. *To Pray, Pay and Play: The Cultural Structure of Japanese Domestic Tourism.* Aix-en-Provence: Centre des Hautes Etudes Touristiques.

———. 1983b. "Tourism and Prostitution: A Review Article." *Annals of Tourism Research* 10: 437–456.

———. 1995. "The Past in the Present in Japan: Nostalgia and Neo-traditionalism in Contemporary Japanese Domestic Tourism," in *Changes in Tourism: People, Places, Processes,* ed. Richard W. Butler and Douglas G. Pearce, 47–70. London: Routledge.

Hale, Charles. 2002. "Does Multiculturalism Menace? Governance, Cultural Rights and the Politics of Identity in Guatemala." *Journal of Latin American Studies* 34 (3): 485–524.

Hamada, Tomoko. 1980. "Winds of Change: Economic Realism and Japanese Labor Management." *Asian Survey* 20 (4): 397–406.

Hammar, Tomas. 1999. *Denizen to Kokumin-kokka* [Permanent Residents and the Nation State]. Tokyo: Akashi Shoten.

Hatsuse, Ryûhei. 1985. *Uchinaru Kokusaika* [Internal internationalization]. Tokyo: Sanryô Shobô.

Hilger, Inez. 1971. *Together with the Ainu: A Vanishing People.* Norman: University of Oklahoma Press.

Hudson, Mark. 1999. *Ruins of Identity: Ethnogenesis in the Japanese Islands.* Honolulu: University of Hawaii Press.

Ishii, Yoneo, and Masayuki Yamauchi. 1999. *Nihonjin to Tabunka Shugi* [The Japanese and multiculturalism]. Tokyo: Kokusai Bunka Kôryû Shuisin Kyôkai; Hatsubai Yamakawa Shuppansha.

Ivy, Marilyn. 1995. *Discourses of the Vanishing: Modernity, Phantasm, Japan.* Chicago: University of Chicago Press.

Iyotani, Toshio. 1995. *Cross-national Labour Migration in Asia and Regional Development Planning: Implications for Local Level Management.* Nagoya: University of Nagoya Centre for Regional Development.

Kaneko, Anne. 1998. *Overstay* [73 minute video]. Los Angeles: Pacific Rim Center.

Kaner, Simon. 1996. "Beyond Ethnicity and Emergence in Japanese Archaeology." In *Multicultural Japan: Paleolithic to Postmodern,* ed. Donald Denoon et al., 46–59. Cambridge: Cambridge University Press.

Kelsky, Karen. 2001. *Women on the Verge: Japanese Women, Western Dreams.* Durham, NC: Duke University Press.

Kingston, Jeff. 2004. *Japan's Quiet Transformation: Social Change and Civil Society in the Twenty-First Century.* New York: RoutledgeCurzon.

Komai, Hiroshi. 1978. "Non-White Immigrants in Toronto." *Shakaigaku Journal* 3: 1–7.

———. 1979. "Beikokujin Rôdôsha to Nihonteki Rômu Kanri—Nikkei Kigyô no Rôdôsha Ishiki Chôsa [American worker and Japanese style labor management—research on workers' consciousness in Japanese corporations in America]." In *Nihon no Taibei Chokusetsu Toshi ni Kansuru Kenkyû,* ed. Nikko Research Center. Tokyo: National Institute for Research Advancement.

———. 1990. *Gaikokujin Rôdôsha o miru Me* [The view towards foreign workers]. Tokyo: Akashi Shoten.

———. 1994. *Imin Shakai Nihon no Kôsô* [Japan as a multi-ethnic society]. Tokyo: Kokusai Shoin.

———. 1997. "The Role of Buddhism in the Reconstruction of the Cambodian Rural Village." Paper presented in Phnom Pen.

———. 1999. *Nihon no Gaikokujin Imin* [Japan's foreign migrants]. Tokyo: Akashi Shoten.

———. 2001. *Foreign Migrants in Contemporary Japan.* Melbourne: Pacific Press.

———, ed. 2002. *Kôza: Gurobaru suru Nihon to Imin Mondai* [Japan and the immigration issue in globalization series] (6 volumes). Tokyo: Akashi Shoten.

———. 2003. *Tabunka Shakai e no Michi* [The road to a multicultural society]. Tokyo: Akashi Shoten.

Komai, Hiroshi, ed. 2000. "Joint Statement by Scholars Demanding the Retraction of Govenor Ishihara's Remarks Viewing Undocumented Foreigners as Dangerous." http://www.geocities.co.jp/CollegeLife-Labo/8108/ishihara-e.htm

Komai, Hiroshi, and Ichiro Watado, eds. 1997. *Jichi-tai no gaikokujin Seisaku: Uchinaru Kokusaika e no Torikumi* [Local government policies towards foreigners: the struggle towards domestic internationalism]. Tokyo: Akashi Shoten.

Kondo, Dorinne K. 1990. *Crafting Selves: Power, Gender and Discourses of Identity in a Japanese Work Place.* Chicago: University of Chicago Press.

Leach, Edmund. 1951. "The Structural Implications of Matrilateral Cross-Cousin Marriage." *Journal of the Royal Anthropological Institute.* 81: 22–55.

Lebra, Takie. 1993. *Above the Clouds: Status Culture of the Modern Japanese Nobility.* Berkeley: University of California Press.

Levi-Strauss, Claude. 1949. Structures élémentaires de la parenté. Paris: Presses Universitaires de France. [1969. *Elementary Structures of Kinship.* Boston: Beacon Press.]

Lie, John. 2001 . *Multiethnic Japan.* Cambridge: Harvard University Press.

MacCannell, Dean. 1976. *The Tourist: A New Theory of the Leisure Class.* New York: Schocken Books.

Mainichi Wire Reports. 2003. "1 in 3 Japanese Don't Want Foreign Tourists." *Mainichi Wire Reports,* 3 November.

Manzenreiter, Wolfram, and John Horne. 2004. *Football Goes East: Business, Culture and the Peope's Game in China, Japan and South Korea.* London: Routledge.

Matsubara, Hiroshi. 2003. "Crime Crackdown or Xenophobia? Visaless Foreigners Are Easy Scapegoats." *Japan Times,* 21 December.

McCarty, Steve. 1997. Review of *Multicultural Japan: Paleolithic to Postmodern,* ed. Denoon et al. *Japan Journal of Multilingualism and Multiculturalism* 3 (1): 57–59.

McConnell, David L. 2000. *Importing Diversity: Inside Japan's JET Program.* Berkeley: University of California Press.

McCormack, Gavan. 1996. "Kokusaika: Impediments in Japan's Deep Structure." In *Multicultural Japan: Paleolithic to Postmodern,* ed. Donald Denoon et al., 265–286. Cambridge: Cambridge University Press.

Miller, Laura. 2000. "Media Typifications and Hip *Bijin.*" *US-Japan Women's Journal* 19: 176–205.

Mills, C. Wright. 1959. "On Intellectual Craftmanship." In *The Sociological Imagination,* 195–226. New York: Oxford University Press.

Morris-Suzuki, Tessa. 1998. *Re-inventing Japan: Time, Space, Nation.* Armonk, NY: M. E. Sharpe.

———. 2005. "Japan's Hidden Role in the 'Return' of Zainichi Koreans to North Korea." *Japan Focus.* http://japanfocus.org/208.html

Murphy-Shigematsu, Stephen. 1993. "Multiethnic Japan and the Monoethnic Myth. *Asian Perspectives* 18 (4): 63–80.

Nakamura, Akemi. 2005. "Migration Expert Makes Case for Helping Foreign Workers." *Japan Times,* 12 February.

Nakane, Chie. 1973. *Japanese Society.* Harmondsworth: Penguin.

————. 1978. *Tateshakai no rikigaku* [The dynamics of the vertical society]. Tokyo: Kodan-sha.

Neary, Ian. 1997. "Burakumin in Contemporary Japan." in *Japan's Minorities: Illusion of Homogeneity*, ed. Michael Weiner, 50–78. London: Routledge.

Neiburg, Federico, and Marcio Goldman. 1998. "Anthropology and Politics in Studies of National Character." *Cultural Anthropology* 13 (1): 56–81.

Nelson, John. 1996. *Japan's Rituals of Remembrance: Fifty Years after the Pacific War*. Video documentary. Austin: Center for Asian Studies.

————. 2002. "From Battlefield to Atomic Bomb to the Pure Land of Paradise: Employing the Bodhisattva of Compassion to Calm Japan's Spirits of the Dead." *Journal of Contemporary Religion* 17 (2): 149–164.

Nugaido. 1997. *Watashi no Nihon* [My Japan]. Okinawa: Nugaido.

Oguma, Eiji. 2002. *A Genealogy of "Japanese" Self-images*. Melbourne: Trans Pacific Press.

Oguri, Saori. 2002. *Dârin wa Gaikokujin: Gaikokujin no Kare to Kekkon Shitara, Dônaruno? Repô* [My darling is a foreigner: What will happen if I marry my foreign boyfriend? A report]. Tokyo: Mediafakkutorî.

Ohnuki-Tierney, Emiko. 1990. "The Ambivalent Self of the Contemporary Japanese." *Cultural Anthropology* 5: 197–210.

Okubo, Yuko. 2005. "'Visible' Minorities and 'Invisible' Minorities: An Ethnographic Study of Multicultural Education and the Production of Ethnic 'Others' in Japan." Ph.D. diss., University of California, Berkeley.

Pang, Ching Lin. 2000. *Negotiating Identity in Contemporary Japan: The Case of Kikokushijô*. London: Kegan Paul.

Rea, Michael. 2000. "A Furusato Away from Home." *Annals of Tourism Research* 27 (3): 638–660.

Ryang, Sonia. 1997. *North Koreans in Japan: Language, Ideology, and Identity*. Boulder: Westview Press.

————. "Chrysanthemum's Strange Life: Ruth Benedict in Postwar Japan." *Japan Policy Research Institute, Occasional Papers*, 32. http://www.jpri.org/publications/occasionalpapers/op32.html

Sekine, Masami. 2003. "An Introductory Note on the Special Issue on Japanese Society and Ethnicity." *International Journal of Japanese Sociology* 12 (1): 2–6.

Sered, Susan. 1999. *Women of the Sacred Groves: Divine Priestesses of Okinawa*. New York: Oxford University Press.

Shipper, Apichai. 2003. Review of *Foreign Migrants in Contemporary Japan* by Hiroshi Komai (2001). *Social Science Japan Journal* 6 (1): 132–135.

Shôji, Hiroshi, ed. 2004. *Taminzoku Nihon-Zainichi Gaikokujin no Kurashi* [Multiethnic Japan: Life and history of immigrants]. Suita: National Museum of Ethnology.

Sjoberg, Katarina. 1993. *The Return of the Ainu: Cultural Mobilization and the Practice of Ethnicity in Japan.* Langhorn: Harwood Academic Publishers.

Strong, Nathan O. 1978. "Patterns of Social Interaction and Psychological Accommodation among Japan's Konketsuji Population." Ph.D. diss., University of California, Berkeley.

Sugita, Yone. 2001. "Japan's 'Third Wave' Breaks onto Keiretsu Rocks." *Atimes.com.* 27 March.

Suzuki, Nobue. 2000. "Women Imagined, Women Imaging: Re/presentations of Filipinas in Japan since the 1980s." *US-Japan Women's Journal English Supplement* 19: 142–175.

Taylor, Charles. 1994. "The Politics of Recognition." In *Multiculturalism: Examining the Politics of Recognition,* ed. Amy Gutmann, 25–73. Princeton: Princeton University Press.

Tominaga, Ken'ichi, Hiroshi Komai, Hideo Okamoto, and Michoko Ise. 1969. "The Modernization and Industrialization of Thai Society: A Sociological Analysis." *East Asian Cultural Studies* 8: 1–4.

Tsuda, Takeyuki. 2003a. *Strangers in their Ethnic Homeland: Japanese Brazilian Return Migration in Transnational Perspective.* New York: Columbia University Press.

———. 2003b. "Domesticating the Immigrant Other: Ethnic Essentialization and Discourses of Tradition in Japanese Media Images of Nikkeijin Migrants." *Ethnology* 42(4): 289–305.

Turner, Terence. 1993. "Anthropology and Multiculturalism: What is Anthropology that Multiculturalists Should Be Mindful of It?" *Cultural Anthropology* 8 (4): 411–429.

Valentine, James. 1990. "On the Borderline: The Significance of Marginality in Japanese Society." In *Unwrapping Japan: Society and Culture in Anthropological Perspective,* ed. Eyal Ben-Ari, 36–57. Manchester: Manchester University Press.

Van Wolferen, Karel. 1989. *The Enigma of Japanese Power: People and Politics in a Stateless Nation.* New York: Knopf.

Vogel, Ezra. 1979. *Japan as Number One: Lessons for America.* Cambridge: Harvard University Press.

Weiner, Michael, ed. 1997. *Japan's Minorities: The Illusion of Homogeneity.* London: Routledge.

Yamaguchi, Tomoyuki. 2003. The "Building a Multicultural Society-from Tokyo" Symposium. http://www.jca.apc.org/apfs/NL/news_200308.htm

Yoshino, Kosaku. 1992. *Cultural Nationalism in Contemporary Japan: A Sociological Enquiry.* London: Routledge.

Yoshino, Roger, and Sueo Murakoshi. 1977. *Japan's Invisible Visible Minority: The Burakumin.* Osaka: Buraku Kaihô Kenkyûsho.

Yuginuma, Taku. 2000. "Multicultural Explorers Go on Tokyo Adventure." *Yomiuri Shimbun,* 15 September.

Yurchak, Alexei. 2005. *Everything Was Forever, Until It Was No More: The Last Soviet Generation.* Princeton: Princeton University Press.

1

THE GREAT HANSHIN-AWAJI EARTHQUAKE AND TOWN-MAKING TOWARDS MULTICULTURALISM

Yasuko I. Takezawa

OVER A DECADE HAS PASSED since the Great Hanshin-Awaji Earthquake—the most devastating earthquake in postwar Japan—suddenly attacked Kobe and vicinity on 17 January 1995, killing more than 6,400 people. The victims included about 300 non-Japanese nationals in the whole region and 174 within the city of Kobe itself.[1] Kobe has a population of approximately 1.5 million, of which 3 percent are non-Japanese nationals. The destructive impact of the earthquake focused attention on the presence of ethnic minorities, in particular on Koreans as well as on new immigrants such as the Vietnamese refugees and Brazilians of Japanese ancestry. The media provided extensive coverage of these immigrants and minorities, often reporting on their struggles and sudden losses, and on their new relationships with the ethnic Japanese.

Although the depth of sorrow and depression among many residents in the region cannot be overestimated even now, on the other hand, there is widespread recognition in Kobe that the learning experience of the disaster should be utilized to its maximum extent to change Japanese society. One of the hot issues that emerged out of the disaster was *tabunka kyôsei*, or "multicultural coexistence," a concept describing the ideal of coexistence of ethnic Japanese and minorities and immigrants as equal partners rather than as hosts and guests. The diffusion of the idea was one of the outcomes from the discussions between volunteers and activists about how to assist "foreign survivors" after the Kobe earthquake. In fact, the earthquake was a significant turning point in terms of the relationships between the

Endnotes for this chapter begin on page 42.

Japanese and the ethnic minorities in the city. The term is now fashionable throughout Japan, although it is still far from being fully implemented.

The wave of globalization that has swept other parts of Japan has also reached Kobe. In addition to those often called "oldcomers" such as Europeans, Americans, Indians, Chinese, and Koreans who have settled in this attractive city, in some cases, since the late nineteenth century, there are also many "newcomers," including Vietnamese refugees and Brazilians and Peruvians of Japanese descent, who arrived in or after the late twentieth century and have provided mainly unskilled labor to small or middle-sized businesses (see Tsuda, Chapter 6).

In recent years, there has been a great amount of discussion regarding globalization and the cultures associated with space and place. For example, Appadurai's concept of "ethnoscapes" (1990) has added a new dimension to the analysis of "community," while others (e.g., Gilroy 1987, 1993; Hall 1992) have also highlighted the importance of new approaches to community and culture in today's global context to explain the deterritorialization of culture.

In this chapter, I explore how new concepts of local community and *tabunka kyôsei* have emerged among Kobe residents since the earthquake. In particular, I focus on Nagata Ward, an inner-city neighborhood and manufacturing area of plastic shoes where non-Japanese nationals form about one-tenth of the population, because it seems to be a space where a creolized and hybrid culture has been emerging as local residents rebuild their homes together. In the process, I examine how locality has been defined by residents themselves, both ethnic Japanese and non-Japanese, in their struggle to rebuild from ashes and ruins, and in their success in obtaining the support of local governments. I aim to show the process of social changes on a micro level in response to the emerging consciousness of *tabunka kyôsei*, the changes that eventually influence the local government as well as other cities in Japan with high concentrations of immigrants and ethnic minorities.

Kobe and Internationalization

Kobe has enjoyed a reputation as one of the most international and cosmopolitan cities in Japan since opening its port to world trade in 1868. Currently, nearly forty-three thousand people of foreign nationalities from about one hundred countries reside in Kobe. Two-thirds of them are people of Korean ancestry and another one-fifth is of Chinese ancestry.[2] The city government has encouraged internationalization activities, such as entering into sister-city relationships starting with Seattle in 1957, providing assistance to countries in need, and welcoming foreign students. In a sense, the city of Kobe has utilized its image as a cosmopolitan city in its urban development. However, although major Korean and Chinese ethnic organizations have worked together with city and prefectural governments, most municipal attention has been directed outside, towards foreign countries, rather than inside, towards local foreign nationals and ethnic minorities. In other words, "internationalization" was promoted to strengthen the image of the "international" town, not so much to increase the tolerance of multicultural heterogeneity at the local level.

Yet since the late 1980s, new immigrants, most of whom have little understanding of the Japanese language and culture, have become readily visible throughout Japan. Each local government in Japan has started to confront the issue seriously by promoting the slogan *uchi naru kokusaika* (internal internationalization) as well as dealing professionally with issues affecting both ethnic minorities and new immigrants.[3]

The Earthquake and Minority Residents

When the immensity of the earthquake disaster and its potential impact on citizens' lives was realized, many Japanese were worried about the safety of Koreans and other minorities, recalling the experience during the Great Kanto Earthquake that hit Tokyo in 1923. Shortly after the Kanto earthquake, six thousand people, about the same number of the total victims of the Hanshin-Awaji earthquake, were killed, not by fires or the collapse of housings and buildings, but by Japanese after false accusations of arson and deliberately poisoning the water. However after the Kobe earthquake, both Korean and Japanese community activists say that they never even heard any such rumors. They describe instead the deep emotions they felt when they saw Japanese, Koreans, Vietnamese, and other minorities assisting each other smoothly in the chaos despite serious shortages of food, water, and medicine in the temporary earthquake shelters.

Immediately following the earthquake a great number of volunteers from within and outside of Kobe established local NGOs and many individuals concerned about "*gaikokujin*" (foreigners) formed relief organizations and quickly initiated various kinds of services to all foreigners regardless to their "legal" status. To give just a few examples, Gaikokujin Jishin Jôhô Sentâ, the Foreigners' Earthquake Information Center, which later changed its name to the Tabunka Kyôsei Sentâ (Multicultural Coexistence Center), was organized five days after the quake to provide hotline services and distribute short newsletters containing official government information regarding services, the condolence fund, financial assistance, and other programs, translated into 15 languages. Kobe Gakusei-Seinen Sentâ, the Kobe Students and Youth Center, passed out thirty thousand yen in cash to every foreign student whose residence had been totally or partially destroyed[4]; and a total of 767 students received it between 1 February and 31 March 1995 (Gaikokujin Jishin Jôhô Sentâ 1996: 147–157).[5] Hisai Betonamujin Kyûen Renraku Kai, the Network Association to Help Vietnamese

Suffering from the Disaster, set up its office in the Takatori Catholic Church in Nagata Ward, and Hyogoken Teijû Gaikokujin Shien Sentâ, the Center for Rebuilding the Lives of Permanent Foreign Residents in Hyogo, was also established in Nagata soon after the earthquake. These two groups merged together two years later to become Kobe Teijû Gaikokujin Shien Sentâ, the Center for Assisting the Lives of Foreigners. Other organizations provided such services as confirming the safety of individuals, assisting with the official procedures required to receive the compensation payments, and establishing FM radio stations to broadcast information in ten languages and ethnic music to encourage the non-Japanese segment of the population. In February 1995, a couple of weeks after the earthquake, these organizations mentioned above and a few others joined together to form Gaikokujin Kyûen Netto, the Network for Relief of Foreigners.

One issue that became a debate between these NGOs and the local and the national governments was that of who is a "local resident," a term included in a law regarding distribution of disaster compensation to the bereaved. Although both local and national governments paid both legal immigrants and permanent residents five million yen to bereaved families for the death of a breadwinner, and two million yen for the death of a dependent, the national government, specifically the Ministry of Welfare, rejected payments to three foreigners: an overstayer, a short-term sojourner, and a visitor. Another issue regarded medical costs began in February. For all of January after the earthquake, everyone received totally free medical care at emergency medical care centers, regardless of status. After that, foreigners living in Japan less than one year and people who had overstayed their visas were not eligible to join government medical insurance and therefore had to cover all of their medical expenses. Other long-term foreign nationals were treated equally with Japanese and their expenses were fully covered. The Network for Relief of Foreigners found a solution to these problems, paying one million yen out of donations it collected to aid foreigners officially ineligible for the compensation fund,[6] and convincing the prefectural government to pay hospitals for the unpaid medical costs of those foreigners.

The Hyogo branch of the Red Cross in Japan announced on 6 February 1995 that it would pay 100,000 yen from the donations to every undocumented immigrant as well as legally registered foreigners and Japanese nationals who could provide documentation of having sustained damage in the disaster as well as proof of residence such as receipts for utility bills or mail.[7]

In this way, NGO leaders protested the decisions of the local and national governments not to provide particular kinds of financial aid in certain cases. These protests were responses to the government's bureaucratic division of the population in terms of citizenship and status as foreigners. These leaders claimed that the national government was strictly maintaining an exclusive definition of citizenship or permanent resident status, whereas local government responded more flexibly in adopting the NGO proposals. The NGOs achieved many, if not all, of their goals to encourage local governments to consider more seriously the problems faced by foreigners.

It is also noteworthy that as these discussions continued between the NGOs and the city and prefectural governments, an informal regular study group was formed called GONGO (Government Organizations and Non-Government Organizations). GONGO managed to cover the unpaid medical expenses of foreigners at hospitals, and promoted the idea discussed below of an "Asia Town" in Nagata Ward.

Compared with governments, local residents hardly drew any lines between Japanese and foreigners. According to a number of sources, including leaders of minority groups, ethnic Japanese, whether young or old, victims or volunteers alike, made no distinction between minorities and Japanese in the distribution and sharing of goods and in extending assistance.

The newspapers also covered stories of how Japanese neighbors of a Korean ethnic school in east Kobe and Koreans connected to the school managed to break down previous divisions between them to develop closer relationships. When these Japanese, who had no previous contact with the school, found shelter there after the earthquake, the Korean teachers warmly welcomed them and shared their facilities, and later the Koreans offered rice balls and warm soup to everyone. While living together in tents at the school over several months, almost every night the groups talked about each other's history, the prejudice each had against the other, and came to have a better understanding of each other. A 68-year-old Japanese man, who used to believe that this Korean school affiliated with North Korea was teaching terrorism to its students, said to me that it was the first time in history that the Japanese and the Koreans had come to trust each other from the bottom of their hearts and started looking ahead instead of back. He said, "The Quake was indeed a hard and sad experience. But it was a challenge God gave us. We overcame the challenge to develop this relationship." It was a complete 180-degree change in their relationships. Later he became one of the strongest advocates speaking out for the rights of Koreans in the region. Even critical minority activists praised the way in which the Japanese and minorities helped each other and increased their mutual understanding in the process.

Of course, it was not that there was a total absence of conflicts. For instance, some Vietnamese in Kobe were asked, "Why are you Vietnamese here?" In another case, some working-class Japanese, standing behind a Vietnamese shelter, apparently complained that the Vietnamese had not cleaned the toilets during the week when they were on duty. Since many water and sewer lines were either cut or destroyed in the earthquake, the damage to or total lack of toilet facilities was a serious problem in many shelters.

Generally speaking, however, through the difficult life-or-death experience of the earthquake, an almost unanimous consciousness arose that the relationships between ethnic Japanese and minorities and immigrants had shifted after the earthquake and people had become more sensitive to multicultural settings. A 59-year-old Korean man quoted in the local newspaper *Kôbe Shimbun* (1 November 1995) believed that "since the tragedy and disaster was a common, shared experience, we have come to enjoy mutual safety and conversation when we meet on the street. Those people who used to adopt a certain attitude [towards non-Japanese] have stopped assuming it."

Nagata as a Testing Ground

Until the earthquake, most activities related to international exchange, international events, and various services for foreigners were initiated by the city and prefectural governments and were offered in downtown Kobe. In this sense, Nagata Ward was totally marginalized within Kobe. However, since the earthquake, this long-neglected inner city has emerged as a testing ground for a number of new projects of multicultural coexistence in Kobe. This situation was unique because it was not initiated by local governments but by local residents themselves, both ethnic Japanese and Koreans and new immigrants, with the local governments later reacting to residents' initiatives.

In Nagata Ward, almost 10 percent of the population or ten thousand people were of foreign nationality when the earthquake occurred.[8] They represented twenty-eight different countries, although most were Koreans (7.3 percent) and Vietnamese. Although there are geographically defined communities such as "China Town" and a European area near downtown Kobe, there was no "Korea Town" or "Vietnam Town" in Nagata.

It was only a few months after the quake that the idea of an "Asia Town" in Nagata became publicly known. It derived from a plan among Korean permanent residents to build a Korea Town in Nagata, but through the experience of the earthquake the leaders of the original idea and other residents became aware of how many Asians and other foreigners lived together in Nagata. Thus, Ajia Taun Suishin Kyôgikai, the Council for the Promotion of Asia Town, established after the earthquake, became engaged in various projects such as constructing multilingual public signs. The languages provided reflect the makeup of the residential population: English, Korean, Chinese, Vietnamese, and Japanese. There was a strong conviction among council members that multilingual signs and information improve communications between the different nationalities in terms of daily life and promote mutual understanding between different cultures. Furthermore, such multilingual information will allow smoother communications in disaster or emergency situations by assisting residents in evacuating the areas affected and conducting them to safe shelters.

The idea of an Asia Town was to create a "global village" with booths selling various ethnic foods and ethnic crafts, ethnic grocery stores, and small restaurants, as well as a square for ethnic music and dancing. As a prototype, the public market in Nagata, Marugo Ichiba, organized a three-day "Asia Market" in 1997 and 1998, utilizing stalls in the market left vacant after the earthquake. Activities included ethnic dances, music, and the celebration of ethnic cultures. Store guides in five languages were provided by the organizers (Japanese, Chinese, Vietnamese, Korean, and English). As a 52-year-old Korean involved in the Asia Town plan said, "It is not a matter of being Japanese or Korean. We are all the same local residents in this neighborhood" (*Kôbe Shimbun*, 1 November 1995).

Efforts toward a new community building also include FMYY, a ten-language FM station, merging into a single station integrating a Korean FM station and a multilingual FM station mainly targeting Vietnamese residents, both of which started airing after the earthquake. The FMYY provides ethnic music and news with announcers in each language. It too has contributed to generating and strengthening the atmosphere of multicultural coexistence in Nagata.

Membership in the Local Community versus the Nation-State

What we have observed in Nagata Ward is not necessarily an isolated case. For example, regarding the relationship in Nada Ward between the Korean school and its Japanese neighbors, the school has been actively supported by the neighborhood association, a women's group, and other groups and individuals since their new mutual understanding after the earthquake. They have succeeded in fundraising for the school, and in getting a traffic light set up in front of the school, which the school had requested for a long time in vain from the police. Geographically, the school is located at the edge of Chûô Ward, in the middle of a factory area with almost no residents, whereas its Japanese neighbors belong to Nada Ward. Although the official demarcation line cuts between the two, they have formed their own new "local community." In Higashinada Ward, where many universities with foreign students are concentrated, residents and university professors have started a *machi zukuri* (town development) project in their community. Among the various groups involved in relief activities, one young man declared that "Nationality is nothing more than a person's individuality."

Although Nagata is the most symbolic and most active community in initiating various projects for multicultural coexistence, Kobe society as a whole is certainly changing significantly. This is supported by a keyword search of newspaper articles in the *Kobe Shimbun* newspaper. In 1995, I found nearly 500 articles containing the term, "foreigners," and then came a steady increase: there were nearly 700 during 1996 and nearly 900 during 1997.[9] Furthermore, with regard to *tabunka kyôsei* or multicultural coexistence, although I found no instances of the use of the term in titles of articles throughout 1994, there were two articles in 1995, eighteen in 1996, and fourteen in 1997.

Starting before the earthquake and continuing to the present, a large number of local governments throughout Japan have passed resolutions to support the local suffrage of permanent foreign residents, which is at present restricted by national law. In March 1995, the Supreme Court ruled that it is not against the Constitution to grant local (municipal and prefectural) suffrage to permanent foreign residents.

In March 1995, two months after the earthquake, the Hyogo Prefectural Assembly and the Kobe City Assembly unanimously passed a "Resolution on the Local Suffrage of Permanent Foreign Residents." In passing the resolution, the Prefectural Assembly stated, "the occurrence of the earthquake had a major impact on clarifying how Japanese residents could coexist with permanent foreign residents." An editorial in the *Kôbe Shimbun* dated 20 March 1995 entitled "Foreign Residents' Suffrage Needed for Rebuilding" discusses this issue. It is worth quoting at length.

> Indeed, it is not surprising that the landscape dotted with foreigners' residences and foreign embassies has generated the common tourist catchphrase describing Kobe as an exotic town. However, a real international sense in Kobe and its vicinity, I believe, has been nurtured by the foundations of this metropolitan city and in the daily lives of its citizens. Why is it that among Kobe's and Osaka's citizens, they are able to engender a consciousness, a kind of affinity towards Koreans, Chinese, and Filipinos? It is because people of many countries are their neighbors in their daily lives. Without mixing with people from other cultures and experiencing their cultures, we cannot find uniqueness and strength in cities like Kobe and Osaka.
>
> If we think that way, the uniqueness of this international consciousness in Kobe and Osaka is a significant factor necessary to rebuild the areas. We can even go so far as to say that without the cooperation of foreign residents, it would be impossible to rebuild Kobe and Osaka. In order to reconstruct our cities, we need to build a new society of coexistence and choose a path of reconstruction together with our foreign residents. (*Kôbe Shimbun*, 20 March 1995)

This concern is not one-sided. A 65-year-old Korean man stated that prior to the earthquake he had never been concerned about his suffrage rights; yet, after the earthquake, he found searching for employment difficult and felt that he would have no luck in obtaining a temporary apartment subsidized by the city. He now thinks, "If I had the right to vote, I certainly would this time." In his appeal for local suffrage and for full rights of employment and promotion as a government employee, a Korean community leader said, "Local communities share common destinies regardless of the nationalities or ages of their inhabitants. Community people not only live together but also could die together."

In order not to lose the focus of this chapter, I will not discuss here the complexities of the differences in responses to the local suffrage issue between people of South Korean descent and North Korean descent nor the problems that opened up associated with naturalization. However, it should be mentioned here that many people of South Korean descent, if not all, seem to have strong attachments to their locality and identify themselves as members of the local community, and yet many still consider maintaining their Korean citizenship as an important way to maintain their Korean identity after losing many other markers due to cultural integration. Thus, when the president of an association for South Korean residents in Hyogo Prefecture claimed at its tenth anniversary event that it should demand local suffrage in Japan and national suffrage in South or North Korea (*Kôbe Shimbun*, 17 June 1996), his statement was very symbolic.

On a different level, while the national government maintains its position restricting suffrage to Japanese nationals, support for local suffrage by a large number of local governments throughout Japan in a sense questions what membership of Japanese society means at the local level and at the national level. It is obvious that the national government as the ruler of the nation-state is losing its control over a definition of citizenship (or nationality) that some see as sacred and unique to Japan.

Much of the literature on globalization and culture emphasizes fragmentation of local communities, disintegration of community, or deterritorialization while giving close attention to transnational ties, imagined communities, or diaspora. There is no doubt that the Vietnamese, the people of Japanese descent from Brazil and Peru, the Koreans, and the Chinese maintain special attachments to their own "communities" at the global level. The impact of globalization on locality, however, does not necessarily result in dislocation of communities. Such a theoretical model seems to be more suitable to explain "localities" that entail some degree of residential or economic segregation.

In the case of Kobe, although there are concentrations of ethnic populations in certain areas, their housing is integrated without forming ethnic enclaves, unlike Gunma or Shizuoka. According to Komai, since new immigrants provide the labor force for small or middle-sized businesses, what is called the "double split labor market" did not come into existence (Komai 2000). As a result, as far as new immigrants are concerned, the coworkers (or employers) and neighbors with whom they interact in everyday life are mainly Japanese, though the degree of interaction may vary in each context.

There are also other factors that should be taken into account. The significance of the many decades of struggles and the achievements of ethnic minorities, especially the Koreans and the Chinese, should not be underestimated, as there would have been no foundation on which to develop relationships of coexistence with new immigrants. It is the sudden increase in the number of immigrants, most of whom have limited understanding of Japanese language and culture, that has had an impact on Japanese society as a whole and on local governments throughout Japan.

Furthermore, the age of globalization has affected the ethnic Japanese as much as it has immigrants and ethnic minorities. The NGO leaders mentioned earlier have varied experience with globalization, such as working for international organizations, traveling around the world as backpackers, marrying non-Japanese, and having close ties with foreign neighbors. For ordinary Japanese, too, foreigners' faces are not foreign any longer as they see them almost everywhere in Japan, and the distance from foreign countries in time and space has been compressed through the media and the changing speed and cost of travel.

Of course, Kobe is still far away from becoming the type of society where different ethnic groups coexist as equal partners in a real sense, as there is overt or covert discrimination in employment, housing, and other domains of social life. However, what we see in Kobe after the great earthquake is that local communities, especially in areas hard hit by the quake, are the main arenas for interaction, friction, negotiation, and cooperative planning for local residents, both ethnic Japanese and minorities or immigrants. Thus, using Hannerz's (1996) definition of culture as a "phenomenon of interactions," local communities have started to produce a hybrid and creolized culture by synthesizing other culture and transforming themselves. They have, in turn, been putting pressure on local governments to change their definitions of who is a member of society. Japanese society is therefore changing from the bottom up.

Epilogue

The tenth anniversary of the earthquake was marked in January 2005, and a number of ceremonies and events were planned to commemorate the tragedy and review the past ten years of rebuilding. I served on a review committee dealing with the issue of foreign residents and multicultural coexistence. Among a number of the features observed, I would like to note that over the past few years, the cooperation between Hyogo Prefecture and local NGOs has dramatically increased in relation to activities to assist foreign residents, especially new immigrants. Also one of the most urgent and serious problems involving new immigrants is the estimated low rate of enrollment to schools among school-aged children, especially those from Latin America. Another issue, related to this education problem, is the need to assist the development of leadership among new immigrants, so that the immigrants can become more independent and mutually supportive of each other. It should be also mentioned, however, that some NGOs in Nagata have become role models in *tabunka kyôsei* throughout Japan. Leaders in these NGOs visit upon request many different cities and towns to share their know-how in providing such services and consultations as multilingual information on disaster, education, medical and health care, and legal services. Overall, the activities assisting minorities and immigrants and developing relationships with ethnic Japanese are not diminishing but have kept growing in both quantity and quality since the earthquake.

Notes

1. About two-thirds of the foreign victims were Koreans and a quarter were Chinese, in line with the composition of the foreign population in Kobe.
2. Statistics from the end of 2003 show that Koreans (approximately 24,000) are the largest group, followed by Chinese (12,000), Americans (1,200), Indians (1,000), Brazilians (700), Vietnamese (1,000), and Filipinos (700).
3. For example, the city of Kobe established a Division of International Relations within the Department of International Relations under the direction of the Mayor's Office in 1991, and Hyogo Prefecture established the section for Local Internationalization within the Department of International Exchange in 1995.
4. There were other associations and NGOs that provided financial aid to foreign students. As a result, each foreign student whose residence was totally or partly destroyed received approximately 500,000 yen.
5. The international volunteer organization SESCO (Sekai no Kodomotachi ni Gakkô wo Okurou Kai [The Organization for Providing the World's Children with Schools]) also provided extensive assistance to foreign students, such as donating 100,000 yen to forty-three foreign students who were attending university schools without fellowships in Hyogo Prefecture.
6. The government paid 5 million yen each to families who had lost breadwinners, and 2 million yen each to those who had lost dependents if the victims were Japanese nationals, permanent residents, or legal immigrants who had resided in the area for more than one year.
7. However, perhaps a misunderstanding regarding this assistance program prevented undocumented or overstayed immigrants from going to the city hall to register their names and addresses in order to receive the documentation. Some NGO leaders had to go through a difficult negotiation process with government bureaucrats in order to obtain compensation for these illegal immigrants. They later reported that they eventually received this money for all the cases they worked on.
8. As of the end of 2003, legal foreign residents number approximately 8,100 in Nagata Ward.
9. No data from 1994 in this respect was available.

References

Appadurai, Arjun. 1990. "Disjuncture and Difference in the Global Cultural Economy." *Public Culture* 2 (2): 1–24.

Gaikokujin Jishin Johô Center, ed. 1996. *Hanshin Daishinsai to Gaikokujin* [The Hanshin great earthquake and foreigners]. Tokyo: Akashi Shoten.

Hannerz, Ulf. 1996. *Transnational Connections: Culture, People, Places.* London: Routledge.

Komai, Hiroshi. 2000. "Immigrants in Japan." *Asian and Pacific Migration Journal* 9 (3): 311–326.

2

GLOBALIZATION AND THE NEW MEANINGS OF THE FOREIGN EXECUTIVE IN JAPAN

Tomoko Hamada

Introduction

THIS CHAPTER DISCUSSES THE CULTURAL meanings of the foreign executive in the recession-ridden Japanese economy during the 2000s. A foreign executive in Japan has been called *gaijin-jûyaku*, or an executive from an outside or foreign country. The term *gaijin* (outsider or foreigner) has been considered derogatory by some who have pointed out the ethno-centrism and xenophobia of the Japanese corporate world. However, this author observes that Japanese managers are producing new *uchi-soto* or "inside-outside" worldviews at the start of this century, and their "center-periphery" discourses have shifted, particularly among those working for firms that face intense international competition. This chapter focuses on a new symbolic treatment of the foreign executive in Japan in the 2000s that contrasts greatly to the negative 1990s portrayal of the *gaijin-jûyaku* as ruthless job-choppers from the outside. The makeover of the image of the foreign executive is directly related to the recent growth of multiculturalism in Japan's popular imagination and in social arrangements in the community.

The ethnographic case study presented here is based on field research at Nissan Motors in the automobile industry, which is arguably one of the most competitive sectors of Japan's economy. The author interviewed middle-level managers at Nissan, which merged with Renault, a French company, in 1999, and formed the so-called Nissan-Renault Alliance. In the midst of the ensuing organizational shakedown during the merger, Japanese middle-level managers attempted to make sense of their working lives and the future of the company. While many middle-level managers suffered

Endnotes for this chapter begin on page 59.

from the consequences of the ongoing personnel cuts to save money (Nissan cut the number of its employees by twenty-one thousand in 2001), they nevertheless gave an overall positive image of Nissan's multiculturalism at the beginning of the merger. In fact they were often critical of the Japanese top executives' style of management and their corporate governance in the past. In their stories, the newly arrived foreign executive from Renault was portrayed as an agent of change, who could bring forth much-needed reforms in order to revive the company. Their stories suggest an intriguing symbolic transformation of the *gaijin-jûyaku* from villain to new business hero, and then to normal and ordinary business executive. In conclusion, the ethnographic case study presented here will be related to the current theoretical debates on globalization, modernity, and capitalism.[1]

The Myth-Making of the Japanese-Style Management

Until the end of the Japan's economic growth in the early 1990s, top executives as well as social scientists often listed such characteristics as respect for the employee welfare and long-term orientation as significant components of the Japanese corporate ideology and normative value orientation. However, in an article published more than two decades ago, I predicted that environmental changes would force Japanese management to reconsider conventional managerial practices. Five important factors in the environment I listed then were as follows: (1) reduction in the growth rate of Japan's economy; (2) change in the Japanese industrial structure; (3) demographic change: the aging of society; (4) trends toward higher education; and (5) growing competition with other nations in the global economy (Hamada 1980). This article predicted that "To the average Japanese white collar worker, the company will no longer be a community based on paternalism and familism, but an arena of fierce competition.... This is an inevitable consequence for Japanese management if they are to prosper in the new global economic order" (Hamada 1980: 406).

The Globalization Debate and
the Critique of the Japanese Style of Management

The Japanese business environment underwent tremendous changes during the 1990s, reversing the economic conditions of the 1980s. Japan's real estate market soared to its highest level in 1988, and the stock market peaked in 1989. Then, in February 1991, Japan's bubble burst. By 1992, the Nikkei stock index dropped by more than 40 percent of the 1989 value, and Japan entered a long period of economic recession.

Critical discussions of the "Japanese-style" of employment relations began in Japan in the early 1990s, when top business leaders themselves began to express doubts about its continued financial feasibility and validity.

Business elites began to discard phrases such as "the company as the family" or "the commitment to employee job security." Instead, more attention was focused on increased competition, costs, and profit. "Previously taboo words such as "restructuring," "rationalizing," and "human cost reduction" began to appear more often during the 1990s. It seemed that the Japanese management had forgotten their previously avowed obligations to the welfare of the employees of several years before.

In order to defend its position, Japanese leadership, including both corporate top management and politicians speaking through various surrogates, emphasized the necessity of responding to globalization pressure. In their cost-cutting efforts, the management used the threat of *gaiatsu* (foreign pressure) as reasons to eliminate formerly conventional corporate practices such as "life-long employment" and internal promotion and salary increases based upon seniority rules. Instead of familial or social bonds, employer-employee relations were increasingly characterized as economic transactions undertaken in the interests of the investors, to be terminated at will by the employer, whenever circumstances dictate.

Until rather recently, the conventional Western emphasis on creating good returns for investors never really existed in Japan in the same way. While Japanese firms in extreme financial difficulty do let go of workers, in general, when they experience a few months of poor sales, they tend to resort to other measures. Companies will cut annual bonuses, reduce salaries of managers, reduce overtime, and work on further cost reduction before they resort to layoffs. They continue to protect the full-time workers on their payroll and look for different work they can do or new products for them to produce, rather than lay them off outright. They reduce new hires of regular employees, and cut back to a smaller core of full-time employees who benefit from long-term employment. In order to cut the cost of human labor they increasingly rely on non-regular workers who are part-time, dispatched workers (employed by temporary worker agencies), and temporary and short-term contract employees. This practice creates a larger group of peripheral workers who do not have guaranteed job security through life-long employment, and who often make substantially less money than their full-time counterparts while doing the same or similar work.

An important shift toward this type of dual employment structure is a new perception of employment that is much more transactional and based on economic interests. It is moving away from the normative social contracts created by shared commitment and willingness to make sacrifices for the collective good, and by the perceived common organizational culture between management and labor. In the increasingly difficult environment of intense competition, the inefficient and incapable will be eliminated. A good example is Japan's automobile manufacturers, which need efficiency, sophistication, advanced technology, and administrative ability to prosper and capture the global market. The following section examines Japan's auto industry in some detail.

Foreign Capital Participation in Japanese Auto Manufacturers

Competition has intensified for automobile manufacturers partly because of a global overcapacity as more production facilities are coming on line, particularly in China. Automakers are facing many challenges that include excess inventories, new inspection standards, new demands for fuel efficiency, the need for new sales channels, and advancing technology. Profit margins are shrinking while price competition is becoming very severe. Japan's automakers consider that the world has become a single market, thus making domestic industry concerns indistinguishable from international issues.

The intense internationalization in the auto industry creates an interesting issue for the Japan Automobile Manufacturers' Association (JAMA). Until 2002, there were about twelve Japanese vehicle makers that were JAMA members. However, today only a few vehicles makers, such as Toyota and Honda, have 100 percent Japanese management control. The rest have become partially or fully foreign-owned, some with foreign executives on their corporate boards. The following table shows the capital participation of foreign companies in major Japanese auto companies in 2003.

Table 1: Foreign Capital Participation in Japanese Auto Firms as of 2002.

Name of Japanese Auto Firm	*Foreign Firm's Capital Participation*
Fuji Heavy Industries, Ltd. (Subaru)	20.0% owned by General Motors
Isuzu Motors	12.0% owned by General Motors
Mazda Motor Co.	33.3% owned by Ford Automotive Intl.
Mitsubishi Motors Co.	33.7% owned by DaimlerChrysler A.G.
Mitsubishi Fuso Truck & Bus Co.	43.0% owned by DaimlerChrysler, 42.0% owned by Mitsubishi Motors
Nissan Motors	44.3% owned by Renault
Nissan Diesel Motor Co.	22.5% owned by Renault
Suzuki Motor Co.	20.3% owned by General Motors
Toyota Motor Co.	No large percentage owned by foreign capital
Daihatsu Motor Co.	No large percentage owned by foreign capital (51.4% owned by Toyota)
Honda Motor Co.	No large percentage owned by foreign capital

Toyota entered into several alliances with General Motors (GM) and signed agreements to share parts with Volkswagen. However, after having operated a joint-venture named New United Motor Manufacturing Inc. (NUMMI) with GM in the United States, Toyota was not interested in acquiring a foreign auto maker because the firm saw potential demerit of cultural clashes in that approach. The firm recognized that it is very difficult to proceed with different corporate cultures. Therefore, instead of forming international mergers and joint ventures, Toyota went forward with Japanese companies such as Daihatsu and Yamaha. Meanwhile, Daimler and Chrysler merged to form DaimlerChrysler, and the newly created DaimlerChrysler took a stake in Mitsubishi Motors.

During the 1990s and 2000s, Toyota built a number of new factories in such locations as Kentucky, West Virginia, Alabama, and Texas, despite heavy initial start-up costs. As of 2007 Toyota owned thirteen vehicle, engine, and parts production facilities in nine US states, Canada, and Mexico. The geographical dispersion of Toyota's North American plants is quite a contrast from the geographical concentration of its domestic manufacturing facilities, near Toyoda City. What is more, each North American plant has only one or two product lines, which on the surface does not make good economic sense. Toyota has spread its manufacturing operations to different states mainly due to political concerns. By positioning itself as a powerful corporate citizen among diverse constituencies, often in economically depressed regions of the United States, Toyota has created goodwill in local communities. The company so far has deterred American protectionism despite the fact that it has been in head-to-head competition with Detroit automakers. Toyota's newest American plant began operating in Mississippi in 2007.

Vehicle manufacturers—whether they are foreign or domestically owned—are more likely to rely on local suppliers because they are better able to meet their requirements in terms of inventory control, rapid delivery, and interface flexibility. In such a dynamic political-economic environment, automakers and their supplier networks should no longer be identified simply in terms of corporate nationalities and reciprocal trade flows.

Foreign Executives and Their Style of Managing Japanese Companies

In tandem with the globalization of Japan's corporate structure, the faces of carmakers' top personnel have become more diversified in recent years. In 2000, about 6 percent of all the employees in Japan (3.79 million) were executives (Kurosu 2003). In the same year, about 600,000 foreigners worked in Japan, of which about 40,000 were board members (6.7 percent). Combining these two sets of statistics, we learn that less than 1 percent of all executives in Japan were non-Japanese in 2000. The majority of these non-Japanese board members worked for foreign enterprises in Japan. Until rather recently, foreign heads of big Japanese corporations were unheard of in Japan. However, changes are happening in this area.

In 1997 Ford Motor Company bought a controlling stake in Mazda Motor Corporation and brought in a Ford executive, Mark Fields, to be the CEO of Mazda. Fields graduated from Rutgers University (New Jersey) in 1983 with a degree in economics and then received an MBA from Harvard in 1989. He then joined the Ford Motor Company and served in a variety of positions. Prior to arriving in Japan he was the managing director of Ford Argentina SA. Fields led Mazda's Millennium Plan, announced in November 2000, in order to implement a financial overhaul, to revitalize Mazda's image, and to introduce a new generation of cars. In 2002 Fields moved on to a new position as group vice president of Ford's Premier Automotive Group, and Mazda selected Lewis Booth as its new CEO. Lewis had worked for Mazda as Senior Advisor in charge of corporate strategy. From January of 2000 Booth was the president of Ford Asia Pacific and Africa Technical Staffs he had operational responsibility for South Africa, Australia, New Zealand, and India and for developing Ford's strategy in the Asia-Pacific region. Born in England, Booth earned a bachelor degree in mechanical engineering from Liverpool University in England and subsequently qualified as a chartered management accountant.

The story of Nissan Motors was even more dramatic than that of Mazda. In July 1999, Renault SA of France bought a 36.8 percent stake of Nissan for US $5.4 billion. At that time, the Japanese automaker had shown its seventh loss in eight years to the amount of US $571 million. In order to revive the ailing Nissan, Renault sent Carlos Ghosn, a man of Brazilian-Lebanese heritage, to Tokyo. Born in Brazil, Ghosn received a master's degree from Paris National High Level Mineralogy Institute after graduating from the National Institute of Technology in France. He joined the Michelin Tire Company and was appointed president of Michelin Brazil at the age of 31. He was promoted to president of Michelin Tire of North America when he was 35. Seven years later, Ghosn was hired by Renault. He reconstructed the company and succeeded in turning around the troubled Renault in record time. He was nicknamed "the Cost Cutter" (Magee 2003).

The arrival of Ghosn as Nissan's new CEO in 1999 generated tremendous fear among the Japanese. The Japanese media immediately introduced the nickname the French gave to him, "*le* Cost-Cutter." The Japanese media then altered the nickname as "*kubikiri gôn*" (Head-Cutter Ghosn). Ghosn became one of the most closely watched executives in Japan. Many Nissan insiders predicted Western-style layoffs, ruthless plant closures, and relentless cost slashing; they believed Ghosn had come to Japan to enforce a management overhaul in order to revive Nissan for its new French owner. In 2001, debt-ridden Nissan did slash the number of workers by 21,000. But in the same year, Ford eliminated 35,000 workers, and GM and Daimler-Chrysler also slashed 26,000 jobs (Associated Press 2001).

In spite of the Japanese media's hype about the cruelty of foreign business methods, the expectations for Ghosn were high, especially among younger Nissan managers within the company. Middle-level managers said in private that Nissan's problems had become so serious that it actually helped to bring in a *gaijin,* an outsider. A manager noted that President Ghosn could implement any new plan as he saw fit because he was not perceived as someone who had been involved in the past board decisions that had led Nissan to its financial disaster.

Indeed Ghosn's management approach differed in many ways from the traditional Nissan style of management. For example, early in his tenure at Nissan he decided to reduce the number of suppliers and chose global suppliers on the basis of quality and cost, rather than sticking to the traditional *keirestu*-related companies out of the loyalty that was once a pillar of how business was done in Japan. Ghosn also set up teams of workers to draw ideas from the younger ranks, another drastic departure from the hierarchically formed decision-making patterns of Japan's corporate world. Executive meetings with Ghosn at the helm were conducted in the English language, marking a tremendous change in corporate communication. As serious debates in English were encouraged, junior executives and middle-level managers for the first time could express their candid opinions and critiques of past actions in English without utilizing polite, status-sensitive Japanese expressions.

Three months after his arrival, in October 1999, Ghosn revealed the Nissan Revival Plan (NRP), a three-year plan to turn the company around. Younger Nissan managers agreed with Ghosn that Nissan had been too complacent, failing to act on such obvious problems as the need to streamline its broad selection of models, cut costs, and design more attractive cars. The company was not selling automobiles, and yet it had not eliminated its excess production capacity. Consequently, efficiency was declining and the cost of maintaining plants was becoming a terrific financial burden to the company.

To the amazement of the Japanese public, Ghosn even predicted that Nissan would return to profitability within a year. Many took such a direct declaration of his ability and showmanship as rather brash. The president was very visible, both inside and outside of the company, again different from the rather opaque methods of communication in the old Nissan structure. Ghosn promised to streamline Nissan's broad selection of models, cut costs, and design more attractive cars. He announced that the purpose of the NRP was to overhaul Nissan's product plan, create brand power, invest in plans for the future, reduce costs, and sell assets for Nissan's resurgence. It is important to note that the Nissan auto workers' union, consisting of 40,000 members, never raised its voice to object to Ghosn's NRP and conducted no protest actions against the plan. It was not only the Nissan autoworkers' union that failed to raise its voice. The Nissan workers' union had set up the Confederation of Nissan Workers' Union (200,000 members) with Nissan-related companies and dealers, which joined the

Confederation of Japan Automobile Workers' Union, or JAW (800,000 members). Neither the Confederation of Nissan Workers' Union nor the JAW lodged protests against the plan.

The Nissan workers' union and the Confederation of Nissan Workers' Union made a public announcement: "… considering the current situation surrounding Nissan Motor Company, as well as the Nissan group, it is unavoidable to accept the structural reform plan of the company" (Asian Labour Update 2003). Nissan workers and managers alike accepted the NRP, which was extremely painful. The company closed three Japanese plants, dropping Nissan's production capacity in Japan to 1.65 million units from 2 million by 2002. Nissan slashed 14 percent of its workforce worldwide, down to 127,000 by the fiscal year beginning 1 April 2002. Of the 21,000 jobs cut in the three-year restructuring, about 16,500 were in Japan, 2,400 in Europe, and 1,400 in the United States. Nissan offices in New York and Washington were closed. Though the large size of Nissan's cuts stood out in Japan, it was not unusual in the global auto industries. For example, in March 2002 Ford announced that it would eliminate 35,000 jobs. Nissan also utilized the restructuring like other Japanese companies by decreasing personnel through attrition, an increase in part-time and flextime schedules, contractual workers, spin-offs, and early retirements. Nissan also decreased its cost base vigorously, resulting in cumulative purchasing cost reductions of 18 percent in one year.

One Nissan middle manager stated that before Ghosn's arrival, the majority of his fellow managers had been quite upset because the old top leadership had done little to save the company, even when everyone had known about the decline of profits every year. These middle managers felt that top executives had been concerned only with their own interests. In addition, according to some of my informants, Nissan's system of employee performance appraisal had sometimes been intentionally used as a means of discriminating against "undesirable" employees who had criticized the top management. The use of the performance appraisal system as a tool of employment discrimination is prohibited by law in the United States. However, Japanese employees had few means to correct such situations.

My informants agreed that the *Gôn senpû* (the whirlwind of Ghosn) was necessary, and that was why they were willing to participate in the creation of the NRP. The managers also stated that because the meetings with the new chief operating officer (COO) were conducted in English and older managers and directors could not speak English well, this gave younger managers opportunities to speak out in English more directly and honestly. Although it was quite difficult at first, they came to welcome the Ghosn approach.

One year after its near-death experience Nissan began to revive, at least in terms of bottom-line numbers, as the result of severe restructuring and governance reforms. In October 2001, the second year of the NRP, Nissan reported its third consecutive half-year of record profits. Its expected operating income was ¥187 billion (US $1.56 billion), a jump of 39 percent from the previous year, reflecting an operating margin of 6.2 percent. Ghosn also reported that Nissan had reduced consolidated net automotive debt by ¥149 billion (US $1.24 billion) in the previous six months to ¥804 billion (US $6.70 billion). He expected net income after tax to come to ¥230 billion (US $1.92 billion), for a return on net sales of more than 7.5 percent. Nissan Motor forecasted a net profit of US $2.3 billion for the fiscal year ending 31 March 2002. Nissan's performance in the following year was nothing short of spectacular: by the end of the 2002 fiscal year that ended on 31 March 2003, the operating profit had exploded to ¥737 billion, up from ¥83 billion three years before. Prior to forming its alliance with Renault in 1999, Nissan's net automotive debt was a staggering ¥2.1 trillion, but by the end of March 2003 the corporate debt had been completely eliminated, with ¥8.6 billion in cash reserves.

Middle-level managers praised Ghosn's leadership. Their stories implied that a *gaijin* executive such as Ghosn had acquired a new and positive status as their business hero. This new image of *gaijin-jûyaku* was rather unprecedented, and it differed greatly from the 1990s portrayals of the ruthless villain or outsider/job chopper.

Changes in Corporate Governance

Japanese corporate governance and auditing systems are also changing. Critics of conventional corporate governance point to opaque decision-making practices and lack of accountability at the pinnacle of the organization. In traditional Japanese firms that allow long-term tenure for managers, directors who have been internally promoted are handpicked by the CEO to sit on the corporate board. Once there, they therefore frequently enjoy fraternal and cozy relations with one another and with the CEO. Board decision-making processes in such an environment may lack transparency and accountability, partly because there are few outside members, and partly because no separation of power exists between the board and the executive office.[2] However, the new visibility of *gaijin-jûyaku* and the rapid internationalization of large Japanese firms has brought a demand for increased transparency in corporate governance and for standardized and globalized corporate auditing systems across affiliates and subsidiaries.

In April 2003 a revised Commercial Code finally came into effect, which allowed Japanese firms to adopt American-style corporate governance by transferring power from auditing officers to directors from outside the company (Japan Institute of Labor 2003). Under the new system called "Company with Committees," three committees would be established within the board of directors: (1) a nomination committee for appointing candidates for directors, (2) a compensation committee to determine compensation for corporate executive officers, and (3) an auditing committee responsible for auditing management. Because more than half the board members in each committee can be directors from outside the company, it is expected that business operations will become more transparent. More outsiders, including foreign executives, would sit on the corporate boards. While many large Japanese firms may still wish to maintain the current audit system, large electronic manufacturers such as Sony, Hitachi, Toshiba, and Mitsubishi have decided to adopt corporate management based on the three-committee system. These firms plan explicitly to separate management supervision and executive duties. Sony will adopt a unique system of corporate governance and separate the post of the chairperson of the board of directors from the post of the CEO, even though laws in the United States and Japan allow these posts to be combined. Hitachi, with eighteen group and related companies, will also establish a committee system in an attempt to strengthen its supervisory function over individual group companies. The new option may shift traditional intracorporate management relations, which have been based upon the long-held assumption that top executives are chosen from inside. Outside executives and *gaijin-jûyaku* will have more opportunities to play key decision-making roles inside multinational enterprises as a result.

The Language of Business

One interesting aspect of the Nissan recovery story is the fact that the new COO could not speak Japanese and therefore insisted that all board meetings and important business meetings be conducted in English. The company doubled the corporate financial support for English lessons. Within the corporate culture of Nissan, the ability to speak English became an important job qualification for managers.

It has been said many times that a major obstacle to Japan's internationalization (*kokusaika*) is a lack of English language ability. An increasing number of Japanese businessmen and women are learning English, and some speak English proficiently enough to conduct international business. In January 2001, Recruit Company conducted a questionnaire survey of thirteen thousand company employees in Tokyo and found that while the Japanese still have a long way to go in mastering business English an increasing number of younger employees are overcoming the linguistic barrier: 22.9 percent of those aged between thirty-five and thirty-nine years said that they can converse in English well enough, and 5.8 percent said that they can conduct business in English. However, among those aged fifty-five to fifty-nine only 12.6 percent can converse in English at all and only 3.4 percent can conduct business in English. In general, those 35- to 39-year-olds who can speak business English are likely to be junior managers working at the frontier of international business. The Japanese company used to rely on English specialists who worked in international or overseas departments to handle international issues. However, high-stake international competition has led companies to develop and favor those who can conduct business in English throughout the corporate structure. The demand for English is increasing in a wide range of business activities, including computer graphics, technological transfer, marketing, and executive decision making.

The Test of English for International Communication (TOEIC) is a widely used English proficiency test developed by the Educational Testing Service of the United States in 1979 and published by its subsidiary, the Chauncey Group International. According to the Institute for International Business Communication, which administers TOEIC examinations in Japan, 2,200 firms, schools, and organizations used the standardized test in fiscal year 2002. When this exam was first introduced to Japan in fiscal year 1979, only three thousand people took the test. In fiscal year 1990, the number grew to 332,000 and then to 1.3 million in fiscal year 2002.

In January 2003, the Institute sent a questionnaire to 1,803 organizations, 655 of which responded (Test of English for International Communication 2003). They found that roughly half of these firms (54 percent) already use TOEIC scores as hiring criteria, while 22.6 percent (148 companies) would like to use TOEIC in the future when hiring new employees. Out of all the companies, 16 percent reported that they currently use TOEIC scores as a prerequisite for promotions, but this figure reaches 50 percent if companies that would like to use scores as a prerequisite are also included. For example, Fujitsu Limited, Japan's biggest computer manufacturer, set a target TOEIC score of 600 for engineers, researchers, planners, and salespeople who deal with overseas clients. Those who use English regularly must score at least 730, while production-line employees and others require a minimum of 500. Fujitsu requires all new employees to take the TOEIC exam, and those who score lower than 600 have to study eighty hours of basic English.

Matsushita Electric Industrial Company (Panasonic) uses TOEIC scores as a basis for promotion. In fiscal year 2002, Matsushita employed 245,922 people, only 28 percent of whom were Japanese. In 2002, Matsushita decided that employees would need a TOEIC score of at least 450 in order to be promoted to a *shunin* (coordinator). In addition, new employees are encouraged to attain a score of 650 within three years of joining Matsushita, and those who are expected to work overseas need to obtain a score of at least 730 (Yanagawa 2003).

Globalization of Automakers in the mid 2000s

After several years of spectacular financial recovery, in 2007 Nissan reported a 3.3 percent decrease in global sales over the previous year, which constituted the company's first negative-turn since Ghosn took the helm in 1999. Although Nissan retained a very respectable 7.4 percent consolidated operating profit margin, it was nevertheless a drop from 11.1 percent in 2003. At this time, the market competition had shifted dramatically. Detroit's big three, particularly Chrysler and Ford, faltered while Toyota, Honda, and some European and Korean car manufacturers made a stride both in the US market and elsewhere. Chinese automakers also picked up speed, and in 2007 they were getting ready to introduce low-cost cars to the US market.

The competition in the 2000s was no longer simply that of domestic versus foreign automakers, nor that of Japanese versus Detroit's Big Three. Global strategic and operational systems began to emerge, in terms of procurement, manufacturing, sales, marketing, accounting, human resources, R&Ds, capital formation, and even recycling and sustainablity. Successful automakers replaced the traditional mechanism of exporting and importing assembled vehicles across national boundaries.

Over the last decade Toyota, Honda, and Nissan have doubled their overseas production from just over 5 million in 1998 to over 10 million units. In the US they now supply 67 percent of their total sales from their North American plants, compared with less than 12 percent a decade ago. For example, in 2002 Toyota implemented a global supply chain based in Thailand through its Innovative International Multi-Purpose Vehicle (IMV) project. The IMV project aimed to build a global operating platform for vehicles and components entirely outside of Japan. In 2005 Toyota expanded the IMV series not only in Thailand but also in Indonesia, South Africa, and Argentina in order to ship the assembled vehicles to more than 140 countries and regions worldwide. Toyota's push for global plants has been phenomenal; the company has doubled the number of its overseas plants to fifty-one and has increased its presence from eighteen to twenty-six countries over the past ten years.

Nissan on the other hand attempted to take advantage of its alliance with Renault. In 2005 Carlos Ghosn became CEO for both Nissan and Renault. By then Renault owned 44 percent of Nissan, while Nissan owned 15 percent of Renault. The French government also owned 15 percent of Renault. Nissan and Renault closely coordinated their operations and strategies. They collaborated on building common platforms, components, and engines. Renault built cars in Nissan's Mexico plants, and Nissan used Renault's Brazil plant and distribution networks. By forming an alliance they increased global purchasing power because the alliance could buy components for six million cars instead of three. Nissan halved its Japanese suppliers from 1,450 a decade ago to 700. It then asked the remaining Japanese suppliers to implement relentless cost-cutting. Critics argued that Nissan's over zealous cost-cutting weakened the group solidarity and would undermine quality. They pointed out Toyota's strong links with its suppliers, which included the highly successful Denso Corp and Aisin Seiki Co. Ltd., supported by the famous Toyota kanban system as well as its *esprit de corps.*

In the mid 2000s, Nissan experienced recalls. In April 2004, they recalled 27,000 minivans (Quest) in the United States due to some defective mounting brackets that caused the minivan's sliding door to open while it was being driven. Then in June 2006, Nissan recalled 128,000 passenger vehicles (Altima) in the United States because of defective piston rings that had caused some 120 engine fires. Nissan was also slow in introducing hybrid cars partly because of Renault (European) interest in diesel fuel. Both Toyota and Honda introduced hybrid vehicles and quickly captured the market. In 2007 Toyota sold one million hybrid cars worldwide, including 541,210 units in the United States.

Toyota achieved record-high net revenues, operating income, and net income. Toyota's net revenues for the fiscal year ending March 2007 on a consolidated basis totaled ¥23.94 trillion, an increase of 13.8 percent compared to the previous fiscal year. Toyota's consolidated vehicle sales for the period reached 8.52 million units, an increase of 550 thousand units compared to the previous year. In North America, vehicle sales reached 2.94 million units, an increase of 386 thousand units, due to strong sales of models such as RAV4, Camry, FJ Cruiser, and Yaris.

Nissan's net revenue for the fiscal year ending in March 2007 was ¥10.4686 trillion. Its operating profit was ¥776.9 billion; ordinary profit, ¥761.1 billion; and consolidated net income, ¥460.8 billion. The operating profit margin came to 7.4 percent. Nissan's global sales were down 2.4 percent (3,483,000 units). In the United States, sales were down 4.0 percent at 1,035,000 units. In Japan, sales were down 12.1 percent at 740,000 units. In Europe, sales came to 540,000 units, down by 0.2 percent. Sales in General Overseas Markets were 1,168,000 units, an increase of 5.1 percent. In 2007, Nissan globally launched eleven all-new products in order to improve its product mix, but none of them was hybrid. Nissan continued to invest in its future, especially in research and development of breakthrough technologies.

Growing Income Inequity in Japan

During the 2000s, income inequality and relative poverty in Japan rose above the average of that of fourteen members of the Organization for Economic Cooperation and Development (OECD) (Jones 2007). The fourteen members were Australia, Canada, Denmark, Finland, France, Germany (old Länder only), Italy, Japan, the Netherlands, New Zealand, Norway, Sweden, the United Kingdom, and the United States. The Gini coefficient for Japan was 0.317 in 1984, which was well below the OECD average of 0.401. It rose 9.4 percent to 0.41 in 2000, closer to the OECD average of 0.443. The

Gini coefficient of zero corresponds to perfect income equality (i.e., every-one has the same income) and one corresponds to perfect income inequal-ity (i.e., one person has all the income while everyone else has zero income). The proportion of the population in relative poverty, defined as less than one-half of the median household disposable income, surpassed 15 percent in 2000 in Japan, the fifth highest in the OECD area and well above the average of 10 percent.

This type of relative poverty and income inequality is due in part to the increasing propotion of non-regular employees in the work force and the rising unemployment and under-employment of younger people. Non-regular workers include part-time and dispatched workers (employed by temporary worker agencies) and temporary and short-term contract em-ployees. The proportion of non-regular workers has risen from 19 percent of employees a decade ago to over 30 percent. Part-time workers earn on average only 40 percent as much per hour as full-time workers, and only a very small portion of non-regular workers have chances to become reg-ular workers. As a reflection of the increasing dualism in employment, Japanese terms such as *kachigumi* (group of winners) and *makegumi* (group of losers) began to circulate among the general public. *Kachigumi* describes successful members of Japanese society who are winning today's tough competition. In reference to corporations, it means profitable and growing companies. The new winner-loser demarcation directly relates to the Jap-anese people's awareness of a class-based society. The new identification of societal bifurcation is quite a departure from the images of homogene-ity in the preceeding era, ranging from the notion that all Japanese belong to the middle-class to the notion of xenophobic distinction between the Japanese people and the rest.

In explaining the meanings of *kachigumi* and *makegumi,* Japanese man-agers of Nissan described the strengths and weaknesses of their company, one that must compete worldwide with strong winners such as Toyota. The Nissan-Renault Alliance must face not only the Toyota juggernaut but also General Motors, Ford, Honda, and the Chrysler Group, as well as European, Korean, and Chinese automakers. The corporate executives of Nissan, whether they are *gaijin* or non-*gaijin,* face formidable challenges worldwide.

Discussion: Globalization and the Representation of the Foreign Executive

I have described the changing image of the foreign executive in Japan and Japanese firms' new push for English language training. In this section, I try to connect these phenomena to the concepts of globalization. The term "globalization" refers to the increased mobility of goods, services, labor, technology, and capital throughout the world. Although globalization is not a new phenomenon, its pace has increased with the advent of new technologies in recent years. Robertson defines globalization as "the compression of the world and the intensification of consciousness of the world as a whole" (1992: 9). Waters defines globalization as "a social process in which the constraints of geography on social and cultural arrangements recede and in which people become increasingly aware that they are receding" (1995: 3). Waters sees three different but interacting types of exchange in the social process of globalization: material, political, and symbolic exchange. The third of these, symbolic exchange, includes "oral communication, publication, performance, teaching, oratory, ritual, display, entertainment, propaganda, advertisement, public demonstration, data accumulation and transfer, exhibition and spectacle" (1995: 8). Many writers have frequently associated globalization theory with the theme of modernity. Giddens declares that "modernity is inherently globalizing" (1990: 63).

The present study shows that the Japanese discourse on globalization surrounding the foreign executive is intimately related to the Japanese constructs of modernity and capitalism, all of which incorporate the idea of progress. Their notion of progress has been closely linked to their images of Anglo-American hegemony in the economic arena and intensified competition in the global market. It is important to note that Nissan was taken over not by an American but a French company and that Nissan's new CEO was a Brazilian who speaks Portuguese and French. English is not his native language. And yet, when Japanese middle managers talked about their need to learn a foreign language to move ahead and to be winners, they were almost exclusively talking about English, not French or any other language. Discussions of the use of business English also neglect other non-Western languages spoken in Japan. Japanese is spoken by some 125 million individuals, although no legislation defines Japanese as Japan's official language. This makes Japanese the seventh most widely spoken language in the world. There are at least two other native languages besides Japanese spoken in Japan: Okinawan and Ainu. There are also several foreign languages other than English that are more regularly and frequently spoken in Japan. Although official statistics on various language usages in Japan are not readily available, one could use the numbers of foreigners on record as a reference.

In the year 2000, there were 1,686,444 foreigners registered in Japan. A vast majority of these foreigners were Korean (635,267) and Chinese (335,575), followed by Brazilian (254,394) and Filipino (144,871). There were relatively few English-speaking foreigners in Japan. There were 44,856 North Americans and 16,525 British living in Japan in 2000—less than 4 percent of all foreign residents (Tsukahara 2002).

Japanese businessmen's current enthusiasm for English is directly related to neglect of the "other" native languages and a dominant foreign language (Korean) in Japan. Okinawans and Ainu have been "minorities" throughout Japan's modernization process and Korean is the language of the ex-subjects of the Japanese colonial empire. The relative indifference towards these languages and enthusiasm for English are two extremes of the same rule that gauges the value of a language by its market and commercial value. Totally absent in their discourses for business English are Japan's need for linguistic diversity and Japan's need for protecting the linguistic rights of the speakers of minority languages.

Japanese people are now speaking of the "English Divide." According to Tsukahara, the "English Divide" is a new phenomenon in Japan where individuals with knowledge of English have superior economic status. English in this sense becomes a discriminating factor, professionally, economically, and politically, as it is directly linked to Japan's class structure (Tsukahara 2002). This divide often overlaps the divide between those working for Japan's most successful multinationals, and the rest of Japanese workers. It also overlaps the generational gap between older and younger Japanese employees within one firm. Since older Japanese employees rarely speak English fluently, the traditional age-based status structures are being undermined. There is a paradox of incommunicability in this age of communication.

The adoption of English goes beyond mere linguistic and communication issues. Language is one of the most powerful resources for transmitting values and ideas. The decision to speak in one language instead of another is not only about communicating in a different manner, but it is also to accept a novel way of thinking about the world over alternative worldviews, and to make sense of reality in a different way.

In the past, Japanese managers' everyday work practice and sociolinguistic behavior were deeply rooted in their strong sense of nationalism and territorial identity. However, their new positive image of *gaijin-jûyaku*, the new concepts of winners and losers, and their wholehearted acceptance of business English reflect an ongoing cultural makeover.

As car makers rush to extract the maximum advantage from global opportunities, they are in effect collectively increasing competitive pressures upon one another. The automotive industry is already experiencing excess capacity, operating at 74.5 percent of operational capacity in 2003, representing close to 20 million units of excess light vehicle capacity. Despite this fact of global overcapacity, the top ten largest enterprises have added more than 5.5 million additional units of capacity between 2003 and 2006, and such levels of investment are expected to continue through the end of this decade.

Looking ahead, global automotive assembly is expected to increase by nearly 17 percent, topping 67 million units by 2011. Of this expected growth, Asia-Pacific will contribute 45 percent, North America 20 percent, East Europe 14 percent, South America 9 percent, and West Europe around 7 percent. There is a strong possibility that automakers will face diminishing returns on investment, razor-thin margins, high capital requirements, intense competition, and a significant amount of excess capacity globally. It is also anticipated that many of today's automakers and their alliances will inevitably change form, re-align, or perhaps even disappear as a result. The high-stakes, competitive environment is forcing managers to mentally rearrange organizational, informational, socioeconomic, and communicative space and create a new supraterritorial strategy for the company's survival. They have realized that in order to stay alive and prosper, they must conform to the US-based corporate rules for standardization and enforce corporate governance for efficacy over multiple local realities. They believe that they must adopt the English language as the lingua franca for everyday business communication. Thus, in their narrative, their regards for territoriality, nationality, and diversity bow to their manifest desire for accepting universal consistency, global penetration, and uniform economic logic. Japanese managers are constructively adapting to a specific type of internationalism that is linguistically more English, socio-ideologically more Anglo-American, and economically more market-based capitalist. The *gaijin-jûyaku* exemplifies this globality at home and abroad.

Notes

1. The term "capitalism" refers to an economic system characterized by private ownership of goods, by investments that are outcomes of informed privateers' decision-making processes, and by prices, production, and the distribution of goods that are determined by competition in a free market. According to many, including Karl Marx, a society is capitalist only if production is carried on by employees working with means of production that belong to their employer(s), producing commodities that belong to the employer(s). Max Weber argued that in order for a particular manner of life so conducive to capitalism to become dominant, it had to originate somewhere, as a way of life common to a large number of people.
2. None of these practices is wholly absent from US firms, but they have come under increasing scrutiny in the wake of corporate scandals like those of Tyco and Adelphia, where executives were accused of looting the company. Moreover, institutional investors such as pension and mutual funds investment managers, representing millions of stockholders, sit on boards of large US corporations. Their increasing insistence on transparency and accountability has been driving governance reforms at the corporate board level. The US Securities and Exchange Commission (SEC) has also demanded more openness. Large Japanese automakers such as Toyota and Honda, as New York Stock Exchange (NYSE) member companies, are subject to SEC regulations, at least for their US operations.

References

Abbeglen, James C. 1958. *Japanese Factory: Aspects of its Social Organization.* Glencoe, IL: Free Press.

Asian Labour Update. 2003. "Nissan Revival Plan and Autoworkers in Japan." Paper presented at Automobile Workers in Globalising Asia, the Center for Education and Communication and Asia Resource Centre, New Delhi, 30 November–1 December.

Associated Press. 2001. "DaimlerChrysler to Lay Off 26,000 Workers." 30 January.

Ballon, Robert J. 1972. *Foreign Competition in Japan: Human Resource Strategies.* Tokyo: Sophia University Press.

Clark, Rodney. 1979. *The Japanese Company.* New Haven: Yale University Press.

Cole, Robert E. 1967. "Japanese Blue Collar Worker: A Participant Observation Study." Ph.D. diss., University of Illinois.

————. 1971a. *Japanese Blue Collar: The Changing Tradition.* Berkeley: University of California Press.

————. 1971b. "Permanent Employment and Tradition in Japan." *Economic Development and Cultural Change* 20: 47–70.

Dore, Ronald P. 1973. *British Factory-Japanese Factory: The Origin of National Diversity in Industrial Relations.* London: George Allen and Unwin.

Drucker, Peter. 1973. *Management: Tasks, Responsibilities and Practices.* New York: Harper & Row.

Giddens, Anthony. 1990. *The Consequences of Modernity.* Stanford, CA: Stanford University Press.

Hamada, Tomoko. 1980. "Winds of Change: Economic Realism and Japanese Labor Management." *Asian Survey* 20 (4): 397–406.

————. 1997. *Absent Father, Feminine Son, Selfish Mother, Disobedient Daughter: Revisiting the Japanese Ie Household.* Japan Policy Research Institute Working Paper Series No. 33: 1–6. San Diego, CA: Japan Policy Research Institute.

Hamaguchi, Eshun. 1977. *Nihon rashisa no sai-hakken* [Rediscovery of Japanese-ness.] Tokyo: Nihon keizai shinbun-sha.

Hazama, Hiroshi. 1963. *Nihonteki keiei no keifu* [Genealogy of Japanese style management]. Tokyo: Nihon keizai shinbun-sha.

————. 1964. *Nihon rômu kanri-shi kenkyû* [Study of the history of Japanese labor management]. Tokyo: Nihon keizai shinbun-sha.

————. 1974. *Nihon-teki keiei; shûdan-shugi no kôzai* [Japanese style of management: Merits and demerits of groupism]. Tokyo: Nihon keizai shinbun-sha.

Iwata, Ryushi. 1977. *Nihonteki keiei no hensei genri* [Organizational principle of the Japanese management]. Tokyo: Bunshin-dô.

———. 1978. *Gendai nihon no keiei fûdô* [Climate of management in contemporary Japan]. Tokyo: Nihon keizai shinbun-sha.

Japan Institute of Labour. 2003. "General Survey: Revised Commercial Code Introduces US Style Corporate Governance." *Japan Labor Bulletin* 42 (5): 2–3.

Jones, Randall S. 2007. "Income inequity, poverty and social spending in Japan." *OECD Economics Department Working Paper* No. 556. Paris: OECD.

Johnson, Richard T., and William G. Ouchi. 1974. "Made in America (Under Japanese Management)." *Harvard Business Review* 52 (5): 61–69.

Kawashima, Takeyoshi. 1950. *Nihon shakai no kazoku-teki kôsei* [The familistic composition of Japanese society]. Tokyo: Nihon hyôron-sha.

———. 1957. *Ideorogii to shiteno kazoku-seido* [The family system as an ideology]. Tokyo: Iwatani-shoten.

Keizai Dôyûkai. 1999. *The Declaration for the 21st Century.* Tokyo: Keizai Dôyûkai.

———. 2001. *The Beginning of the Year Message.* Tokyo: Keizai Dôyûkai.

Koike, Kazuo. 1988. *Understanding Industrial Relations in Modern Japan.* New York: St. Martin's Press.

———. 1994. *Nihon no koyô shisutemu: Sono fuhensei to tsuyomi* [Japanese employment system: Its universality and strengths]. Tokyo: Toyo keizai shinpo.

Kurosu Masashi, ed. 2003. *Japan Almanac 2004.* Tokyo: Asahi Shinbun.

LeVine, Solomon, with Kazuo Okochi and Bernard Karsh, eds. 1973. *Workers and Employers in Japan: The Japanese Employment Relations System.* Princeton, NJ: Princeton University Press.

Lincoln, James R., with Hon Olson and Mitsuyo Hanada. 1978. "Cultural Effect on Organizational Structure: The Case of Japanese Firms in the United States." *American Sociological Review* 43: 829–847.

Magee, David. 2003. *Turnaround: How Carlos Ghosn Rescued Nissan.* New York: HarperBusiness.

Marsh, Robert M., and Hiroshi Mannari. 1976. *Modernization and the Japanese Factory.* Princeton, NJ: Princeton University Press.

Nakane, Chie. 1969. *Kazoku no kôzô; shakaijinruigaku-teki bunseki* [Structure of family: A social anthropological analysis]. Tokyo: Tokyo Daigaku Tôyô Bunka.

———. 1971. *Japanese Society.* Berkeley: University of California Press.

———. 1978. *Tate-shakai no rikigaku* [The dynamics of the vertical society]. Tokyo: Kôdan-sha.

Noda, Kazuo. 1975. *Nihon no keiei* [The Japanese management]. Tokyo: Daiamondo-sha.

Robertson, Roland. 1992. *Globalization: Social Theory and Global Culture.* London: Sage.

Test of English for International Communication (TOEIC). 2003. *The 12th Trends Survey of TOEIC Utilization (July 2003).* Tokyo: TOEIC Steering Committee of the Institute for International Business Communication. http://www.toeic.or.jp

Tsukahara, Nobuyuki. 2002. "The Sociolinguistic Situation of English in Japan." *Noves SL:* Autumn. http://cultura.gencat.net/llengcat/noves. Accessed 10 March 2002.

Waters, Malcolm. 1995. *Globalization.* London: Routledge.

Yanagawa, Shinichi. 2003. "English, the Lingua Franca of Business." *Daily Yomiuri,* 10 August.

Yoshino, Michael. 1968. *Japan's Managerial System: Tradition and Innovation.* Cambridge, MA: MIT Press.

———. 1975. "Emerging Japanese Multinational Enterprises." In *Modern Japanese Organization and Decision Making,* ed. E. Vogel, 146–166. Berkeley: University of California Press.

———. 1976. *Japan's Multinational Enterprises.* Cambridge, MA: Harvard University Press.

3

(Re)Constructing Boundaries: International Marriage Migrants in Yamagata as Agents of Multiculturalism

Chris Burgess

Migration Studies in Japan

THE TERM "NEWCOMER" DESCRIBES POST-WAR flows of migrants to Japan (Shimizu and Shimizu 2001: 3).[1] The first "newcomers" were the ten thousand or so Indo-Chinese refugees who arrived from the mid to late 1970s (Komai 2000: 314). Sellek (1997) identifies three further waves of newcomers: female "entertainers" from Asia from the late 1970s to 1986; male undocumented migrant workers from South and Southeast Asia, China, Korea, and Iran from the mid 1980s; and the *Nikkeijin* from 1990. However, it was only in the latter half of the 1980s that migration started to receive media attention. The influx of male workers in the second wave of postwar migration was dubbed the "new migration" (Sassen 1994) or the "second opening of Japan" (Lie 2001: chapter 1). It has been suggested (Douglass and Roberts 2000b: 3–37; Lie 2001: 7–18) that the reason the second wave got so much attention, despite the relatively small numbers, was because the social visibility of such racially different workers posed a potential (though largely symbolic) threat to prevailing notions of Japan as an ethnically homogeneous society.

Ishii (2003) notes that migration remained a foreign worker issue (*gaikokujin rôdôsha mondai*) until the middle of the 1990s, with the belated recognition that newcomers were not guests who would simply go home but residents (*jûmin*) and settlers (*teijûsha*) who might stay (Douglass and

---

Endnotes for this chapter begin on page 77.

Roberts 2000a; Komai 1995; Miyajima and Kajita 1996a; Weiner and Hanami 1998). Subsequent work on migration has tended to focus on issues of living (*kyojū*) and lifestyle (*seikatsu*) of newcomers rooted in families, communities, and localities. These kinds of studies are typically of the microsociological/anthropological type characterized by fieldwork in ethnic communities at the grassroots level (Ikegami 2001; Kawakami 2001; Yamanaka 2002). A central feature of this scholarship has been the idea that newcomers are more than just a source of labor (Piper and Roces 2003). As an increasingly visible and permanent population in Japanese society, newcomers have the potential to shape fundamental social change (Komai 2001: chapter 7). In order to understand their capacity to effect change, Hirano and colleagues (2000: 251) stress the importance of framing migrants in the context of wider global flows and transformations. As local agents operating in a global environment (Harzig 2001; Mato 1997), the different ways of thinking and being that newcomers bring with them from their countries of origin may be the key to the emergence of "new designs for collective life" (Appadurai 2001: 6), leading to changes in Japanese society.

The Present Study

The aim of this chapter is to contribute to the shift in contemporary scholarship on migration that is appearing as Japanese society begins to reorganize and reconceptualize itself as a multicultural society. The data presented here gives voice to a group of female marriage migrants in Yamagata, Northeast Japan. In comparison with metropolitan areas, most of the foreign residents in Yamagata are permanent migrants, particularly marriage migrants. Spouses rooted in an extended family, a neighborhood, and a local community have infiltrated local society in a way that many temporary or circular "transnational" migrants in other areas have not. As permanent migrants, these settlers may be more motivated than temporary migrants to make an investment both in society and in their own identity, sowing the seeds of multiculturalism in the regions.

The main focus is how newcomers interviewed for this study talked about engagement with their own identity and with society. As such, this study examines newcomers' own accounts, experiences, and perceptions of migration. In particular, I look at how they perceive their presence and actions will change (or have changed) Japanese people and national identity. The wider argument is that Japan may have reached or be about to reach some kind of turning point in terms of changing representations of national identity. While migrants in Japan may still lack the material requirements to instigate significant concrete transformations, they can engage in "cheaper" symbolic exchanges (Ching 2001: 285) that challenge and transform conventional images and stereotypes of Japanese and non-Japanese.

The increasing visibility of migrants in Japanese society also makes visible the processes behind the social construction of national identity and difference. Permanent migrants in particular can help make representations such as "Japanese" and "foreigner" *visible* as specific identities, depriving them of their assumed naturalness, which is vital to their functioning (Rathzel 1995: 59). Putting the spotlight on previously taken-for-granted national representations and stereotypes opens them up to challenge and transformation. This is not to say that subjects directly or consciously "challenge" or "resist" conventional categories of identity. Although the intention to change Japanese society comes across strongly in the data, not all behavior that has the potential to impact on systems of representation is necessarily carried out (or said to be carried out) for that purpose. Nevertheless, whether intended or not, the argument is that stereotypes of "Japanese" and "foreigner" are inevitably challenged as newcomers negotiate and navigate their own self-representations in their new homeland.

The Research Site: Yamagata Prefecture

Yamagata Prefecture (hereafter Yamagata) is located in the Northeast (Tôhoku) region of Japan, along the Japan Sea. Although only two and a half hours from Tokyo on the bullet-train, many of the smaller towns and villages in the regions become virtually cut off during winter. The population of Yamagata peaked in 1950 at 1,357,347. In 2001, it stood at 1,240,714, down 1 percent from 1996 (Tôkei Kyôkai 2003: 4–16). In terms of population, Yamagata ranks thirty-third out of forty-seven prefectures. However, in terms of area it ranks ninth (Tôkei Kyôkai 2003: 22). This gives it a population density of 133.2 people/km^2, considerably below the national average of 340.4 people/km^2 (Japan Almanac 2001: 279–285).

The population of Yamagata is older than the national population. In Yamagata, the number of people aged sixty-five years or older exceeded those aged fourteen years or younger in 1994; this ratio was reached nationally in 1997 (Data Book of Japan 1995: 25; Japan Almanac 1998: 59). In 2000, the prefecture had the highest percentage of households with parents aged over sixty-five, the lowest percentage of nuclear households, and the greatest number of three-generation households in the whole of Japan. Yamagata also has the highest rate of husband and wife working (Table 1). The implication for foreign spouses is that they will likely live with one or both of their in-laws and participate in the labor force.

The high number of three-generation households reflects the continued influence of the traditional *ie* (household) system. Indeed, the desire of some *ie* to reproduce themselves and the associated agricultural way of life resulted in local governments, concerned at the increase in unmarried eldest sons, implementing *kôkeisha taisaku* (measures to retain heirs) (Tamanoi 1998: 200). One manifestation of this policy was the "importation" of

Table 1: Demographics, Living, and Working Patterns in Yamagata and Japan, 2000

	Japan	Yamagata	Rank
People aged 15–64	67.9%	62.1%	(45th)
People aged over 65	18%	23.5%	(4th)
Households with parents 65 or over	32.16%	49.75%	(1st)
Nuclear households	58.42%	45.79%	(47th)
Three-generation households	10.1%	28.1%	(1st)
Average no. of household members	2.67	3.25	(1st)
Households where husband and wife work	28.09%	49.2%	(1st)

Source: Tôkei Kyôkai (2003: 17, 22, 24); Yamagata Prefecture (2001, 2003)

Note: The figures for people aged over 65 are for 2001.

foreign brides (Suzuki 2000: 147). In 1985, Asahi-Town in Yamagata became the first place in Japan to bring in brides from abroad (Shukuya 1988). This sparked a steep rise in the number of international marriages nationally, from more than one in a hundred in 1980 to one in twenty-two in 2000 (Japan Almanac 2002: 36–37). In Yamagata especially, the number of international marriages has skyrocketed, standing at one in fourteen in 2000 (*Asahi Shimbun* 2002) and fueling the rapid growth of the foreign population in the prefecture (Table 2).

Table 2: Registered Foreigners in Japan and Yamagata by Number, 1989–2001

	1989	1991	1993	1995	1997	1999	2001
Japan	984,455	1,218,891	1,320,748	1,362,371	1,482,707	1,556,113	1,778,462
(percent increase)		(24%)	(8%)	(3%)	(9%)	(5%)	(14%)
Yamagata	1,381	2,171	2,726	3,122	4,080	5,368	6,853
(percent increase)		(57%)	(26%)	(15%)	(31%)	(32%)	(28%)

Source: Sôma (2003: 161)

Note: Figures are for December of the relevant years. "Percent increase" is from the previous year.

There were three reasons for choosing Yamagata as a research site. The primary reason is the high proportion of newcomers who settle there. Yamagata has a high ratio of foreign-born spouses to total foreign residents, 34.6 percent compared with 15.8 percent nationally as of December 2001 (Sôma 2003: 160). This translates into substantial numbers of foreign residents with a long history of residence, deep family connections in the prefecture, and a personal investment in the society at the grassroots level. "Internationalization is occurring at the very basic unit of society, the family," begins a Yamagata University report (Yamagata University Education

Department Planning Committee 1997: i), "and [the migrants'] influence on local society can be said to be more than any other locality in Japan." Young and often adventurous, foreign spouses can bring new energy, life, and ideas to conservative rural communities affected by rural depopulation.

The second reason for selecting Yamagata is the well-developed nature of the support organizations. This is particularly true of NGOs and small volunteer groups in rural areas. The spread and the quality of support organizations, such as the nationally renowned Yamagata Nihongo Nettowâku (Japanese-Language Network), was a big factor in Yamagata City's selection as a model Japanese-teaching locality for the period 1995–1997, ranking it alongside cities like Hamamatsu, which have far greater foreign populations (Yamagata City 1996: 1). With Yamagata as the first prefecture to invite marriage migrants back in 1985, both public and private organizations have an unparalleled level of experience in helping newcomers settle in.

The third reason for choosing Yamagata is the rapid pace of change. As Table 2 showed, the year-on-year percentage increase in the number of foreigners in Yamagata has been much higher than it is nationally. The fact that change is more rapid and therefore more visible in nonmetropolitan areas like Yamagata may be one reason why the regions have been quicker to grasp the realities of life in Japan for foreigners (Miyajima and Kajita 1996b: ii). Machimura (2000: 176) argues that local communities are becoming the frontier of Japan's internationalization and the arena for political debate on the reception of foreign migrants. Similarly, Pak (2000) argues that the autonomy of regional governments in Japan has allowed local or "inward internationalization" (*uchinaru kokusaika*) to flourish.

Together, the three reasons for choosing Yamagata as a research site give the impression of an extremely progressive locality. However, Yamagata should not regarded as some international utopia, welcoming the foreign and understanding the position of newcomers. The widespread acceptance at many levels for international marriage and foreigners conflicts with and contradicts established notions of Japanese identity as a homogenous one based on "blood" (Nakamatsu 2002: 148–153). The subjects' narratives reveal that even close family members tend not to be interested in learning about the foreign. In fact, people in Yamagata are some of the least traveled in the whole of Japan: only 0.05 percent of the population traveled abroad in 2001 compared with 13 percent nationally (Japan Almanac 2002: 252; Yamagata Prefecture 2003). Gender roles remain quite conservative as well. It is not the case, then, that Yamagata offers an environment that welcomes change and thrusts newcomers into proactive roles. Rather it is a place where local agents can be seen operating in a rapidly but reluctantly globalizing environment. As such, Yamagata may offer a microcosm of the situation in Japan as a whole and provide a unique snapshot of the future.

Methodology

A number of scholars of migrants in Japan (Faier 2003; Nakamatsu 2002; Piper 2000; Suzuki 2003) have found international marriage migrants a particularly valuable object of research.[2] Because of their relative visibility and permanence, this segment of the migrant population has contributed greatly to an understanding of the processes of integration and settlement in Japan. In this study, I introduce a segment of interview data gathered during a period of fieldwork in Yamagata from September 2001 to March 2002. While the data as a whole also covered a range of nonmarriage migrants and Japanese, here I focus on marriage migrants who had lived in Japan for a number of years.

Table 3: Biographical Profiles of Interviewees

Name	Ethnicity	Arrived	"Official" role upon arrival	Children	Current visa status	Current work in Japan	Interview duration (mins.)
Jane	Filipino	1982	spouse	2	natur.	Language education group; English teacher at a college	120
Soo-Min	S. Korean	1997	spouse	0	spouse	Language education group	
Huiyung	Chinese	1986	spouse	2	natur.	Language education group	
Meilin	Korean-Chinese	1993	spouse	2	PR	Language education group; court interpreter	
Cindy	Brazilian	1988	trainee	2	spouse	International association	80
Hye-Sook	S. Korean	1990	spouse	3	PR	Japanese language teacher	45
Chin-Ja	S. Korean	1991	spouse	2	PR	Court interpreter; NGO	85

Note: 'natur.' is 'naturalised' and 'PR' is 'permanent resident'. The 'language education group' There was a translation and home teaching service set up by Jane in October 2000 at the local international salon. Jane recruited a number of other foreign-born women in the locality, including Soo-Min, Huiyung, and Meilin. The group provides fee-based services such as home language teaching for students and translation for the local authorities in Chinese, English, Tagalog, and Korean.

The focus is on this small group of settlers because, having acquired linguistic and cultural skills, these individuals were the ones who had the resources to (and the most to say about) change in Japanese society. Interviewees were recruited through two local foreigner-support organizations that I was affiliated with during fieldwork. Apart from the members of the language education group, who were interviewed together, interviews were one-on-one. The ethnic mix roughly reflected that in Yamagata, where, despite enduring stereotypes of the "Filipino bride," two-thirds of foreign residents are Chinese and Korean (Sôma 2003: 162). Respondents had a range of work histories and all except Chin-Ja were university educated. All but Cindy had come to Japan for the specific purpose of marriage.

Data and Discussion

When subjects talked about their engagements in Japanese society, they frequently framed them in terms of how their actions broadened or "internationalized" the consciousness of the Japanese around them. Words like "to contribute" (*kôken suru*), "help" (*tetsudau*), and "educate" (*oshieru*) were common. This sense of making a difference is often portrayed as mutually beneficial: "For Japan to develop more than it has is difficult on its own. China is the biggest economy in Asia—in lots of ways isn't it better to deepen relations? This is good for the sake of Japan too I think. In this respect, if there is something we Chinese can do, then I want to try and do it" (Meilin).

For Meilin, it was her very "Chinese-ness" that allowed her to act as a kind of cultural ambassador, investing in both China and Japan. She seemed to consider the role of what she called "private diplomat" (*minkan-gaikôkan*) important because it is an exclusive role that Japanese cannot perform. Meilin's asking if there is something she (as a Chinese) can do is a rhetorical assertion of agency. The women frequently asserted or confirmed their agency using such "can-do" language. "Is there really nothing I can do?" asked Jane at the beginning of the interview, "I can do something, can't I?" Although not always framed in terms of change, there is a strong recognition amongst many of the women of the need to be proactive—to be an active agent:

> At the beginning, I'd go home and while saying to my husband, "What sort of place did you bring me to?!" [*laughs*] [we'd] argue.... But, look, the people living here don't understand at all, so for me to be angry towards those people would be really stupid, wouldn't it, I thought. Rather the [initiative] from me, "the things you think and your way of thinking is different, you know." From me, even just bit by bit, the feeling of "let's teach [them]." Bit by bit, while being active, discussing/explaining various things.... In the first place, (the initiative) from me, positively (considering) what to do. Pride from back "home" and all that—throw that sort of thing away. [I've/we've] come to this country called "Japan" so let's start from zero. Do this, coming together and talking, one thing at a time, with those around me about whatever history I know and the various experiences I've had. We really enjoy doing that sort of thing. (Soo-Min)

The repetition of "from me" (*watashi no hô kara*) is important as it makes it clear that if she/they don't take the initiative then nothing will happen.

"Even if I'm not invited," says Soo-Min later, "the initiative [should come] from me." Many of the women considered agency—the capacity to act— as central in tackling perceived exclusion. The emphasis on self-help was not only practical. It also replaced conventional stereotypes (passive, pitiable victims who need help) with alternative representations (active agents who can make a contribution). "*We* have to do something," says Hye-Sook, "after all, we are the ones who are in difficulty." Mere presence is not enough. One has to be active, visit local schools, and educate the local populace, especially children:

> Now, I want young children to know more and more. Rather than just [being aware] that there is a Korean or Korean children in the neighbor-hood. What kind of country is Korea? What kind of people are Koreans? ... There is some study of the colonial period [in Japanese schools]. But, in Japanese textbooks, there are only about six lines! This is all that is written. Looking at the Korean [textbook], this much is written, a [text]book this thick! [*Gestures with thumb and finger to show thickness.*] The study of history is that different. ... With a correct understanding of history, feelings can change, can't they? (Chin-Ja)

Chin-Ja notes how the project of creating knowledge, understanding, and recognition (*ninshiki*) is aided by external events. She talks about how the 2002 World Cup saw a surge in interest, which produced an environment increasingly open to things Korean. As mentioned earlier, it is important to recognize that the presence and increasing visibility of migrants in Japan is only part of wider global movements. Nevertheless, it is the individual agents themselves, rooted in local communities, who have the role of exploiting the favorable conditions and taking advantage of the many opportunities presented to engage in what Chin-Ja calls "PR." In turn, the women can act as catalysts in making conditions even more favorable.

The importance placed on being agents is reflected in a strongly imperative vocabulary accompanying talk of action. This comes through clearly in many of the narratives. Soo-Min says she "has to" educate the local populace; Huiyung comments that she "had to" do something after quitting her job; Jane observes that foreigners "have to do" something; and Meilin demands that she "has to be" allowed to teach and rectify misunderstandings. In one short stretch of speech, Hye-Sook comments seven times on the need to change the consciousness of the Japanese. Although these statements carry a strong sense of agency, at the same time the sense of "having to do something" underlines the women's relative lack of power and choice. It is their very lack of resources that motivates them to act to change the status quo.

As Hye-Sook suggests, change is central in understanding what it is the women have to do and why. Agency is not just about doing for the sake of doing. As the capacity to formulate and enact projects within societal constraints it contains the idea of change. This is not transformation through revolution but a "calculated conformity" (Scott 1985)—an acceptance of the need to (appear to) accept certain customs and values—hiding a quiet determination to effect change. Soo-Min epitomized this in her previous statement when she recognized, despite the obvious frustrations, that it would be "stupid" to rail against the people around her. She recognized that "resistance," in the sense of open defiance, insubordination, or confrontation towards dominant power structures that restrain, may not be the best way to further her interests. But lack of resistance does not mean passivity. Jane makes it clear that bitterness and resignation are not options. She says, "it's all over" if you start thinking you hate society and the way things are done in society. On the contrary, genuine change comes through the careful and strategic exercise of agency:

> If (they) can understand (our culture) bit by bit, those people too can come to comprehend, "Ahh—there's this kind of culture as well!" So, bit by bit, on our initiative—if we don't make a move then nobody will move for us, you see. We have to do something—this applies to the language too. We're the ones who have difficulties, so it's us who have to act. Waiting for someone to do something—well, the government and that, they have the attitude that it's "difficult." Towards action, yeah? (Hye-Sook)

Hye-Sook, like Soo-Min earlier, is arguing that if migrants want to sustain and transform their social and cultural universe they can't wait for someone to do something for them. But neither can change be effected immediately:

> Obviously, it's impossible to reform how Japanese people have been thinking up to now in one fell swoop. So, the first step, as foreigners too, is to talk together with Japanese about various things at the sites of daily life. (Meilin)

> Obviously, you can't really, you know, [change] things such as daily customs and manners [that] have flowed through history from way back. The way of thinking has hardened over time, you see, so it's impossible to [change things] overnight. It takes time. (Soo-Min)

> Up until now, [Japanese] have come along without knowing or understanding different cultures. Suddenly, from somewhere, those different cultures are brought in. At first, there is resistance, yes? After once, twice, three times [they] slowly get used to [it]. ... [But] while the door is shut, however much [we] try to get in, we won't be able to get in of course—it's impossible! Therefore, the first step is to internationalize the consciousness [of the Japanese]. (Hye-Sook)

The influence of migrants in instigating gradual change in the consciousness, thinking, and ideas of the Japanese is a manifestation of the kind of symbolic change that can transform systems of representation. As Hye-Sook makes clear, migrants must first "internationalize" the conscious-ness of those around them if they are to be accepted in Japanese society:

> First, what [I] want most is for everyone—those in the cities and in the pre-fecture—their consciousness must change. I think it must change to an in-ternational person's consciousness ... if that happens [society becomes] easy to enter.... Therefore, first that consciousness must change to an inter-national consciousness.... A consciousness that says, "Ahh, from now on [it's] an international society." Everybody, from various countries, has to as-sociate. People from various different countries must get along. The con-sciousness must change, you see. (Hye-Sook)

This kind of change in the consciousness of those close to the migrants can help set the conditions for more concrete change. Change may be slow in coming but for those who have been in Japan for some time, signs of change have begun to emerge. This is a mutual process. The women recog-nize that they have changed, becoming "more Japanese" or Japanese-like. They also recognize that, thanks to their presence, others around them have changed. Chin-Ja tells how her husband's conservative view of human relations changed as he witnessed her success in the local commu-nity using a direct and open style of socializing. One recent arrival related how her husband's stereotype of a "poor" Korea was dispelled over the course of several visits to Korea. In terms of his way of thinking and even clothing she noted a significant change. Similarly, Jane talks about the change in her mother-in-law after visiting the Philippines and experienc-ing its hospitality: "After that [she] slowly changed.... Inside the home, you have to teach about the good points of the Philippines, for the sake of the kid's education too. Thanks to [me], my mother-in-law has gradually become more generous.... She's changed it seems, being around me ... she's become like a Filipino! Probably, it's my influence, isn't it? ... On the other hand, I've become more stingy! [laughs]" (Jane).

Soo-Min interrupts with the comment that this is micro-international-ization—internationalization within the home (*chîsana kokusaika, katei no naka no kokusaika*), a form of internal (*uchi naru*) internationalization. Hye-Sook suggests that this broadening of the worldview of those around them is possible precisely because they are "insiders" living locally. "It is not something that can be done from outside," she argues, "Those of us in the locality are really resources." Similarly, Cindy argues that the changes that are undoubtedly occurring in Japan are more the product of internal rather than external pressures: "Now, even in the center of Japan, it's changing, don't you think? Women, in the center of Japanese society, Japanese women must do this or that, walking three steps behind the men—that's changing. It's not the influence from abroad, but we are changing, [we] are making changes. That's a good thing I think" (Cindy).

In this instance, Cindy seems to be positioning herself not so much as a foreigner but as a woman "in the center of Japanese society" who is both changing and instigating change. Change is not a one-way process but a mutual one. Just as Jane noted the change in her mother-in-law, she also recognized that she herself has become more "stingy" and quieter. Chin-Ja accepts that change is often initially one-sided:

> All countries are cautious (about newcomers).... I think that's the same everywhere, so Japanese people not accepting (us) at first is natural, (I) guess. I have a feeling that basically everyone thinks like that maybe.... My husband's aunts and uncles were cold (towards me at first). Whenever they came over and I offered them food they would just ignore me.... At that time they felt uncomfortable (around me). Inside me, I recognize that this was probably natural. Therefore, (they) couldn't accept me just like that, you see? Now they treat me really well, (those) old people.... Most people will accept you if you make an effort. That's my personal philosophy. (Chin-Ja)

For Chin-Ja, patience with and understanding of the difficulty all people have in accepting outsiders eventually leads to acceptance. Acceptance of difference is itself evidence of a change in consciousness to a more "internationalized" way of thinking. Hye-Sook also accepts the need to be patient and willing to adjust to Japanese norms. However, in contrast to Chin-Ja who stresses "sacrifice" and "reconstruction" as necessary elements of being a newcomer, Hye-Sook emphasizes that the hosts too need to be willing to change:

> We came here, after all, so I think [we] intend to gradually live and adjust. [But] everybody has to change. It's a feeling that everybody has to change. In other words, it's a case [for us] of gradually coming to absorb the customs and habits of Japan. But the [Japanese] people who live here don't [adjust]. At first, [they] resist, I think, because it's unpleasant ... if there's an event or something and you ask them if they want to go they say, "No way—I'm not going." ... Through various [international exchange] events, what is called *tan('itsu) minzoku*[5] [weakens and] multiculturalism is adopted bit by bit. In the future, those [Japanese] people will change. The consciousness will change, won't it? (Hye-Sook)

The presence of permanent migrants in families and communities can sow the seeds of tolerance for other cultures in the minds of those whose lives they touch. Activity carried out by individuals embedded in a social context can be a transforming behavior that changes both self and other. It is not only the women adapting to household practices, local customs, and Japanese culture but family members, neighbors, and Japanese society in general learning from the women:

> Japanese people generally know a lot about America, but concerning countries which are less developed than their own they don't know much. For

that reason—because I'm a foreigner living here—those things they don't know, because there are things Japanese don't know about foreign countries, there are many misunderstandings towards foreigners. In order to get rid of those misunderstandings, here I have to be allowed to teach, I think. Me, as well, I'm here so I'm studying about the good points of Japan too. If this happens, as [we] mutually learn and teach, I think things will get better for both of us. As I said before—I said I wanted to become a bridge between China and Japan—for the sake of Japanese people, for the sake of Chinese people, teaching Chinese people about Japan, teaching Japanese people about China. Not only Japanese, not only Chinese. From that specific and narrow scope, a wider scope. Everybody [is] developing. In the middle of that [I] want to do what I can do, I think. (Meilin)

Hye-Sook reflects on the concrete changes since 1989 that have occurred in her local society in terms of attitudes towards "foreigners." She puts this down partly to her international exchange (*kokusai kôryû*) activities:

[I've] been doing a lot of *kokusai kôryû*, going to various places, talking about Korean dancing, songs, and other things. Because of that, it's become pretty much the norm now.... Being looked at strange—"Ahh, a foreigner!"—[nobody] looks at me like that [now].... [I] don't feel that from the people around me.... It's different [now compared with ten years ago]. In other words, bit by bit I think, yeah, with exchange of our culture as the medium, a lot of people are coming to realize, "Ahh, there's that kind of culture too," or "In Korea they have this fabulous thing." (Hye-Sook)

When I ask her if she still feels like an outsider (*yosomono*), as she described herself on first arriving in Yamagata, she replies that she doesn't feel like that now. When I ask if she has gradually been accepted, she answers as follows:

Yeah. I wouldn't call it accepted. I think [I've] become used to it I guess. Others too have become used to us too. To our culture. We're getting used to Japanese culture as well. I think it's important to become familiar with each other. Consciously getting used to things and unconsciously getting used to things are different. Getting used to things without realizing it is absorption. I personally have been permeated [by the environment.] (Hye-Sook)

Here, Hye-Sook again stresses the importance of mutual accommodation. Accommodation, when it is returned (mutual), is often appraised positively. However, when it is one-sided it is generally appraised negatively. Chin-Ja uses the example of food to illustrate the importance of mutuality:

Inevitably, both parties have to [make an effort]. Recently, selfishness is increasing. [People] think everybody should adapt to them.... [Saying] unreasonable things like, "This is Japan so get used to it."... "I'm Korean so I live the Korean way ... you people are Japanese, live like Japanese please."... For example, preparing dinner. "I'm Korean and can only make Korean food, so everybody please eat Korean"—that kind of thing is distressing. Moreover, mother-in-laws who make nothing but Japanese food, saying to the bride "eat this"—that's distressing too. Therefore, if mother-in-law makes Japanese food, I can make Korean food and we can share.... It's a mutual problem I think ... more effort is needed. (Chin-Ja)

Mutual accommodation of the "let's try each other's food" variety can lead to "externalization" where transformation becomes possible for both parties. This is not to say that change results only from mutual accommodation. The change the women only recognize they have undergone when they go back to the country of origin suggests an unconscious reproduction of Japanese norms and values, as was the case with Jane becoming quieter and more careful with her money. However, as a prominent psychologist (Kuwayama 1995, 1996) in Yamagata has pointed out, imposed or forced accommodation is more likely to produce resentment and mental health problems. For example, I sometimes heard Filipinos describe Christmas and New Year as the saddest time because families often did nothing special to mark this period. As Kuwayama (1993: 151) concludes, mutual accommodation is important in bringing about genuine change.

The acknowledgment that the first step in instigating change has to come from within shows the importance of internal resources. In criticizing other Korean women in her locality who ghettoize themselves and don't attempt to "take the initiative and positively interact," Soo-Min stresses the importance of an outgoing, positive attitude in improving one's position in society. A sense of humor may also be important. In the group interview, the four women have great fun and laughter impersonating Japanese customs such as holding the rice bowl up to the mouth, loudly slurping noodles, or bowing on the telephone, admitting that now they too do these things. This is not to say that migrants do not, at times, refuse to conform. Subjects talked of customs they disliked, of expressing this displeasure to husbands, and arguing with in-laws suggesting the existence of at least a low-level conflict or confrontation. The point is that they recognize that the path of refusal and nonconformity is not the best path to take if they want to improve their lot in society, gain recognition and influence, and begin to set change in motion. At base is the simple desire of those investing their future in Japan to be accepted into Japanese society:

Japanese people have taught me a lot. Conversely, from my side I have something to teach them, too, I think. Bit by bit the world is getting smaller—it's the age where national borders are disappearing. So, which country, which region—it's not a question of that now. It's the twenty-first century! So [we should move towards] opening our hearts, accepting and recognizing everybody: "Ahh, there are different people." ... It's a feeling of wanting people to accept others for what they are, you see? That's what I wish for most. (Soo-Min)

In mobilizing social resources and formulating and enacting projects in society, the potential for both individual and social transformation emerges. Many of the women were very articulate about their long-term goals to transform Japanese society—and transform themselves—while keeping a low accommodating profile. Huiyung suggests that the goal of constructing a society that accepts "foreigners" inevitably requires a reconstruction of the way identities are typically represented in Japan. This kind of comment indicates an understanding of Hall's (1996: 4) point that identities are about mobilizing resources—of history, language, and culture—in the process of becoming.

Conclusion: The Changing Face(s) of Japan

Not all marriage migrants in Japan are potential agents for change. Some spouses assimilate, completely adopting Japanese norms and blending in with the local environment. Others strongly resist assimilation, something that can lead to conflict between Japanese and foreigners. Tsuda (2003) argues that while the influx of foreigners may have disrupted patterns of homogeneity, transnational migration can also maintain and reinforce local ethnic identities and nationalist discourses. The women here, however, seem to adopt a position somewhere between the extremes of assimilation and nonassimilation, a practical strategy of calculated conformity. As Nakamatsu (2002: 202) puts it, becoming an essential member of a receiving family "does not necessarily require complete cultural assimilation." Similarly, becoming literate in the language and culture of the host society does not necessarily imply unilateral assimilation (Allendoerfer 1999; Suzuki 2002: 115).

Because the data focused on the ways a complex and diverse number of subjects talked about engagements with their own identity and with society, it is not clear exactly how their presence and actions will change (or have changed) Japanese people and national identity. Further research, using interviews with those Japanese touched by the presence of migrants, would paint a more complete picture of the kind of symbolic changes that are argued to be taking place. In this sense, the conclusion to be drawn is that migrants are talking like people who might be agents for change— that is, potential agents of multiculturalism—without going so far as to say that they are agents of change.

The shifts in systems of representation the narratives suggest are occurring under the surface today are likely creating conditions ripe for change that will enable future newcomers to have a louder voice in determining how Japanese society might evolve in the coming years. The main purpose of this chapter has been to shed light on these important but largely invisible processes occurring in Japanese society at the local level. The chapters in this volume all argue that there are already signs of dramatic changes in the nature of these Japanese and non-Japanese boundaries within Japan. While it is too early to claim, as some have (see Douglass and Roberts 2000a), that the multicultural age has already come to Japan, it is possible to say, as Yamanaka (2002: 2–22) does, that "Japan stands at the crossroads of becoming a multicultural society … the dawn of becoming a multi-ethnic society." As such, it is future events—perhaps a rapid and sudden explosion of very overt change—that will determine whether the arguments for a "new Japan" stand or fall. In this sense, the work here is not an end but a starting point for further research.

Notes

This chapter is adapted from a larger work (Burgess 2003). I would like to acknowledge the support received from the Monash University Postgraduate Publications Award in the preparation of the manuscript.

1. It is interesting to note that, outside of academia, the term *imin* (migrant) is rarely used to describe those recent arrivals to Japan. As Douglass and Roberts (2000b: 8) observe, foreigners coming to Japan are not "[im]migrants" but "entrants" (temporary residents). The emphasis on entrants reflects the dominant official position that Japan has neither minorities nor migrants and is not (and has no intention of becoming) a migrant society. Pak (1998:140–142) calls this position the "no immigration principle," an institutionalization of the *tan'itsu minzoku* (homogeneous people) idiom that underlies the state system for controlling foreigners.
2. Figures for "international marriages"—what Kamoto (2003) describes as an "original Japanese concept"—include marriages involving a non-Japanese who was born and brought up in Japan but has not naturalized. Although such marriages are technically "international," they do not involve migration. Consequently, I adopt the narrower term "international marriage migration" (IMM) to exclude such cases. IMM is used to mean the marriage of a Japanese with a non-Japanese (although either party may at a later date change their nationality), the "non-Japanese" someone who was not born and brought up in Japan. IMM includes both those who come to Japan for the specific purpose of marriage and those who come for different reasons and end up marrying.
3. The organizations were the Association for International Relations in Yamagata (AIRY), a prefectural government body (http://www.jan.ne.jp/~airy/), and the International Volunteer Centre Yamagata (IVY), a private nonprofit organization (http://www.dewa.or.jp/IVYama).
4. As defined in the first end note, the term means "homogeneous people." It features in those discussions of Japanese uniqueness (*Nihonjinron*) that portray Japan as a mono-ethnic nation (*tan'itsu minzoku kokka*).

References

Allendoerfer, Cheryl Margaret. 1999. "Creating a 'Vietnamerican' Discourse: Ethnic Identity Construction in the English-as-a-Second-Language Classroom." Ph.D diss., University of Wisconsin, Madison.

Appadurai, Arjun. 2001. "Grassroots Globalization and the Research Imagination." In *Globalization,* ed. Arjun Appadurai, 1–21. Durham, NC: Duke University Press.

Asahi Shimbun. 2002. "Kokusai Kekkon Futatabi Kyûzô Chû" [International marriage once again in the middle of a steep increase]. February 28.

Burgess, Chris. 2003. "(Re)Constructing Identities: International Marriage Migrants as Potential Agents of Social Change in a Globalising Japan." Ph.D. diss., Monash University, Melbourne.

Ching, Leo. 2001. "Globalizing the Regional, Regionalizing the Global: Mass Culture and Asianism in the Age of Late Capital." In *Globalization,* ed. Arjun Appadurai, 279–306. Durham, NC: Duke University Press.

Data Book of Japan. 1995. *IMIDAS Data Book of Japan.* Tokyo: Henei-sha.

Douglass, Mike, and Glenda S. Roberts, eds. 2000a. *Japan and Global Migration: Foreign Workers and the Advent of a Multicultural Society.* London: Routledge.

Douglass, Mike and Glenda S. Roberts. 2000b. "Japan in a Global Age of Migration." pp. 3–37, in *Japan and Global Migration: Foreign Workers and the Advent of a Multicultural Society,* eds. Mike Douglass and Glenda S. Roberts, London: Routledge.

Faier, Lieba. 2003. "On Being Oyomesan: Filipina Migrants and Their Japanese Families in Central Kiso." Ph.D. diss., University of California, Santa Cruz.

Hall, Stuart. 1996. "Introduction: Who Needs Identity?" In *Questions of Cultural Identity,* ed. Stuart Hall and Paul Du Gay, 1–17. London: Sage Publications.

Harzig, Christiane. 2001. "Women Migrants as Global and Local Agents: New Research Strategies on Gender and Migration." In *Women, Gender, and Labor Migration: Historical and Global Perspectives,* ed. Pamela Sharpe, 15–28. London: Routledge.

Hirano, Kenichiro, Stephen Castles, and Patrick Brownlee. 2000. "Towards a Sociology of Asian Migration and Settlement: Focus on Japan." *Asian and Pacific Migration Journal* 9 (3): 243–253.

Ikegami, Shigehiro, ed. 2001. *Burajiru-jin to Kokusai-ka suru Chiiki Shakai: Kyôiku, Iryô* [Brazilians and Internationalizing Communities: Housing, Education, Medicine]. Tokyo: Akashi Shoten.

Ishii, Yuka. 2003. "Imin no Kyojyû to Seikatsu: Genjyô to Tenbô" [Migrant living and lifestyle: The current situation and future prospects]. In

Imin no Kyojyû to Seikatsu [Migrant living and lifestyle], ed. Yuka Ishii, 1–22. Tokyo: Akashi Shoten.

Japan Almanac 1998. 1999. Tokyo: Asahi Shimbun Publishing Company.

Japan Almanac 2001. 2002. Tokyo: Asahi Shimbun Publishing Company.

Japan Almanac 2002. 2003. Tokyo: Asahi Shimbun Publishing Company.

Kamoto, Itsuko. 2003. "Kokusai Kekkon in Late 19th Century Japan." Presented at Japanese Studies Association of Australia 13th Biennial Conference, Brisbane.

Kawakami, Ikuo. 2001. *Ekkyô Suru Kazoku - Zainichi Betonamukei Jyûmin no Seikatsu Sekai* [Families crossing borders: The life-world of Vietnamese residents]. Tokyo: Akashi Shoten.

Komai, Hiroshi. 1995. *Teijyûka Suru Gaikokujin* [Foreigners settling down]. Tokyo: Akashi Shoten.

———. 2000. "Immigrants in Japan." *Asian and Pacific Migration Journal* 9 (3): 311–326.

———. 2001. *Foreign Migrants in Contemporary Japan*. Trans. Jens Wilkinson. Melbourne: Pacific Press.

Kuwayama, Norihiko. 1993. "Yamagata-ken Zaijyû no Gaikokujin Hanayome to Nihonjin Kazoku" [Foreign brides who live in Yamagata Prefecture and their Japanese families]. *Japanese Journal of Clinical Psychology* 22: 145–151.

———. 1995. *Kokusai Kekkon to Sutoresu* [International marriage and stress]. Tokyo: Akashi Shoten.

———. 1996. "Borantia no Shiten—Seishinkai no Tachiba Kara" [The volunteers' point of view: From the standpoint of a psychiatrist]. In *Kokunai no Nihongo Kyôiku Nettowākuzukuri ni Kansuru Chôsa Kenkyû: Chûkan Hôkokusho* [Survey research regarding the construction of Japanese language networks in Japan: Midterm report], ed. Nihongo Kyôiku Gakkai, 107–143. Tokyo: Nihongo Kyôiku Gakkai (Nettowāku Chôsa Kenkyû Iinkai).

Lie, John. 2001. *Multiethnic Japan*. Cambridge, MA: Harvard University Press.

Machimura, Takashi. 2000. "Local Settlement Patterns of Foreign Workers in Greater Tokyo." In *Japan and Global Migration: Foreign Workers and the Advent of a Multicultural Society*, ed. Mike Douglass and Glenda Roberts, 176–195. London and New York: Routledge.

Mato, Daniel. 1997. "On Global and Local Agents and the Social Making of Transnational Identities and Related Agendas in 'Latin' America." *Identities* 4 (2): 167–212.

Miyajima, Takashi, and Takamichi Kajita, eds. 1996a. *Gaikokurôdôsha Kara Shimin e: Chiiki Shakai no Shiten to Kadai kara* [From foreign workers to citizens: From the perspective of local society]. Tokyo: Yûhikaku.

Miyajima, Takashi and Takamichi Kajita. 1996b. "Hashigaki (Preface)," pp. i–v in *Gaikokurôdôsha Kara Shimin e: Chiiki Shakai no Shiten to Kadai kara* [From Foreign Workers to Citizens: From the Perspective of Local Society,] eds. Takashi Miyajima and Takamichi Kajita. Tokyo: Yûhikaku.

Nakamatsu, Tomoko. 2002. "Marriage, Migration, and the International Marriage Business in Japan." Ph.D. diss., Murdoch University.

Pak, Katherine Tegtmeyer. 1998. "Outsiders Moving In: Identity and Institutions in Japanese Responses to International Migration." Ph.D. diss., University of Chicago.

———. 2000. "Foreigners Are Local Citizens Too: Local Governments Respond to International Migration in Japan." In *Japan and Global Migration: Foreign Workers and the Advent of a Multicultural Society,* ed. Mike Douglass and Glenda Susan Roberts, 243–274. London: Routledge.

Piper, Nicola. 2000. "Globalization, Gender, and Migration: the Case of International Marriage in Japan." In *Towards a Gendered Political Economy,* ed. Joanne Cook, Jennifer Roberts, and Georgina Waylen, 205–225. London: Macmillan Press Ltd.

Piper, Nicola, and Mina Roces, eds. 2003. *Wife or Worker? Asian Women and Migration.* Boulder, CO: Rowman and Littlefield.

Rathzel, Nora. 1995. "Images of Heimat and Images of 'Auslander'." In *Negotiating Identities,* ed. Aleksandra Alund and Raoul Granqvist, 45–70. Amsterdam: Rodopi.

Sassen, Saskia. 1994. "Economic Internationalization: The New Migration in Japan and the United States." *Social Justice* 21 (2): 62–81.

Scott, James C. 1985. *Weapons of the Weak.* New Haven: Yale University Press.

Sellek, Yoko. 1997. "Nikkeijin: The Phenomena of Return Migration." In *Japan's Minorities: The Illusion of Homogeneity,* ed. Michael Weiner, 178–210. London: Routledge.

Shimizu, Kokichi, and Shimizu, Mutsumi. 2001. *Nyûkama? to Kyôiku: Gakkô Bunka to Esunishiti no Kattô wo Megutte* [Newcomers and education: On the conflict between school culture and ethnicity]. Tokyo: Akashi Shoten.

Shukuya, Kyôko. 1988. *Ajia kara Kita Hanayome Mukaeru Gawa no Ronri* [The logic of those inviting the brides from Asia]. Tokyo: Akashi Shoten.

Sôma, Kenichi. 2003. *Yamagata-ken Nenkan 2003* [Yamagata Prefecture yearbook 2003]. Yamagata: Yamagata Shimbun-sha.

Suzuki, Nobue. 2000. "Women Imagined, Women Imaging: Re/presentations of Filipinas in Japan since the 1980s." *US-Japan Women's Journal English Supplement* 19: 142–175.

Suzuki, Nobue. 2002. "Gendered Surveillance and Sexual Violence of Filipina Pre-migration Experiences to Japan." In *Gender Politics in the Asia-Pacific Region*, ed. Brenda Yeoh, Peggy Teo, and Shirlena Huang, 99–119. London: Routledge.

Suzuki, Nobue. 2003. "Battlefields of Affection: Gender, Global Desires, and the Politics of Intimacy in Filipina-Japanese Transnational Marriages." Ph.D. diss., University of Hawaii.

Tamanoi, Mariko Asano. 1998. *Under the Shadow of Nationalism: Politics and Poetics of Rural Japanese Women.* Honolulu: University of Hawaii Press.

Tôkei Kyôkai, Yamagata-ken. 2003. *Yamagata Kenmin Techô* [Yamagata citizen's handbook]. Yamagata: Yamagata-ken Tôkei Kyôkai [Yamagata-Prefecture Data Association].

Tsuda, Takeyuki. 2003. *Strangers in Their Ethnic Homeland: Japanese Brazilian Return Migration in Transnational Perspective.* New York: Columbia University Press.

Weiner, Myron, and Tadashi Hanami, eds. 1998. *Temporary Workers or Future Citizens? Japanese and U. S. Migration Policies.* New York: New York University Press.

Yamagata City. 1996. *Yamagata Chiiki Zaijyû Gaikokujin Seikatsu Jyôkyô Chôsa Hôkokusho* [Report on the conditions of resident foreigners in the local regions of yamagata]. Yamagata: Yamagata-shi Chiiki Nihongo Kyôiku Suishin Iinkai [Yamagata City Council for the Promotion of Local Japanese Education].

Yamagata Prefecture. 2001. *Tôkei Kara Mita Yamagata-ken no Sugata* [The shape of Yamagata Prefecture through statistics]. Yamagata: Yamagata-ken Kikaku Chôsei Bu Tôkei Chôsa Ka [Yamagata Prefecture Planning and Regulation Department, Data Investigation Section].

———. 2003. *Tôkei Kara Mita Yamagata-ken no Sugata* [The shape of Yamagata Prefecture through statistics]. Yamagata: Yamagata-ken Kikaku Chôsei Bu Tôkei Chôsa Ka [Yamagata-Prefecture Planning and Regulation Department, Data Investigation Section].

Yamagata University Education Department Planning Committee, ed. 1997. "Introduction." In *Rikai Kara Kôzô e: Yamagata no Kokusaika to Ibunkakan Kyôiku* [From understanding to structure: Yamagata internationalization and intercultural education), ed. Yamagata University Education Department Planning Committee. Yamagata: Yamagata University Education Department Planning Committee; Yamagata Regional "Recurrent" Council for the Promotion of Education.

Yamanaka, Keiko. 2002. "Transnational Activities for Local Survival: A Community of Nepalese Visa-Overstayers in Japan." Presented at the Annual Meeting of the American Sociological Association, August 16–19, Chicago, IL.

4

INTERNATIONAL PERIPHERIES: INSTITUTIONAL AND PERSONAL ENGAGEMENTS WITH JAPAN'S *KOKUSAIKA* MOVEMENT

John Ertl

Introduction

THIS CHAPTER EXAMINES THE THEME of multiculturalism in Japan through the example of Ishikawa Prefecture and the provincial town of Rokusei,[1] a community with only a score of foreign residents. Located in the Noto Peninsula in northern Ishikawa, Rokusei is a small textiles community rich in "traditional" culture, kinship, religion, and folkways, and as such it may seem an unusual candidate for examining this issue. However, as a "typical" township it offers insights as to how and why multiculturalism is brought about in a place that is seemingly homogeneous in terms of its culture and ethnicity. The term "multiculturalism" is not used here as a descriptive condition in which people of diverse ethnic, linguistic, and national backgrounds live together and influence each other, but rather as an ideology that shapes the worldview and actions of the civic body, including public policy. Taking multiculturalism as an ideology that emphasizes the unique characteristics of different cultures and encourages mutual respect, tolerance, and recognition of such difference, its practical manifestations include indigenous or minority rights movements, cultural revivals, and the formation of civic groups aimed at supporting these movements. This essay examines a range of these groups and institutions that, spawned out of the ideals of multiculturalism, are designed to form connections with "foreign" cultures and people. These institutions are only partially meant to create an internationally minded civic body or form peaceful coexistence with foreign residents, as they are also aimed at build-

---

Endnotes for this chapter begin on page 96.

ing strong local (municipal and prefectural) identities through select and carefully directed international exchanges.

Today in Japan there are over five thousand registered nonprofit organizations (NPOs) that participate in "international cooperation" (*kokusai kyôryoku*) activities,[2] with many other informal groups that have no recognized status. While several of these institutions are national or global in scale, such as the Buraku Liberation League (Neary 1997) and the Worldwide Uchinanchu Conference (Ueunten n.d.), the large majority of "international" organizations are geographically limited to the prefecture or municipality of residence.[3] One segment of these groups is formed "top-down" by government authorities and includes the prefectural and large municipal "international associations" (*kokusai kôryû kyôkai*), formed at the behest of the Ministry of Internal Affairs and Communications (*sômushô*), that conduct services (language, legal, and residency) for foreign residents. This approach contrasts with most small-scale, municipal-based internationalization groups, which are founded from personal desires to increase interactions with an international population or are initiated by the community to address very specific "problems" relating to foreign residents.

Set along the Japan Sea, Ishikawa Prefecture is relatively isolated from the economic growth and transnational flows of people and goods that can be found in the metropolitan areas along the Pacific coast of Japan. This is reflected in the proportion of registered foreign residents in Ishikawa, which at 0.5 percent of total population (6,321 total) in 2000 was comparatively lower than the major metropolitan areas of Tokyo (1.8 percent), Osaka (1.9 percent), and Aichi Prefecture (1.5 percent). Despite these low numbers of foreign residents, Ishikawa and its constituent municipalities are engaged in many internationalization activities ranging from prefecture-run assistance programs to sister-city programs, business exchange enterprises, foreign student homestays, multinational scholarly cooperative projects, and community-based friendship associations. This chapter introduces several international outreach activities within Ishikawa Prefecture focusing on how such projects are generally set within broader place-making enterprises that attempt to naturalize the municipality and prefecture as distinct "cultural" entities (e.g., Bailey 1991). From this perspective, these internationalization projects are parallel in intent to the *furusato-zukuri* (hometown building) projects of the late 1980s and early 1990s (Ivy 1995; Knight 1994; Robertson 1991) and the ongoing decentralization drive (Kitagawa 2001; Rozman 1999) that aims at creating a nation of culturally unique and administratively independent localities.

Rokusei Town, located approximately eighty kilometers north of Ishikawa's capital city Kanazawa, offers an up-close investigation of how these organizations operate "on the ground." Unlike many urban centers, Rokusei has been isolated from foreign immigration and attempts to stimulate the economy through international business ventures and tourism.

Their involvement with multiculturalism has been limited largely to the realm of concerted internationalization (*kokusaika*) projects that "import" foreigners. In 2002, Rokusei took part in a summer internship program for graduate students arranged through the Japan Local Government Center (JLGC), New York office, which places advanced students at a municipal office where they conduct research on some aspect of Japanese local government. I was introduced to Rokusei through this program and for the town administration it was the first time they had hired and worked with a foreign employee. The effect of this program was threefold: it furthered international education initiatives in foreign language and cultural studies; it introduced Rokusei to the outside world through the research I conducted; and it stimulated local residents to think about and reinterpret their culture through their dialogic exchanges with an outsider. In this light, I argue that multiculturalism should be examined foremost as a local or personal issue, rather than a problem of national-ethnic relations, as encounters with foreign "others" take place between individuals in specific contexts.

Manifestations of Multiculturalism in Japanese Public Policy

The politics and policies of multiculturalism take a different shape in Japan than in other parts of the world. This is due largely to the fact that Japan's renegotiation with its own diversity and its interactions with the world came about out of foreign pressure (*gaiatsu*) from the early 1980s, rather than any form of radical movements within the nation. One set of critics from the political and business world claimed that Japan had become an economic superpower on the backs of the international community, failing to adequately participate in world politics or open its markets to the nations that enabled Japan's success (Van Wolferen 1989). Another form of pressure came out of the Western social sciences, with the critique of the production of scholarly and popular texts on "Japanese national character," ubiquitously called *Nihonjinron*, which are based upon the assumptions of "Japanese uniqueness" and ethnic homogeneity (Befu 1983; Dale 1986; Mouer and Sugimoto 1986; Yoshino 1992). Japan's response to the calls to become a more active international political and economic partner was the adoption of *kokusaika* (internationalization) as national public policy, with the aim of gaining acceptance into the international community by opening the nation to the global economy and showing tolerance and receptiveness to that which is foreign (Soroos 1988: 19). The basis for including internationalization in cultural policy also included the belief that part of the distinctiveness of Japanese society is the way it has continually adopted, transformed, and meshed with foreign culture and traditions (Watanabe 1999: 104).

On the other hand, the recognition of Japan's internal diversity has been slow to develop. Japan continued to declare to the United Nations as late as 1980 that it had no minority populations, and with the case of the Ainu it was only after local leaders began participating in international forums for indigenous rights that Japan began to seriously consider granting them recognition as such (Siddle 1997). Scholarship, public interest, and activism regarding foreign immigrants to Japan has flourished since the 1995 Hanshin earthquake that brought local Japanese and foreign residents together in communal struggle (Takezawa, chapter 1). In 2004, an exceptional exhibit at the National Museum of Ethnology (*Minpaku*) in Osaka on Japanese multiculturalism featured many locally initiated projects that recognize the concerns of international residents, including programs that address health issues of foreign workers and illegal immigrants, provide differential education for ethnic minority populations, and encourage interaction between international and Japanese residents through community classes, foreign language radio programs, and festivals (Shôji 2004).

Multiculturalism in Japan takes form as public policy primarily through the dual projects of internationalization (*kokusaika*) and decentralization (*chihô-bunken*). At a glance, these two movements appear to move in opposite directions, with the first leading towards openness and increased interactions with the outside world and the second oriented inwards, to protect and strengthen the constituent parts of the nation. But together these movements form a pair of responses to the critiques of Japan's long-standing myth of homogeneity by showing that Japan is ever increasingly international, that is, open to foreign peoples and ideas while at the same time emphasizing and building upon the internal diversity that exists between regions in Japan. Furthermore, in the context of municipal planning initiatives, distinctions between these two movements are blurred as many internationalization efforts are aimed more at revitalizing local society than creating a cosmopolitan citizenry, and efforts aimed at increasing autonomy or creating unique tourist attractions often mimic foreign examples or depend upon international investment and recognition.

Both movements have a long history in the postwar era, but the contemporary shape of these movements and their relation to multiculturalism took form during Nakasone Yasuhiro's tenure as prime minister (1982–1987).[4] During Nakasone's administration he developed four major initiatives to change Japan's image and relationship with the world (Pyle 1987). The first was based on the idea that since Japan had "caught up" economically and began to surpass the rest of the world it needed to change roles from follower to world leader, particularly by demonstrating to Asian nations how industrialization and capitalism can improve the quality of life (Witteveen 2004: 36). Second was his determination to become active in global strategic affairs, which included a call to increase defense spending past the 1 percent barrier. The third dimension was to turn Japan into an "international state" by reforming its institutions to meet global expectations, with a particular emphasis on educational reforms. The fourth aim was to form a new liberal or "cosmopolitan" nationalism, arguing for "an appreciation of Japan's special strengths and abilities within an international framework that combined national pride with appreciation for the cultures and traditions of other nations" (Pyle 1987: 261). One of the key ideas behind this was that in order to become more "international" it was necessary for Japanese to become more educated about the positive aspects of their history and culture.[5] A relative of this drive was Nakasone's 1984 "Proposal for Furusato Japan" (*Nippon rettô furusato ron*), which adopted the idea of *furusato-zukuri* (hometown building) as a means to revitalize and reaffirm "native" and "traditional" elements of local and regional cultures (Robertson 1991: 26).

In terms of identity politics, internationalization and decentralization share a homologous structure, where the former reorders the relationship between Japan and other nations, and the latter redefines the relationship between center and periphery (city and countryside) within Japan. The narratives of Japanese homogeneity are opened for questioning as the national population becomes increasingly multinational through immigration (Douglass and Roberts 2000), and Japanese people increasingly live and work overseas (Goodman 2003). The global spread of mass media and popular culture has created a growing cultural complexity for majority and minority populations alike as they are consumed and refashioned based upon individual tastes or local culture (Allison 2006; Appadurai 1996; Mathews 2000). Japanese cultural identity has become mixed through diverse regional and municipal place-making strategies that may stress the exotic or foreign cultures of the countryside (Ivy 1995) or build upon a particular historical and contemporary multiethnic or international heritage (Guo et al. 2005). The boundaries of these diverse Japanese identities are primarily based on state-sanctioned precincts (the municipality or prefecture) but such identity construction can also be taken up by regions, neighborhoods, or even by civic interest groups with no territorial basis (Robertson 1999).

The Worldly Province:
Internationalization Projects in Ishikawa Prefecture

The drive to become more "international" has become a central element of the development and promotional activities of Ishikawa Prefecture and its municipalities. The rhetoric in support of international outreach clearly reflects multicultural ideals such as hosting goodwill exchanges with foreign countries, supporting immigrants, contributing to world peace, and advancing the international outlook of residents. Behind the rhetoric, however, are very powerful political and economic objectives aimed at changing the image of Ishikawa from that of a backwards and remote prefecture to that of a progressive and world-renowned center of both traditional and cosmopolitan culture. This posturing is directed on two fronts: towards foreign ambassadors, economic leaders, and tourists; and at central government politicians and officials in Tokyo. By increasing international relationships between the prefecture and foreign provinces, leaders in Ishikawa hope to inspire further international tourism and industrial cooperative projects, and by establishing such relationships bolster their petitions to Tokyo to invest in their economy and infrastructure as would be appropriate for an "international" region. The process of shaping Ishikawa into an international prefecture, spearheaded by a campaign to turn its capital city Kanazawa into a "world city," involves both concrete steps to increase political, corporate, and cultural exchanges as well as the construction of fantastic or imaginary narratives, albeit based on scientific inquiry and historical reconstruction, that reinforce and authenticate their claims to internationalism.

In September 1984, local authorities in Ishikawa organized a three-day conference called the Kanazawa Pan-Japan Sea International Symposium, to which several dozen scholars from Japan, Korea, China, the Soviet Union, and the United States were invited to discuss the historical, economic, and cultural features that link the coastal regions of the Japan Sea. The symposium committee consisted primarily of scholars from across Japan, and its directors were political and economic leaders such as the governor of Ishikawa, the mayor of Kanazawa, the president of the Kanazawa Chamber of Commerce, and the director of the Hokuriku Economic Research Council. Thus, underpinning the ideals of improving mutual understanding and building peaceful relations was a clear economic motivation to form the Japan Sea region into an economic cooperative zone. Under the theme "Urban Culture and Cultural Exchange in the Japan Sea Coastal Regions," the conference largely consisted of historical, literary, and archeological studies of early exchange between Japan and its coastal neighbors. The apparent aim was to form a comprehensive narrative that explains the interrelated history and cultural heritage of the Japan Sea coastal region, and to create a new genre of area studies that bypasses present-day national barriers. By forming a research field on the culture of the Japan Sea region, these scholars effectively naturalized and reified the region as a distinct cultural entity that deserves be studied and fostered.

The development of the Japan Sea coastal research grew substantially in 1994 with the establishment of a regional studies group called the Association for Japan Sea Rim Studies and a publicly sponsored foundation called the Economic Research Institute for Northeast Asia (ERINA) in 1993. Research projects conducted by ERINA, which are commonly contracted by prefectural or city governments along the Japan Sea coast, often examine the possible impacts and benefits of cooperative economic ventures. However, most of the locally initiated endeavors by Ishikawa and other prefectures to create Japan Sea coastal trade and corporate partnerships throughout the 1990s met with little success in terms of actual economic growth, largely due to the lack of investment by Tokyo and continuing political tensions between East and Northeast Asian nations. Thus, despite ongoing diplomatic and cultural exchanges between Japan Sea coastal cities and regions, they are unable to resolve international political tensions or investment issues on their own, and therefore are limited to efforts to build trust and interpersonal solidarity as a precursor for economic ties that may evolve in the future (Rozman 1999: 29).

The promotion of international cultural tourism has been an effective means of both forming human relations and feeding the economy in Ishikawa, especially in Kanazawa City, which has popularized its traditional heritage through the production of large-scale festivals and clear tourism circuits. To turn Kanazawa into a world city and global tourist destination, community leaders have engaged in a number of enterprises to make the city friendlier and more accessible to foreigners, increase the numbers of foreign residents (including international students of Japanese and foreign language teachers), and garner international prestige for the city through diplomatic envoys and petitioning for global recognition of their heritage. As may be expected, these initiatives include the production of foreign language living guides, city signs, and travel brochures, as well as the provision of translation services. They have built a number of international business and cultural convention centers and established guest facilities for foreign travelers. One of the main hurdles has been building a suitable transportation infrastructure for international trade and travels, which involves building new highways, extending the bullet train line (*shinkansen*) to Kanazawa, and increasing international flights through Komatsu Airport. Rather than seeking to attract international visitors solely via Tokyo or Osaka, Ishikawa has invested in establishing direct routes and chartered flights to several foreign cities.

A series of charter flights was arranged between Ishikawa and Taipei following the production of a Taiwanese television series based upon the life of Kanazawa native Hatta Yoichi (1886–1942), who is renowned as the "father of modern agriculture" in Taiwan due to his leadership in building the Wushantou (Coral Lake) Dam and irrigation project finished in 1930.[6] While considered the greatest Japanese figure in the modern history of Taiwan, Hatta is relatively unknown in Japan, even in his hometown of Kanazawa. Local interest in Japan-Taiwan relations was stirred when former Taiwan President Lee Teng-hui visited Kanazawa in December 2004 to visit the opening of a display on Hatta at the Great People of Kanazawa Memorial Museum (Kanazawa-shiritsu furusato ijinkan). Even though Lee came as a "private citizen," on condition that he would make no public speeches or meet with politicians, this visit further damaged the already troubled relations between China and Japan—leading China to remove Japan from the list of candidates to build their new high-speed rail line. China viewed Lee's visit as an attempt to garner Japanese support for Taiwanese political independence, but in fact his trip was more immediately aimed at furthering local trade and interpersonal relations. Where the television drama on Hatta had spurred tourism to Kanazawa, this visit was used to raise local interest in Taiwan by bringing attention to the "positive" relations formed out of Hatta's devotion to the country. Charter flights between Taipei and Komatsu continued after his trip and to reassert the relationships formed by his visit, a delegation from the Ishikawa Prefecture Assembly traveled to Taiwan in January 2006 to meet with Lee Teng-hui.

The earliest form of local internationalization activities in Japan were sister-city programs, the oldest of which is the arrangement between the cities of Nagasaki and St. Paul, Minnesota, dating back to 1955 (Muto 1996: 79–80). In 2004 Ishikawa Prefecture had 11 municipalities with a combined total of twenty-four official sister-city relationships from 11 different countries, along with several other unofficial arrangements (Ishikawa Foundation for International Exchange 2004). These relationships generally form out of historical interactions between influential individuals or because of some perceived similarities between the culture, economy, or climate of the cities. An example of this is the relationship between Unoke Town (recently merged into Kahoku City) and Messkirch, Germany, which developed out of their histories as the respective hometowns of philosophical greats Nishida Kitaro and Martin Heidegger (Okamoto 1992: 171–186). Another example is the city of Nanao, which started a sister-city relationship with Monterey, California because of their similar bay area environments. The first exchanges took place in 1986 after trips by Nanao officials looking to build a Fisherman's Warf modeled on the one in Monterey. Nanao City has since developed tourism activities that mirror those of Monterey, including their own version of the Monterey Jazz Festival. There has even been an influence in the area of social services, as the Noto Public Hospital (kôritsu Noto sôgô byôin) was rebuilt in 2000 based on designs, facilities, and patient care techniques from a Monterey area hospital.

The Pressures and Pleasures of Internationalization in Rokusei Town

Rokusei is a small township in the lower Noto Peninsula approximately eighty kilometers north of Kanazawa. It is located along a long valley region called Ôchi-gata, which in the past was a shallow freshwater lagoon that has since been fully reclaimed to make rice fields. This topography made the area surrounding Rokusei one of the earliest rice agricultural areas in the Noto Peninsula, evidenced by many archaeological sites dating from the Yayoi era (300 B.C. to A.D. 200). The constituent villages (*buraku*) of Rokusei, however, share only a narrow stretch of this fertile land and only a few families in the recent past have depended solely on farming income.

In modern times the major industry in Rokusei has been textiles, beginning with a light linen product called *noto-jôfu* from the 1870s and switching to plain cotton fabric in the 1950s. During the peak of production, nearly all families had either their own small-scale factory or family members who worked for a larger company. With the textiles industry shifting to mainland Asia from the 1980s, the economy of Rokusei has taken a decided turn for the worse as people scramble to find niche textiles markets or abandon their factories to pick up manufacturing or service industry jobs. Despite the recent downturn, Rokusei is comparatively fortunate as its strong economy in the postwar years allowed the town and its traditional folkways to persist and flourish while neighboring communities dwindled.

In this light, the motivation for Rokusei Town to engage in internationalization as a public project has been quite different than that of Kanazawa, whose leaders have tried to build an economy based on cooperative business endeavors and global tourism. In Rokusei there are only a few international business undertakings. One was started by the owner of the largest textiles company in town, who opened a factory outside of Shanghai and set up a training program to bring young female employees to work in his Rokusei factory for a period of six months or one year. These girls, who can be seen riding bikes around town, make up around half of the foreign population in Rokusei at any one time (eight to ten in number); the other half consist mostly of "foreign brides" from China and the Philippines.[7] In Rokusei Town there is one international civic group called the Rokusei Town Japan-Brazil Goodwill Exchange Association (Rokusei-Machi Nichihaku shinzen kôryû kai), which formed in the late 1980s and continued to be active until the late 1990s. The group formed out of the desire to continue personal friendships between Rokusei residents and Brazilians from Jacarei, Sao Paulo, who are *Nikkei* (of Japanese descent) and who originate from Rokusei. Several families left for Brazil in the early 1900s and, despite the separation, managed to continue relationships with their natal villages, notably by seeking brides from the homeland or by bringing their children back to Japan for schooling. The founders of this association were classmates of one such "returnee," who attended elementary school in Rokusei (then called Notobe Town) during the Second World War, following which he went back to his family in Brazil. The most ambitious activity the group arranged was a goodwill kendo tournament held in Jacarei in 1993, where eleven Rokusei residents assisted with the organization and judging, and in the process rekindled old friendships and were introduced to distant relations.

Internationalization projects in Rokusei have been rather subdued and comparatively late in coming despite regular participation by residents in overseas travel, international volunteer and aid projects, and student exchanges organized by prefectural associations and other municipalities.

For the Rokusei Town administration, their involvement with internationalization has been less about stimulating the economy or responding to changing demographics than it has been a response to national demands to establish a *kokusaika* program and prefecture and municipal (peer) pressures to participate in various initiatives. One such program is Japan Tent, run through an NPO called Japan Tent Network, which since 1988 has brought approximately 350 foreign students (*ryūgakusei*) living in Japan each year to Ishikawa for a weeklong program that includes a two-night "homestay" in one of the 41 municipalities.[8] The program is the brainchild of the president of the Hokkoku Newspaper Company, the largest newspaper company in Ishikawa, and is enabled due to large public and corporate sponsorship. Each municipality is not required by the prefecture to participate in the program, but with the Governor of Ishikawa sitting as the president (*sōsai*) of the organizing committee it is impossible to decline the invitation. Rokusei has hosted three or four students each year of the program at a cost of several thousand dollars to the town. One family that has acted as host family multiple times has developed long-lasting personal relationships with several of the students, even attending the wedding of one student in Indonesia several years after the student stayed with them in Rokusei.

This motivation for the town administration to "keep up" with expectations was behind the project that brought me to Rokusei during the summer of 2002. Rokusei Town hired me through a program administered by the Japan Local Government Center (JLGC) located in New York. JLGC is the overseas branch of the Council of Local Authorities for International Relations (CLAIR), an organization established in 1988 to promote and provide support for local-level internationalization projects throughout Japan. The program I participated in was a "short-term internship" designed to give graduate students from the United States and Canada an opportunity to conduct independent research on some aspect of local government while working in a municipal office. For Rokusei Town, I was the first foreign employee they had hired or worked directly with. The initial range of my duties was quite limited to teaching English at the town's schools but grew decidedly during the months I worked there, and again over the year I conducted fieldwork in 2004–2005, as local officials learned how to utilize their resident foreigner. Soon after my arrival, I asked the administrative manager of Rokusei Town Board of Education why they decided to hire someone through this program. He explained that Rokusei Town had joined the wave of international education much later than their neighbors and with the upcoming amalgamation many of the town leaders felt that they needed to "try it out" (*tameshite miru*) themselves to show that they too could be international.

The program that brought me to Rokusei was a much smaller sister program to the Japan Exchange and Teaching (JET) program, arguably the most prevalent form of local internationalization in Japan. The JET program "imports" young foreign-national university graduates on yearly contracts (renewable up to three years) to work for prefectural and municipal governments. Beginning in 1987 with 848 participants from four countries, the program grew to 5,853 participants from forty-four different countries in 2005, with nearly half from the United States. The primary role of JET participants is to provide English language education and advice for internationalization projects. CLAIR is the central administrative unit of JET and its main functions are to facilitate communication between the three Ministries[9] responsible for operations, determine participant placement with the contracting localities, provide guidance for the local authorities, and offer counseling and training for participants.

In some ways, the JET program functions similarly to the Meiji-era employment of foreigners by the government, collectively called *oyatoi gaikokujin* (hired foreigners), who were brought to Japan to assist in its early modernization project (Cazdyn 1995; McConnell 2000). Somewhere between three and four thousand foreign teachers, technicians, mercenaries, and other specialists were hired by the government during the first twenty years following the Meiji Restoration (Beauchamp 1975: 423; Jones 1968). Several of these hired foreigners went on to become the first generation of Japanologists, including figures like Basil Hall Chamberlain, Edward S. Morse, Lafcadio Hearn, and William Griffis. Their continued studies and teaching of Japan following their tenure shows how immensely influential this program was, not only for Japan to build modern institutions, but also for introducing Japanese ideas and concepts to the West. While the prominent stereotype was that Japanese were predisposed to imitation rather than innovation (Lowell 1888), these *oyatoi* found many traits worth emulating in the realms of art and architecture, poetry and literature, and more importantly in providing an alternate value system counter to the egocentric Western mentality (Rosenstone 1980: 573).

The JET program is similarly aimed at bringing Japan into line with global expectations and building an international populace. Furthermore, it may be argued that the program in the long run has helped perpetuate this legacy of Western "orientalist" scholarship that perpetuates a whitewashed image of Japan's unique culture and characteristic qualities, and in turn suppresses discussions of politically sensitive issues (Cazdyn 1995: 137). One reason for this is the rather homogenous selection of participants from mostly White, educated, upper-middle-class backgrounds and who have some interest in Japan and are thus predisposed to view Japan positively. Furthermore, their relatively high pay, light work schedule, and generally affluent living conditions help stimulate positive impressions of Japan that these teachers relay upon returning to their home countries. All participants are required to have a university degree and selection preference is given to recent graduates. As a result, one substantial subset of participants goes on to graduate school, and influenced by their experiences many choose to study some aspect of Japan. Japan's desire to be investigated by foreign scholars, especially from the United States and Europe, can be seen in their generous funding opportunities for graduate students and postdoctoral researchers through the Monbukagakusho Scholarship program, the Japan Foundation, and the Japan Society for the Promotion of Science, which together fund several thousands of young foreign researchers each year.[10]

The program that introduced me to Rokusei was directed at these two objectives of teaching local residents about the world and to introduce Japan and specifically Rokusei Town to the rest of the world. It also had a third unanticipated influence in educating residents about their own community, as my presence and inquiries forced locals to think about aspects of their society and history that might otherwise have been taken for granted. These different roles were expressed during three different conversations with the mayor of Rokusei. On my first day of work in June 2002, I was brought into the mayor's office where he explained his excitement about having their first American in Rokusei and he requested that I "speak plenty of English" to the children to help them learn the language. During that initial summer the mayor developed a keen interest in my research on the folkways, kinship patterns, festivals, and material culture of Rokusei. When it came time for me to leave Rokusei in August, I was again brought to the mayor's office where he expressed his gratitude that I made such a strong effort to learn about Rokusei and conveyed his hope that I will go on to "make Rokusei famous" back in America. The third conversation took place following my return to Rokusei in July 2004, where after hearing more about my research interests the mayor requested that I write a regular column in the town newsletter under the general theme, "Rokusei as seen in the eyes of a foreigner" (*gaikokujin kara mita Rokusei-Machi*).[11]

The impact of the "Western gaze" upon Japanese self-images is particularly well documented in regards to the influence Ruth Benedict's (1946) *Chrysanthemum and the Sword* had in raising awareness of how outsiders view Japan and in stimulating the postwar genre of *Nihonjinron* national character studies (Ryang 2004: 47–48). This influence is not limited to the scholarly world either, as my daily interactions with Rokusei residents forced them to rethink and express their understandings of their culture in response to my inquiries and suppositions. Dialectic exchanges regarding Rokusei history, culture, and identity took place daily at work, in residents' homes, and on the streets. One continuing conversation of this nature was with my coworker at the Board of Education. Our daily conversations, which took place as we drove together across town between schools, were characterized by his intent interest in American music and popular culture and my persistent questions about various places, events, and customs in Rokusei. As a young man in his early twenties, my supervisor consistently felt unable to adequately answer my questions. When I asked about a festival or a local tradition, my supervisor would willingly describe his experiences but was generally unable to answer my persistent questions about the history and rationale behind them. He would often take my questions to his father or grandfather and return the next day with their answers. In this way our encounters forced him to question his culture and identity in new ways and enter into conversations with his elders that he may never have otherwise—and in a similar fashion I learned much from him about Britney Spears and her place in the history of American pop music.

As the town's "hired foreigner," I was obliged to participate in a wide range of events outside of teaching that put me on "display" and allowed residents to meet and interact with me. This included, amongst other things, attending sports competitions, singing in the town karaoke contest, acting as a master of ceremonies for public cultural events, attending various dinner parties, giving lectures and public speeches, and dressing as Santa Claus at the senior citizens' center Christmas celebration. One of the more interesting requests I received was to act as the Rokusei representative for a locally produced television commercial publicizing the newly formed Nakanoto Town. From 2002 the Hokuriku Asahi Broadcasting Company (HAB) has held a yearly "Hometown CM Contest" (*furusato CM taishô*) that solicits commercials from municipal authorities throughout Ishikawa Prefecture. The contest is aired on television and local celebrities and media professionals judge the commercials. There are six categories of awards, and the winners have their commercials aired on HAB frequently throughout the following year. The commercial made by Nakanoto Town officials featured three families, one from each of the former towns, and was filmed at a park ground that intersects the borders of all three towns. The commercial showed three families at different stages of growth; the first family had a wife who was visibly pregnant, second was my family with a single infant child, and we were followed by a third family with several young children. The basic idea was to reflect the imminent birth and development of the new Nakanoto Town in the growing families that live within it. I assumed that my family was invited to showcase the diversity and progressiveness of the town. When I questioned the town official he said that was not his intent, but rather he invited me because I was one of the most visible people in town that he knew, and furthermore the only person with a family that was an appropriate fit for their commercial.

Conclusion: The Personalities of Multiculturalism

The JET program complicates the issue of multiculturalism as the participants, regardless of nationality or ethnicity, come to Japan quite privileged, receiving enviable amounts of community support and preferential treatment—including a salary higher than most junior teachers. Perhaps the key difference between JET participants and many other foreign immigrants is that program participants are invited by the local administration and work directly with the community members where they live. This alone grants the participants a great deal of acceptance, as their "official" introduction to the community and daily contact with residents goes a long way to overcome linguistic and cultural barriers. Regardless of one's ethnicity, people that come "uninvited" into a neighborhood unable or unwilling to interact with their neighbors, work in unusual settings or hours of the day, or fail to follow common rules and customs are likely to be treated with suspicion and disdain. This is why many international civic groups and NPOs work to create opportunities for personal interactions between new and old residents and provide written materials and translation assistance to assist in integration. In this light, issues of discrimination and xenophobia in Japan may stem more from unpleasant personal interactions, class differences, and lack of community participation than any overt forms of "racism."

Research on Japanese multiculturalism has been dominated by a bias towards investigations of ethnic diversity and minority rights. This chapter has examined how multiculturalism, as a political ideology, manifests in Japanese public policy, especially in locales that are arguably ethnically "homogenous." One of the key critiques of multiculturalism is that in the process of promoting cultural understanding and exchange there is a danger of reifying the ethnic "other" as a separate entity with its own internal homogeneity (Turner 1993: 412), and in turn forcing individuals to culturally conform to the dominant group's understanding of their ethnicity (Okubo 2005). Such descriptive practices form pictures of the nation where several discrete ethnic groups (Japanese, Korean, Okinawan, and Brazilian) interact, rather than exploring how individuals distinctly experience their ethnicity and form their identity as a result of their personal "multicultural" encounters. The study of multiculturalism in Japan has generally been limited to discussions of indigenous or foreign ethnic groups and their relations with "ethnic" Japanese (Tsuda 2003) or the range of their rights in the Japanese state (Weiner 1997). The aim of this chapter has been to respond to deficiencies in the scholarship on multiculturalism in Japan, first by focusing on "multicultural" initiatives in fairly remote and comparatively homogeneous localities, and second by complicating the category of "Japan" and "the Japanese" by illustrating how local identity politics work to create diverse and independent localities sometimes marked by their unique international makeup.

An irony occurs in this shift away from national-ethnic identity politics to local place-making practices in that a similar type of "homogenization" takes place as residents are formed into a different solidarity, one based in this case upon residency rather than race. The municipality is thus contrasted to other municipalities—as one ethnicity may be compared with another—each with its own internal consistency, history, and culture. Internationalization activities over the past decades in Japan have been fundamental in the construction of these identities, as municipalities seek to rationalize their identities as constituent of their foreign-national residents, aid in the "assimilation" of new immigrants (Japanese and foreign) into the local community, and form partnerships with localities in other nations that share a similar culture or climate. From this perspective, one can claim Japan is a multicultural nation, not only because of the presence of ethnic and indigenous minority populations, but also because of the internal divisions within the Japanese nation. The solidarity that is formed by the municipal place-making practices described in this chapter attempts to overcome and erase distinctions of class, ethnicity, sex, and nationality in order to unify a populace with a shared vision and hope for the future. This is precisely what multiculturalism, as both an ideology and public policy, aims to accomplish.

Notes

1. As of March 2005 Rokusei Town ceased to exist as a municipal entity when it merged with the neighboring towns of Kashima and Toriya to form Nakanoto Town. The population of Rokusei in January 2005 was 5,202 (Rokusei-Machi 2005: 817).
2. The exact number as of 31 December 2005 was 5,255, or 21.2 percent of the 24,763 total registered NPOs in Japan. There are seventeen different categories of recognized NPO activities and any one organization can belong to multiple categories (83.2 percent fall into two or more categories). These statistics are collected by the Cabinet Office, Quality of Life Policy Bureau, which maintains a website on NPO policies and guidance for prospective NPO groups (http://www.npo-homepage.go.jp/data/bunnya.html).
3. In Ishikawa Prefecture alone there are over 150 reported prefecture- and municipal-based international groups, only a small fraction of which are registered as NPOs (Ishikawa Foundation for International Exchange 2004).
4. This claim that Nakasone was responsible for spurring Japan towards multiculturalism may seem surprising considering his tenure was marked by his nationalist and racist attitude, particularly in his comment that Japan's economic success and "intellectual superiority" were due mainly to the fact that it had no minority populations.
5. One of the major manifestations of this drive was the creation of the International Research Center for Japanese Studies, commonly called *Nichibunken*. This institute was established as a response to criticisms of Japan as a faceless economic giant, but the institute can equally be criticized as a scholarly institute that produces research aimed at improving the image of Japan overseas.
6. The dam was considered the largest in Asia and third largest in the world at the time, providing stable agricultural water for 150,000 hectares of land through 18,000 kilometers of waterways. The story of Hatta and his family is quite dramatic, as they lived in Taiwan from 1920 through the end of the Pacific War where they are said to have developed close ties to the people of Taiwan. Hatta was later assigned to the Philippines where he died at sea. At the end of the war when all Japanese nationals were being returned to Japan,

Hatta's wife Toyoki fell into despair at the thought of leaving her beloved Taiwan and committed suicide by jumping off the dam her husband built.

7. There were twenty-two resident foreigners, including myself, registered in Rokusei Town in January 2005.

8. As a result of the ongoing municipal mergers (*shichôson gappei*), the number of cities and towns has reduced to just nineteen.

9. The JET program is jointly administered by the Ministry of Internal Affairs that provides financial resources and acceptance guidelines, the Ministry of Foreign Affairs responsible for overseas recruitment and selection, and the Ministry of Education, Culture, Sports, Science, and Technology, which conducts seminars and guidance for Assistant Language Teachers (ALTs) in Japan.

10. This funding of foreign scholars is only one-sided, as there are no comparable funding options for Japanese nationals for study overseas. This bias shows that the goal of Japan's international education initiative is to raise exposure of Japan overseas, not to make Japanese more cosmopolitan and competent in international settings.

11. I wrote five short pieces for the town newsletter *Koho Rokusei* between September 2004 and February 2005, which was the last newsletter before Rokusei consolidated (*gappei*) into Nakanoto Town. The topics I examined for these pieces included my impressions of a local festival, my take on the importance of international education measures, and my perspective on the amalgamation process (see Rokusei-Machi 2005).

References

Allison, Anne. 2006. *Millennial Monsters: Japanese Toys and the Global Imagination.* Berkeley: University of California Press.

Appadurai, Arjun. 1996. *Modernity at Large: Cultural Dimensions of Globalization.* Minneapolis: University of Minnesota Press.

Bailey, Jackson. 1991. *Ordinary People, Extraordinary Lives: Political and Economic Change in a Tohoku Village.* Honolulu: University of Hawaii Press.

Beauchamp, Edward. 1975. "Griffis in Japan: The Fukui Interlude, 1871." *Monumenta Nipponica* 30 (4): 423–452.

Befu, Harumi. 1983. "Internationalization of Japan and Nihon Bunkaron." In *The Challenge of Japan's Internationalization: Organization and Culture,* ed. Hiroshi Mannari and Harumi Befu, 232–265. Nishinomiya: Kwansei Gakuin University.

Benedict, Ruth. 1946. *Chrysanthemum and the Sword.* Boston: Houghton Mifflin.

Cazdyn, Eric. 1995. "Uses and Abuses of the Nation: Toward a Theory of the Transnational Cultural Exchange Industry." *Social Text* 44: 135–159.

Dale, Peter. 1986. *The Myth of Japanese Uniqueness.* New York: St. Martin's Press.

Douglass, Mike, and Glenda S. Roberts, eds. 2000. *Japan and Global Migration: Foreign Workers and the Advent of a Multicultural Society*. London: Routledge.

Goodman, Roger, ed. 2003. *Global Japan: The Experience of Japan's New Immigrants and Overseas Communities*. London: Routledge.

Guo, Nanyan, Seiichi Hasegawa, Henry Johnson, Hidemichi Kawanishi, Kanako Kitahara, and Anthony Rausch, eds. 2005. *Tsugaru: Regional Identity on Japan's Northern Periphery*. Dunedin: University of Otago Press.

Hamada, Tomoko. 1985. "Corporation, Culture, and Environment: A Japanese Model." *Asian Survey* 25 (12): 1214–1228.

Ishikawa Foundation for International Exchange, ed. 2004. *Ishikawa-Ken no Kokusai Kôryû Dantai* [The profile of international groups in Ishikawa]. Kanazawa: Ishikawa Foundation for International Exchange.

Ivy, Marilyn. 1995. *Discourses of the Vanishing: Modernity, Phantasm, Japan*. Chicago: University of Chicago Press.

Jones, Hazel. 1968. "The Formulation of the Meiji Government Policy Toward the Employment of Foreigners." *Monumenta Nipponica* 23 (1/2): 9–30.

Kanazawa Pan-Japan Sea International Symposium. 1984. *Nihonkai Engan ni Okeru Toshi-bunka to Kôryû* [Urban culture and cultural exchange in the Japan Sea coastal regions]. Kanazawa: Hokuriku Economic Research Council.

Kitagawa, Masayasu. 2001. "Mie's Bold Bid for Change." *Japan Quarterly* 48 (3): 3–9.

Knight, John. 1994. "Rural Revitalization in Japan: Spirit of the Village and Taste of the Country." *Asian Survey* 34 (7): 634–646.

Lowell, Percival. 1888. *The Soul of the Far East*. Boston: Houghton, Mifflin and Company.

Mathews, Gordon. 2000. *Global Culture/Individual Identity: Searching for Home in the Cultural Supermarket*. London: Routledge.

McConnell, David L. 2000. *Importing Diversity: Inside Japan's JET Program*. Berkeley: University of California Press.

Mouer, Ross, and Yoshio Sugimoto. 1986. *Images of Japanese Society*. London: Kegan Paul International.

Muto, Hiromi. 1996. "Innovative Policies and Administrative Strategies for Intergovernmental Change in Japan." In *Globalization and Decentralization: Institutional Contexts, Policy Issues, and Intergovernmental Relations in Japan and the United States*, ed. Jong S. Jun and Deil S. Wright. Washington, DC: Georgetown University Press.

Neary, Ian. 1997. "Burakumin in Contemporary Japan." In *Japan's Minorities: Illusion of Homogeneity*, ed. Michael Weiner, 50–78. London: Routledge.

Okamoto, Fumiyoshi. 1992. "Unoke no Natsu wa Tetsugaku no Hajimari: Nishida Tetsugaku wo Zenkoku kara Sekai he" [Summer in Unoke is the start of philosophy: Nishida's philosophy from the nation to the world]. In *Machizukuri to Bunka Geinô no Shinkô* [Town planning and the promotion of art and culture], ed. Okamoto Kaneji, 171–186. Tokyo: Gyôsei.

Okubo, Yuko. 2005. "'Visible' Minorities and 'Invisible' Minorities: An Ethnographic Study of Multicultural Education and the Production of Ethnic 'Others' in Japan." Ph.D. diss., University of California, Berkeley.

Pyle, Kenneth. 1987. "In Pursuit of a Grand Design: Nakasone Betwixt the Past and the Future." *Journal of Japanese Studies* 13 (2): 243–270.

Robertson, Jennifer. 1991. *Native and Newcomer: Making and Remaking a Japanese City.* Berkeley: University of California Press.

———. 1999. "It Takes a Village: Internationalization and Nostalgia in Postwar Japan." In *Mirror of Modernity: Invented Traditions of Modern Japan,* ed. Stephen Vlastos, 110–132. Berkeley: University of California Press.

Rokusei-Machi. 2005. *Kôhô Rokusei Shukusatsu-hen Daisankan* [Rokusei newsletter reduced edition, Volume 3]. Rokusei: Rokusei-Machi.

Rosenstone, Robert. 1980. "Learning from Those 'Imitative' Japanese: Another Side of the American Experience in the Mikado's Empire." *The American Historical Review* 85 (3): 572–595.

Rozman, Gilbert. 1999. "Backdoor Japan: The Search for a Way Out via Regionalism and Decentralization." *Journal of Japanese Studies* 25 (1): 3–31.

Ryang, Sonia. 2004. *Japan and National Anthropology: A Critique.* London: Routledge.

Shôji, Hiroshi, ed. 2004. *Taminzoku Nihon-Zainichi Gaikokujin no Kurashi* [Multiethnic Japan: Life and history of immigrants]. Suita: National Museum of Ethnology.

Siddle, Richard. 1997. "Ainu: Japan's Indigenous People." In *Japan's Minorities: Illusion of Homogeneity,* ed. Michael Weiner, 17–49. London: Routledge.

Soroos, M. S. 1988. "The International Commons: A Historical Perspective." *Environmental Review* 12 (1): 1–22.

Responsibilities of States: Learning from the Japanese Experience." *Journal of Peace Research* 25 (1): 17–29.

Tsuda, Takeyuki. 2003. *Strangers in Their Ethnic Homeland: Japanese Brazilian Return Migration in Transnational Perspective.* New York: Columbia University Press.

Turner, Terence. 1993. "Anthropology and Multiculturalism: What Is Anthropology that Multiculturalists Should Be Mindful of It?" *Cultural Anthropology* 8 (4): 411–429.

Ueunten, Wesley. n.d. "Okinawan Diasporic Identities: Between Being a Buffer and a Bridge." In *Being Others in Japan: Multicultural Experiences in Japanese Society,* ed. David Blake Willis and Stephen Murphy-Shigematsu.

Van Wolferen, Karel. 1989. *The Enigma of Japanese Power: People and Politics in a Stateless Nation.* New York: Knopf.

Watanabe, Michihiro. 1999. "Background on Cultural Policies and Programs in Japan: Comparing Cultural Policy—A Study of Japan and the United States." In *Comparing Cultural Policy: Study of Japan and the United States,* ed. Joyce Zemans and Archie Kleingarthner, 61–112. London: Altamira Press.

Weiner, Michael, ed. 1997. *Japan's Minorities: Illusion of Homogeneity.* London: Routledge.

Witteveen, Guven Peter. 2004. *The Renaissance of Takefu: How People and the Local Past Changed the Civic Life of a Regional Japanese Town.* London: Routledge.

Yoshino, Kosaku. 1992. *Cultural Nationalism in Contemporary Japan: A Sociological Enquiry.* London: Routledge.

5

TRANSNATIONAL MIGRATION OF WOMEN: CHANGING BOUNDARIES OF CONTEMPORARY JAPAN

Shinji Yamashita

Introduction

ACCORDING TO THE WORLD TOURISM Organization (UNWTO), 842 million tourists traveled across national boundaries in 2006. This figure is expected to grow to 1 billion in 2010 and 1.6 billion in 2020.[1] As for the international tourism in Japan, 17.5 million Japanese went abroad, while 7.3 million foreigners visited Japan in 2006.[2] In this chapter, within the context of accelerating transnational mobility, I will analyze the process of transnationalization taking place around Japan with special reference to women's border-crossings.[3]

In particular, I will examine three transnational flows of women. The first consists of Japanese women who leave Japan for Bali, Indonesia. They go first as tourists, and later stay for a longer period, and often marry local men after repeat visits. The second consists of those who leave for California in the United States to study abroad (*ryûgaku*). Many of them are OLs ("Office Ladies," a Japanese English word for female office workers), and this phenomenon is therefore termed *OL ryûgaku*. Third, I discuss women guest workers from Asian countries, especially Filipinas, who come to Japan to work, particularly in the entertainment or sex industries, and who sometimes marry Japanese men.

These cases may serve to represent three recent trends in the transnational migration of women to and from Japan. By practicing a sort of "multi-sited ethnography" (Marcus 1998) in Bali, California, and Japan on these transnational flows of women and the resulting cross-border marriages,

Endnotes for this chapter begin on page 112.

this chapter examines the external as well as the internal globalization of Japan today. In so doing, this chapter also suggests more general theoretical insights for the anthropological study of ways of living in the contemporary world-in-motion, what I call "living in-between."

Transnational Human Flows around Contemporary Japan

Let us begin with looking at the statistical data on transnational human flows around Japan. Diachronically, the number of Japanese overseas tourists has been growing continually over the past forty years. In 1964, the year of Tokyo Olympic Games, when restrictions on overseas tourism were removed, only 128,000 Japanese went abroad. In 2006, forty two years later, there were over 17 million Japanese tourists going overseas. The increase was especially rapid in the latter half of the 1980s, from about 5 million in 1985 to 11 million in 1990 (Kokudokôtsûshô 2001: 28). The main reasons for this rapid development of international tourism from Japan were Japanese economic growth and the increased power of the Japanese yen during this period.

It is also interesting to note the fact that the main lifetime goals of Japanese people shifted from housing to leisure in the mid 1980s (Sôrifu 1998: 24). By that time, land and housing in Japan, especially in the metropolitan areas, had become too expensive to buy for most people. In parallel with this change, overseas tourism became popular. In other words, Japanese people gave up their dream of obtaining houses and turned instead to look for happiness in leisure, particularly in overseas tourism.

This trend slowed down slightly in 1998 because of the recession caused by the Asian economic crisis in the previous year, but it recovered in 2000: 17.8 million Japanese people, the highest recorded figure in the history of Japanese tourism so far, went abroad. However, the terrorist attacks of September 11, 2001 in the United States had a considerable impact on international tourism, even in Japan. It was reported that the number of international tourists decreased by 30 percent as a result of this incident. October 2002 saw the Bali terrorist bombing, followed by the Iraq war and the SARS (Severe Acute Respiratory Syndrome) epidemic in 2003, and the second bombing in Bali in October 2005. All of these had a serious impact on international mobility. In 2003 the number of outbound Japanese tourists went down to 13.3 million but recovered to 17.5 million in 2006, as mentioned at the start of this chapter. In this way, international tourism appears very sensitive to the political, economic, and even epidemiological conditions of the world today.

As for the countries that Japanese overseas tourists visit, China became the number one destination in 2006 when 3.75 million Japanese visited China. In that same year, 3.67 million Japanese went to the United States, the number one destination by 2005,[4] with 1.4 million going to Hawaii. In addition, there were 2.3 million visitors going to Korea, 1.3 million to Thailand, 1.3 million to Hong Kong, and 1.2 million to Taiwan. The Asian region constitutes nearly 70 percent of the total outbound destinations.

Turning to inbound flows, 7.3 million foreigners visited Japan in 2006. Compared with the outbound flows, this figure is disproportionately small.[5] Regarding the nationality of international visitors to Japan, approximately 70 percent of them are from nearby Asian countries, particularly Korea, Taiwan, and China.[6]

Furthermore, one of the most remarkable characteristics of Japanese international tourism is the active involvement of young women. Women in their twenties and thirties comprise nearly half (45 percent) of the total number of women tourists. These young, single, "pink-collar" women, according to Karen Kelsky, may be "the most enthusiastic and committed travelers of any demographic group in the world" (Kelsky 1996: 175). In this context of the active involvement of young Japanese women in international tourism, in the next section I focus on one particular phenomenon, that of Japanese women tourists who marry Balinese men.

Japanese Brides in Bali

Bali is the largest and most famous tourist destination in Indonesia. However, Balinese tourism has recently experienced serious challenges, such as the Indonesian economic crisis in 1997, the September 11 terrorist attacks in 2001, and the Bali bombings in 2002 and 2005. In 2003, the year in which the SARS epidemic occurred in Asia, the number of visitors to Bali fell to 993,000, while in 2004 it recovered to 1.46 million, almost the same level as in 2000.[7]

Against this background, the number of visitors from Europe and Australia is in drastic decline, while the number of visitors from Asia, especially from Japan and Taiwan, is increasing. In particular, the visitors from Japan have dominated Bali's international tourism landscape in recent years. Of the 1.46 million visitors to Bali in 2004, 326,000 (22 percent of the total) were from Japan. The number of Japanese visitors to Bali rose sharply in the early 1990s with the introduction of Japan Airlines direct flights, to the extent that the Japanese became the largest group of international tourists in Bali.

Bali is particularly popular among young Japanese women. It is against this background that the phenomenon of Japanese brides in Bali has developed. I have already discussed this phenomenon in detail in a chapter of my book on tourism in Bali (Yamashita 2003: chapter 7). Here I will summarize the main points.

First, many of the thirty women I interviewed during my research[8] were born around 1960. They belong to the generation that grew up during the period of high-speed growth in the Japanese economy. During this period, the Japanese archipelago was transformed drastically, and because of this, these women discovered in Bali the landscapes they had lost—empty spaces and rough and muddy roads—making them think nostalgically of the "old Japan." For example, a 1990s tourist brochure (Jalpak, Japan Airlines group brochure, *I'll, JAL Bali,* 1996 April-September edition) described Bali as "a second homeland," under the slogan "the island touches your heart [*kokoro*]." Here Bali is not exotic. Rather, it is a nostalgic spiritual homeland (*furusato*) for Japanese.[9]

Second, if one looks at the regions that the visitors come from, an overwhelming number come from major metropolitan areas, such as Tokyo and Osaka. The Japanese brides in Bali, therefore, are an urban phenomenon: many of them find that they are unable to adapt to urban life in present-day Japan. Thus they feel that they are rediscovering their true selves in Bali. In this context, it is interesting that a women's magazine, *Rinku* (8 July, 1996), saw Bali as a place for *iyashi* or "healing," where young Japanese women could recover from the battles of the urban workplace in Japan.

Within the relaxed atmosphere of a newfound homeland, they are in search of adventure. This results in a lot of romances in Bali. Shirakawa Tôko, a journalist who writes on women's issues, has pointed out that Balinese men are good at making a Japanese woman feel like a "girl" (*onnanoko*), just like a heroine in girls' comics. They are able to treat women kindly and in a "natural way" that Japanese men completely lack. She mentions a comment by a career woman who once worked in Japan and who is now married to a Balinese man twelve years her junior: "The Balinese men are really skilful in penetrating into the nooks and crannies of Japanese women's hearts" (Shirakawa 2002: 156).

As to the fascination with Balinese men as husbands, here are some of the women's comments taken from my interviews:

"When I was in Japan I didn't want to get married. I thought that marriage led to trouble. But since I experienced the Balinese personality, I changed my mind."

"In married life here, my husband gives me a lot of help with looking after the children and with work."

In this way, these women first woke up to the possibility of marriage and having children when they came to Bali. Their comments also express their dissatisfaction with living in Japan:

"If I am in Japan for about two or three weeks, the energy I bring back from Bali disappears, and I begin to think that I've had enough. Bali is a much cozier place to live."

"Japan is full of gadgets and information, but I always feel they have got things wrong. In Bali there is little information, so you don't get confused. That is a pleasure."

Certainly marriage to a Balinese does not necessarily work out well, and there are also many difficulties resulting from differences in customs. However, these women generally think that life in Japan is not necessarily either prosperous or particularly good. In his book, *Nihonjin wo Yameru Hôhô* (The Way to Stop Being Japanese), the sociologist Yoshio Sugimoto (1993: 175) describes these people as "refugees" in a sense who have lost patience with Japanese society. The idea of refugees from wealthy Japan seems paradoxical, but the refugees here are not political or economic but social and cultural (cf. Yamamoto 1993: 57). Japanese brides in Bali may be a case of this kind. Similar situations can be found in New York, London, and Hong Kong as well. In the next section, I discuss the example of the *OL ryûgaku* in California.

OL ryûgaku in California

OL ryûgaku refers to the phenomenon in which female office workers quit their company after working for several years and go abroad to study and experience change. According to the Study Abroad White Paper (Center for International Cultural Studies and Education [ICS] 1999), the proportion of students abroad who were female increased from 40 percent in 1988 to 70 percent in 1998. As far as the *shakaijin* or adult students are concerned, the female ratio is as high as 80 percent. Therefore, in present-day Japan, it is women, not men, who are keen on studying abroad. The White Paper mentioned the following reasons for study abroad: first, the desire to make a living abroad, and second, the view that the English language is indispensable in today's world. Regarding the destinations for study abroad, the United States ranks first, with 43.7 percent of the total, followed by the United Kingdom (13.7 percent), China (8.2 percent), Canada (6.3 percent), and Australia (5.5 percent).

These motivations and destinations for study abroad may express Japanese women's long-cherished desire or *akogare* for the Western lifestyle and English, the language of power. Following Michel Foucault's idea that "where there is desire, the power relation is already present," Karen Kelsky points out in relation to *akogare* that: "Women's desires for the Occident are embedded in, indeed constituted by, power relations between Japan and the West (exemplified most often by the United States), in an ongoing dialectic of modernity that makes the West the inevitable destination in a unilinial tale of progress" (Kelsky 2001: 10). This kind of asymmetric power relations underlies the phenomenon of *OL ryûgaku*.

Another thing to note is the quality of Japanese students aboard. According to a survey, most of the Japanese students in the United States are enrolled at the undergraduate level, and particularly in lower-ranking schools such as community colleges, while many of the students from China, India, or Taiwan are in graduate school (Recruit America, personal communication, 1999). This difference between the Japanese and other Asian students is interesting in two ways. First, although Japan ranks first in terms of the number of students, Japanese students are not necessarily well qualified, because most of them are often dropouts from the Japanese education or corporate systems. Second, few Japanese enroll in graduate schools because the graduate schools in Japan function reasonably well, while other Asian countries depend on the United States for their graduate education.

In 1999, during my stay at the University of California, Berkeley, I conducted research on Japanese women students in the San Francisco Bay Area.[10] Here are some of their comments from the students I interviewed:

"I was disappointed with the Japanese company after working for one-and-a-half years. I had to make tea ten minutes before men came to the office. The younger men who were employed after me were promoted faster than me. I was shocked when I saw a senior woman colleague of mine in her forties doing the same job as me."

"During my university days in Japan I majored in technology, which was thought of as a male discipline. I always kept up with the men. But I became conscious of being a woman after I began work. I quit the company after many unpleasant things happened to me. Then I went abroad to study in the United States. I am now studying feminism in graduate school."

These voices reflect working situations for women in Japan in which discrimination by sex as well as age is prevalent. Generally speaking, Japanese women nowadays are not discriminated against when they are at school. However, the world changes after they start to work. The feminist sociologist Ueno Chizuko (1996: 315) has pointed out that when the economic bubble appeared to burst, the principle of equal opportunities for women in employment established by the equal opportunities legislation became empty lip service only. Certainly in one-on-one situations, the relationship between men and women is changing. However, in corporations and other organizations, things have hardly changed at all over the last twenty or thirty years. Although recently the Japanese government has been attempting to promote for the realization of *danjo kyôdô sankaku shakai* (a society in which the genders participate equally), it may take time to realize this goal.

In the face of such discrimination and frustration, Japanese women find an escape in overseas tours, by going to "another world" in which they hope to realize their other selves (cf. Kuwa 1998). Next, they plan to leave Japan, and to achieve this they usually enroll themselves in a language school first. Then, if they are successful in gaining a practical command of English, they move to community colleges or universities abroad. Finally, they decide to settle down abroad instead of going back to Japan where the image of jobs and lifestyles remain the same.

As to the reasons why they head for the United States, here are some answers from my interviews:

"It is difficult to find one's real self in Japan. In the United States I really appreciate the fact that there is no discrimination in terms of sex and age."

"I am forty-seven years old and two years ago I was divorced. Because I still have a long time to live, I decided to re-enter university to study psychology. After graduation, I want to be a psychotherapist. I think that America is a country where everyone is able to try again."

These voices convey an image of the United States as a free country without discrimination that may empower Japanese women. In reality, however, discrimination exists in the United States as well. Therefore, even if they manage to graduate from American universities, it is not necessarily certain that they will get jobs in American corporations. Possibly they will have to go back to Japan, because they may not be able to renew their visas. However, it is not certain either that they will make use of their experiences in the United States for making new lives in Japan. The worst scenario is that they will adapt neither to the United States nor to Japan. According to an informant, "They are too Japanese to be American, and too American to be Japanese."

As in Bali, there are many cases in which Japanese women studying in the United States marry local men. In the American "marriage market," Japanese women are usually highly valued. In 1998, the Japanese Consul General in San Francisco recorded 266 cases of such international marriage between Japanese and Americans—most of them between Japanese women and American men. This kind of overseas expansion of Japanese women is a remarkable phenomenon that leads to what Karen Kelsky (1999) has called the "eroticized internationalization" of Japanese women.

There is another thing to note. These new migrants or *shin-issei* from Japan are quite different from older migrants who have become Japanese Americans. *Shin-issei* do not usually associate with Japanese Americans. It seems that they are now different ethnic groups with different modes of thinking, and different associations. And so, for instance, during my stay in Berkeley in 1998–1999, there were two Japanese students associations at the University of California at Berkeley: Tomodachi, consisting of Japanese American students, and CJC (California Japan Club) consisting of Japanese students from Japan.

Asian Brides in Japan

While Japanese women are leaving, women from neighboring Asian countries flow into Japan. This is part of a flow of transnational labor migration in Asia that has accelerated since the 1980s. In 2006, about 2 million registered foreign residents, including 700,000 guest workers, were staying in Japan.[11] About 70 percent of them are from Asian countries such as Korea, China, and the Philippines.[12] These Asian guest workers in Japan have become a part of what Arjun Appadurai (1996: chapter 3) has called the "global ethnoscapes." Therefore, one can observe "Asianized spaces" in some parts of Tokyo as a global city, particularly in such districts as Shinjuku and Ikebukuro (Tajima 1998).

In the global ethnoscapes in Japan, Asian women, particularly women from the Philippines, often called *japayuki* ("going to Japan"), have a special niche: they work in entertainment establishments such as bars and nightclubs (Itoh 1992). The journalist Hisada Megumi in her book about the marriage between Japanese men and Filipinas writes: "1979 was the first year of the *japayuki,* and the Filipinas who came to work numbered over 10,000. Ten years later, in 1989, Filipinas staying in Japan, legally or illegally, numbered over 100,000, and Filipinas married to Japanese men numbered over 10,000" (Hisada 1992: 307–308).[13]

According to Hisada, Japanese men were able to find among the Filipinas the partners that they had not been able to find among Japanese women to help them cope with their lonely and isolated lives, and they ended up marrying them. In her book she described vividly cases of such couples, and writes: "In the close relations between Japanese men and Filipinas through marriage, the Filipinas' powerful Asian energy will change Japanese attitudes toward other Asians in Japanese society" (Hisada 1992: 308–309).

When I interviewed her in 2000, Hisada told me, "It is changing much faster than I ever thought. Now the marriage of Japanese men, even elite salaried men, to women from the Philippines has become so common that it has come to be accepted without any great reluctance by Japanese society."[14] In 2005 the international marriage rate in Japan amounted to 5 percent, ten times as high as the figure in 1970.[15] Most of these spouses are Asians such as Chinese, Filipinas, and Koreans. Of particular interest is the difference in gender. First, about 80 percent of international marriages in Japan are between Japanese males and foreign females. Secondly, there is also a gender difference in the nationality of spouses. In the case of marriages between Japanese males and foreign females, the largest group of wives are Chinese (39 percent), followed by Filipinas (27 percent) and Koreans (19 percent). However, in the case of marriages between foreign males and Japanese females, the largest group of husbands are Koreans (27 percent), followed by Americans (17 percent) and Chinese (13 percent).[16] This difference may be explained in terms of gender and power relations in the contemporary international order to which I will turn later.

Furthermore, there is the phenomenon of the "import" of Asian brides. In Japan today, the marriage age of women is ranked highest in the world.[17] Young Japanese women nowadays often do not seem to find many positive reasons to get married, and so they are reluctant to do so. Tanimura Shiho (1992) has named this *kekkon shinai kamoshirenai shôkôgun,* or the "I may not marry" syndrome.[18] In some villages where depopulation continues, the exodus of women to the towns has led to a dearth of younger women, and it is common knowledge that brides are being "imported" from places such as the Philippines, Korea, China, and Sri Lanka. For example, Ashahi-chô, Yamagata Prefecture, Northeastern Japan, became famous when the mayor of the town led a tour to the Philippines to arrange marriages (Shukuya 1988).[19]

Thus, as the Japanese women who earlier left for the cities start to move overseas, Asian brides are moving into the villages in Japan (see the chapter by Burgess in this volume). What is the significance of this flow of women in the global ethnoscapes?

To answer this question it may be helpful to consider the relations of gender, nationality, and power. In the colonialist discourse, it was common to observe the "orientalizing" gender/power relationship between the colonizing male and the colonized female. This pattern may also apply in the case of contemporary international sex and marriage relations between Western males and non-Western females, even in the postcolonial era. Under the influence of Neferti Tadiar (1993), Lieba Faier, who carried out fieldwork among Filipinas in the Kiso villages of Nagano Prefecture, has observed how relationships between Japan, the United States, and the Philippines are themselves gendered, and how they operate according to a sort of sexualized logic. Within this framework, Faier has discussed the Filipina cases of *oyomesan* (brides) in the Kiso villages as a form of contemporary cultural production in Japan, which has been brought about by what she has termed "the contingency of encounter" (Faier 2003).

Living In-Between: Within Gender/Nationality/Power Relations

Transnational relationships or inequalities between nations, therefore, can take precedence over inequalities based on gender. One might suppose that the existence of such gender/nationality/power relations lies behind the flow of women from the Philippines to Japan, and from Japan to the United States, sometimes resulting in international marriages. In this international circulation of women, the Philippines may appear as female in relation to Japan, just as Japan may appear as female to the United States. Looking at the phenomenon in this way, the flow of women represents the current state of international power relations, mediated by gender.[20]

International marriage is based in a way on this national and racial hierarchy. Kelsky cites the words of the president of an international dating and marriage service in Tokyo: "My opinion is that international marriage is a 'circle of the weak' [*jakusha no wa*]. The weak of the world always look for women outside their own country—weaker women. So weak white men marry Japanese women, who have lower status. Then weak Japanese men marry Thais or Filipinas. Chinese women try to marry Japanese men" (Kelsky 2001: 133). Kelsky also mentions two Japanese women she interviewed who drew similar graphs "illustrating their contention that the majority of women had 'evolved' too far to be content with average Japanese men and were 'forced' to turn their thoughts toward romance and marriage with white men. Most Japanese men, by contrast, were ... only 'good enough' for Southeast Asian and other 'Asian' women" (152).

In this regard, Japanese brides in Bali are particularly interesting, because they do not follow the usual pattern of gender/nationality/power relations. In Bali, the powerful group is the Japanese, but they are women. Balinese men who marry Japanese women are sometimes abused as being *himo* ("pimps"). There is thus a difference in the social and cultural implications of living in Bali and in the United States. In Bali, Japanese are seen as the former colonizers, and holders of economic power. In the United States, Japan is seen as a nation that was occupied (or "colonized") by the United States during the postwar period, and which therefore ranks lower than the United States, politically, economically, and racially. Japanese belong to the Asian minority within multiethnic American society. The keywords for the Japanese who go to the United States are *akogare* ("longing" or "dreaming") and "career-up" (directed towards the future), while the keywords for those who go to Bali are *natsukashisa* (nostalgia), *furusato* (homeland), and *iyashi* (healing), evoking the past. International migration and international marriage are not necessarily free from these kind of power relations in the modern world system.

After their marriages, many of the Japanese wives in Bali work in the tourist sector in places such as souvenir shops, boutiques, restaurants, and "homestay" accommodations. It is interesting that many of them have no idea of giving up their Japanese nationality and becoming Indonesian. They are not conscious of abandoning the country they have migrated from. Therefore, they should perhaps be seen not as migrants, but rather as long-staying tourists searching for a place to which they can belong. In other words, they are what Sato Machiko (2001) has called the new type of "lifestyle migrants" who differ from the former economic migrants.

It could be put another way. According to these women whose lives extend between two countries, the difference between traveling and living, and therefore between tourism and migration, is not all that great. Discussing the people who spend their lives traveling back and forth between the Caribbean and Brooklyn in New York, Clifford has pointed out that the question that has to be asked for them is not so much "Where are you from?" as "Where are you between?" (Clifford 1997: 37). This kind of diaspora lifestyle, which Clifford has termed "dwelling-in-travel," cannot be understood in terms of the static categories of ethnic group and culture in conventional anthropology, in which it is assumed that, if a particular people live in a particular area, they also share a particular culture. Rather than living within their culture, these people live betwixt and between cultures.

As the number of Japanese brides in Bali has increased, Japanese society in Bali, and especially the character of the Japanese Association in Bali, has also changed. Japanese communities in many countries abroad are often very closed and hardly likely to mix at all with the local society. However, in the case of Bali, what is remarkable is that the Japanese women who have married Balinese participate in the Japanese Association, and they are also able to play a role in opening up the Association to Balinese society. During my research in 1995, this was illustrated by an event, the *Bon* Dance (a dance related to the Japanese Buddhist festival), held at the Nusa Dua Hilton Hotel. The Japanese Association in Bali organized the event. The interesting thing about this was that, rather than being the usual expression of Japanese community identity, it expressed the energy of the hybrid community in Bali. The children of mixed parentage danced, while their Balinese fathers took photographs. The Japanese women of the Nyonya-kai (the women's section of the Japanese Association in Bali) performed on the *jegog* (Balinese bamboo instruments), and danced the *joged bumbung* (a type of popular Balinese folk dance) to the music.

It is too early to predict how this jumble of different cultures will work out in the future. However, the next stage in the development of international marriage is apparently that of "hybridization." About 140 children of mixed parentage were registered at the *nihongo hoshûkô* (Supplementary Japanese School) in Bali in 2001 (Shirakawa 2002: 153). In this regard, it seems that the case of California has gone the furthest. During my stay in Berkeley, I came across a group of people who have not only mixed blood but also hybrid identity, called the Hapa Issues Forum. *Hapa* is the Hawaiian word for mixed blood, and Japanese American students at the University of California, Berkeley established the forum in 1992. The Forum's brochure says: "Don't worry, be Hapa! ... In the Twenty-First Century, the typical Japanese Americans will be *Hapa*. With each day we see more Mixed Race Asian Americans who may have green eyes, freckles, and red hair. This is not the end of the community, just an expansion of it" (Hapa Issues Forum 1998).

Even in the "homogeneous" Japanese homeland, the process of hybridization is proceeding. Hisada has observed: "In the Parent Teacher Association meetings at elementary schools which Filipina mothers attend, something happens which makes it possible for closed Japanese society to open to allow fresh air to come in. Some would say that this could result in disorder in society. But in my opinion it would be creative chaos."[21] Japanese society is thus changing its boundaries within, in the sociocultural processes of transnational mobilities today.

Conclusion: An Age of Women

Formerly international migration belonged to the men's domain. Like colonialism and war, it was the task of men who left their families at home. However, today women are moving across national boundaries (Campani 1995; Takezawa 1998: 69–70). In my interview with Aihwa Ong, the author of *Flexible Citizenship* (1999), Ong told me about Asian migrants in the United States:

> "I have noticed among the Asian immigrant groups that it is easier for women than men to adjust to American society. One can look at two factors. American society is generally much more sympathetic to Asian women than Asian men. So they tend to be much more welcoming and they also perceive the women as being more flexible on adjusting to American rules. The other factor is that Asian men have a harder time adjusting to American society, even though they might be highly qualified and get jobs. Perhaps it has to do with a different sense of the role in the family and also the connection between the family and home country. I think that Asian men do feel that they represent their home culture and their home nation. That has some constraint on their flexibility in adjusting to American society."[22]

Of the two factors Ong mentioned as reasons why Asian women are more flexible than Asian men in the United States, the first factor may be related to the orientalism in American society or the sexualized logic of international relations discussed in this chapter. The second factor, that women compared with men do not necessarily bring their home/national identities with them to their new place of residence, is particularly interesting for the examination of gender difference in transnational migration. In other words, women are freed from the nation-state to a greater extent than men because they have less of a stake in nation-states that are created by men.[23]

Therefore, it may be women rather than men who will transcend and remake the nation-state. In this sense, the narratives of transnational migration and international marriage created by women can be used to reconstitute the nation-states created by men. This is particularly the case with Japan, where the salaried man model that has long characterized Japanese society is currently undergoing radical structural reform.

Notes

1. UNWTO Web site: http://www.world-tourism.org
2. Japan National Tourist Organization Web site: http://www.jnto.go.jp
3. An earlier version of this essay was presented at the conference, "Japan: Crossing the Boundaries Within" at the University of California, Berkeley, on 15–16 March 2002, and was entitled "The Exodus of Japanese Women and Brides from Asian Countries: Changing Boundaries of Contemporary Japan." A re-

vised version of the essay was read as a keynote address at the Anthropology and Sociology Section of the Conference of the European Association of Japanese Studies at Warsaw, on 27–30 August 2003, entitled "Circulation of Desire: Transnational Migration of Women to and from Japan." A further revised version of the essay, entitled "Living In-Between: Cross-border Marriages in Transnational Flows of Women from and to Japan," was presented at the conference of Society for East Asian Anthropology, American Anthropological Association, held in Hong Kong on 13–16 July 2006. The Japanese version of the paper was published in 2004 (Yamashita 2004). In this version, I have updated the statistical data and revised the description and notes.

4. Japan National Tourist Organization Web site: http://www.jnto.go.jp. Japanese visitors to China increased from 2.2 million in 1999 to 3.75 million in 2006, while visitors to the United States decreased from 5 million in 1999 to 3.67 million in 2006. This destination shift from the United States to China may reflect Japan's recent economic shift in the same direction as well as the tourism decline in Hawaii after the September 11 terrorist attacks in 2001.

5. The number of inbound flows has been increasing for recent years due to a new policy for promoting inbound tourism introduced by Prime Minister Koizumi in 2003. It aims to receive 10 million inbound visitors by 2013.

6. Japan National Tourist Organization Web site: http://www.jnto.go.jp

7. From the Bali Tourism Board, Web site: http://www.bali-tourism-board.com. The figure is based on the direct fight arrivals in Bali. In 2005, the number of international visitors to Bali went down to 1.39 million due to the second bombing incident occurred in Ocober that year. Regarding the Bali bombings and the "tourism development cycle," see Darma Putra and Hitchcock (2006).

8. The field research in Bali was carried out between August and October 1995, funded by the grant-in-aid for scientific research from the Japanese Ministry of Education, Culture, Sports, Science and Technology, in cooperation with LIPI (the Indonesian Institute of Sciences), Jakarta, Indonesia.

9. "Nostalgia" is one of the keywords for Japanese tourists in Bali. Misa Matsuda (1989: 43–45) suggested that tourism in Bali for Japanese should be analyzed not only in relation to exoticism, but also nostalgia. Regarding "a *furusato* away from home," see also Michael Rea (2002) who discusses Japanese women tourists' attitudes towards England's Lake District and Canada's Prince Edward Island.

10. The research was carried out as part of my research project on "Asians-in-motion in an age of the transnational," funded by an SSRC Abe fellowship, 1998–1999.

11. The Immigration Bureau of Japan Web site: http://www.immi-moj.go.jp

12. According to the statistical data from the Immigration Bureau of Japan, of the registered foreign residents in Japan in 2006, Koreans are the largest group (approximately 600, 000 in number or 29 percent of the total), including the 450,000 *Zainichi* Korean minority residents as a result of colonial labor migration. The second largest group is the Chinese (560,000 or 27 percent), and most of them are newcomers. With the introduction of the 1990 immigration law, the number of *Nikkei* migrants coming to Japan, particularly those from Brazil, increased to the extent that the Brazilian population has become the third largest group (310,000, or 15 percent). The fourth largest group is from the Philippines (190,000 or 9 percent).

13. As was mentioned in note 12, in 2006 the number of the people from the Philippines in Japan amounted to 190,000. The Filipina spouses who married to Japanese males totaled 950,000 for the period from 1989 to 2006. Most of

them were women who came to Japan with entertainers' visas. However, the Japanese government policy towards entertainers changed recently in accordance with the government action plan to fight human trafficking. Under the new policy, which was introduced in June 2006, the government has made the regulations for entertainers' visas stricter (*Kokusaijinryû* [The Immigration Newsmagazine], April 2006). This has made it more difficult for Filipinas to get visas and has placed stricter regulations on who can hire these women in Japan.

14. This interview took place in October 2000 in Tokyo.
15. The Japanese Ministry of Health, Labor and Welfare Web site: http://www.mhlw.go.jp
16. The figure is from the 2004 marriage statistics by the Japanese Ministry of Health, Labor and Welfare. Web site, http://www.mhlw.go.jp. Presumably, most of the American husbands in Japan are soldiers serving at US military bases.
17. According to the Japanese Ministry of Health, Labor and Welfare, the average female age of first marriage in Japan in 2005 was 28 years.
18. Recently, Tôko Shirakawa (2002) has written a book called *Kekkon Shitakutemo Dekinai Ootoko, Kekkon Dekitemo Shinai Onna* [Men unable to marry despite their desire, women who won't marry even though they are able]. This may be an evolving form of the "I may not marry" syndrome.
19. Watanabe Masako (2002) has discussed recent sociocultural changes caused by the dearth of young women and the "import" of foreign wives in rural Japan, especially in the Mogami district, Yamagata Prefecture.
20. Nelson Graburn (1983) wrote about a similar phenomenon in East Asia.
21. See note 14.
22. This interview took place in April 2000 in Berkeley, California.
23. On the marginal position of women in nation-states and its relationship to their transnational migration, see Takezawa (1998: 74) and Lash and Urry (1994: 311–312).

References

Appadurai, Arjun. 1996. *Modernity at Large: Cultural Dimensions of Globalization*. Minneapolis: University of Minnesota.

Campani, Giovanna. 1995. "Women Migrants: From Marginal Subjects to Social Actors." In *The Cambridge Survey of World Migration*, ed. Robin Cohen, 546–550. Cambridge: Cambridge University Press.

Center for International Cultural Studies and Education (ICS). 1999. *ICS Ryûgaku Hakusho* [ICS study abroad white paper]. Tokyo: ICS Kokusai Bunka Kyôiku Center.

Clifford, James. 1997. *Routes: Travel and Translation in the Late Twentieth Century*. Cambridge: Harvard University Press.

Darma Putra, I. Nyoman, and Michael Hitchcock. 2006. "The Bali Bombs and the Tourism Development Cycle." *Progress in Development Studies* 6: 157–166.

Faier, Lieba. 2003. *On Being Oyomesan: Filipina Migrants and Their Japanese Families in Central Kiso*. Ph.D. diss., University of California, Santa Cruz.

Graburn, Nelson H. H. 1983. "Tourism and Prostitution: A Review Article." *Annals of Tourism Research* 10: 437–456.

Hapa Issues Forum. 1998. *Parenting Resources Guidebook*, first edition. Compiled by Sevenju Miki Pepper. Berkeley, CA.

Hisada, Megumi. 1992. *Filipina wo Aishita Otokotachi* [The men who loved Filipinas]. Tokyo: Bunshun Bunko.

Itô, Ruri. 1992. "'Japayukisan' Genshô Saikô: Hachijûnendai Nihon eno Ajia Josei Ryûnyû" [Rethinking the 'Japan-goers' phenomenon: Asian women's migration to Japan in the 1980s]. In *Gaikokujin Rôdôsharon* [The essays on guest workers], eds. Toshio Iyodani and Takamichi Kajita, 293–332. Tokyo: Kôbundô.

Kelsky, Karen. 1996. "Flirting with the Foreign: Interracial Sex in Japan's 'International' Age." In *Global/Local: Cultural Production and the Transnational Migracy*, ed. Rob Wilson and Wimal Dissanayake, 173–192. Durham, NC: Duke University Press.

Kelsky, Karen. 1999. "Gender, Modernity and Eroticized Internationalism in Japan." *Cultural Anthropology* 14 (2): 229–255.

Kelsky, Karen. 2001. *Women on the Verge: Japanese Women, Western Dreams*. Durham, NC: Duke University Press.

Kokudokôtsûshô [Japanese Ministry of Land, Infrastructure and Transport], 2001. *Heisen 13 Nen Ban Kankô Hakusho* [Tourism white paper 2001]. Tokyo: Zaimushô Insatsukyoku [Publishing office, Japanese Ministry of Finance].

Kuwa, Hitomi. 1998. *Nyûyôku De Mitsuketa Atarashii Watashi: Sanjûgosai Karano Ryûgaku Sutôri* [A newfound self in New York: A story of studying abroad after 35 years old]. Tokyo: Daiyamondosha.

Lash, Scott, and John Urry. 1994. *Economics of Signs and Space*. London: Sage.

Marcus, George. 1998. *Ethnography through Thick and Thin*. Princeton: Princeton University Press.

Matsuda, Misa. 1989. *Japanese Tourists and Indonesia: Images of Self and Other in the Age of Kokusaika* [Internationalization]. Master's thesis. Canberra: Australian National University.

Ong, Aihwa. 1999. *Flexible Citizenship: The Cultural Logics of Transnationality*. Durham, NC: Duke University Press.

Rea, Michael. 2000. "A Furusato Away from Home." *Annals of Tourism Research* 27 (3): 638–660.

Sato, Machiko. 2001. *Farewell to Nippon*. Melbourne: Trans Pacific Press.

Shirakawa, Tôko. 2002. *Kekkon Shitakutemo Dekinai Otoko, Kekkon Dekitemo Shinai Onna* [Men unable to marry despite their desire, women who won't marry even though they are able]. Tokyo: Sunmark Publishing.

Shukuya, Kyôko. 1988. *Ajia kara Kita Hanayome* [Brides from Asia]. Tokyo: Akashi shoten.

Sôrifu [The Minister's Office, Government of Japan]. 1998. *Heisen 10 Nen Ban Kankô Hakusho* [Tourism white paper 1998]. Tokyo: Ôkurashô Insatsukyoku [Publishing Office, Japanese Ministry of Finance].

Sugimoto, Yoshio. 1993. *Nihonjin wo Yameru Hôhô* [The way to stop being Japanese]. Tokyo: Chikuma shobô.

Tadiar, Neferti. 1993. "Sexual Economies in the Asia-Pacific Community." In *What Is in a Rim? Critical Perspectives on the Pacific Region Idea,* ed. Arif Dirlik, 183–210. Boulder, CO: Westview Press.

Tajima, Junko. 1998. *Sekaitoshi Tokyo no Ajiakei Ijûsha* [Asian migrants in global city Tokyo]. Tokyo: Gakubunsha.

Takezawa, Yasuko. 1998. "Gurôbarizeishon to Gendai" [Globalization today]. *Imin Kenkyû Nenpô* [Annals of migration studies] 5: 68–81.

Tanimura, Shiho. 1990. *Kekkon Shinai Kamoshirenai Shôkôgun* [The "I may not marry" syndrome]. Tokyo: Kadokawa shoten.

Ueno, Chizuko. 1996. "Heisei Fukyôka no Onna to Otoko" [Women and men in the age of the Heisei recession]. *Gekkan Minpaku* [The National Museum of Ethnology monthly magazine] June: 2–7. Osaka: National Museum of Ethnology.

Watanabe, Masako. 2002. "Nyûkamâ Gaikokujin no Zôdai to Nihonshakai no Bunka Henyô: Nôson Gaikokujinzuma to Chiikishakai no Henyô wo Chûshinni" [The increase of newcomer foreigners and cultural changes in Japanese society: With special reference to foreign wives in rural areas and local social changes]. In *Kokusaishakai 2: Henyôsuru Nihonshakai to Bunka* [International society 2: Changing Japanese society and culture], ed. Takashi Miyajima and Hirokatsu Kano, 15–39. Tokyo: Tokyodaigaku Shuppankai.

Yamamoto, Michiko. 1993. *Deyôka Nippon, Onna Sanjûissai: Amerika, Chûgoku wo Yuku* [Shall I leave Japan: A woman at 31 travels to America and China]. Tokyo: Kôdansha.

Yamashita Shinji. 2003. *Bali and Beyond: Explorations in the Anthropology of Tourism.* Translated by Jerry Eades. Oxford and New York: Berghahn.

Yamashita, Shinji. 2004. "Kokkyô wo Koeru Joseitachi: Bari, Kariforunia, Nihon" [Women's border-crossings: Bali, California, and Japan]. In *Toransunashonariti Kenkyû: Kyôkai no Seisansei* [Studies on transnationality: Productivity of the boundaries], eds. Koizumi Junji and Kurimoto Eisei, 67–81. Osaka: the 21st Century COE Program, Osaka University.

6

CROSSING ETHNIC BOUNDARIES: JAPANESE BRAZILIAN RETURN MIGRANTS AND THE ETHNIC CHALLENGE OF JAPAN'S NEWEST IMMIGRANT MINORITY

Takeyuki "Gaku" Tsuda

Introduction: Internationalization at Home and Abroad

KOKUSAIKA, OR INTERNATIONALIZATION, has become one of the most pervasive ideologies in Japan today. At all levels of Japanese society, it is widely acknowledged that the country needs to free itself from its previously insular mentality and become more engaged in an increasingly globalized world and more receptive to foreign influences at home. Over the last few decades, Japan has internationalized in many respects: Japanese direct foreign investment and international trade has increased exponentially, the economy has become fully integrated into global financial networks, and its corporate offices have become truly multinational (see Hamada, chapter 2). Japan has also begun to assert its political power internationally through a more active foreign policy and in the United Nations and international treaties.

Despite this, Japan's record of internationalizing at home is much more mixed. Although the domestic economy has considerably liberalized since the protectionism of the late 1970s, significant trade barriers still exist. Many domestic industries are not open to foreign competition and foreign investment in Japan remains somewhat restricted. The most problematic aspect of Japan's domestic internationalization is its reluctance to accept foreign peoples. During the labor shortages in the 1970s, Japan continued to insist on its ethnic homogeneity and refused to accept any unskilled for-

---

Endnotes for this chapter begin on page 134.

eign workers, preferring instead to optimize domestic labor productivity and supply to meet its labor needs. However, by the late 1980s, Japan's labor shortage was so acute that it finally succumbed to the pressures of global migration. Despite increasing levels of immigration, the government maintained its long-standing ban on the importation of unskilled foreign workers when it revised the Immigration Control and Refugee Recognition Act in 1989 (hereafter, Revised Immigration Law).[1] Thus, Japan's immigrant population is still miniscule in percentage terms compared with European and American countries.

Nonetheless, Japan currently has well over 800,000 unskilled foreign workers from Asia, Latin America, and the Middle East. Many of these are undocumented or are legally accepted under various official guises (such as "trainees," "students," "entertainers," and ethnic Japanese "visitors"), but actually perform unskilled jobs (see Tsuda and Cornelius 2004). Many immigrants are beginning to settle long-term in Japan and their numbers will dramatically increase if current economic growth and population levels are to be sustained.[2]

This arrival of foreign workers will seriously test the Japanese ideology of domestic "internationalization." Will Japan shed its insistence on ethnic homogeneity and eventually accept these immigrants into Japanese society, embracing multiculturalism and ethnic diversity? Or will it erect ethnic barriers by reacting negatively to the intrusion, excluding immigrants, and intensifying restrictive ethnonationalist ideologies through an increase in anti-immigrant, nativist sentiment?

We can glimpse the future of Japanese immigration by analyzing the reception of the foreign workers currently in the country. This chapter examines how the Japanese have reacted to the most prominent group of immigrants, Latin American *Nikkeijin* (Japanese descendants born and raised overseas), who began "returning" to Japan in the late 1980s in response to a severe economic crisis in South America. Most of these *Nikkeijin* are Japanese Brazilians, whose population in Japan was around 280,000 by the year 2000. It continues to grow despite the prolonged Japanese recession. The Revised Immigration Law, which was implemented in 1990, allowed almost unfettered entry and employment of *Nikkeijin*. Although the Brazilian *Nikkeijin* are seen as relatively middle class in Brazil, they earn five to ten times their Brazilian salaries in Japan as unskilled or semiskilled factory workers. The open immigration policy toward the "ethnic Japanese" up to the third generation and well-established labor recruitment networks between Japan and Brazil have also increased the migrant flow.[3] Most Japanese Brazilians came to Japan to work only for a few years and return with their savings, but many have already brought their families to Japan and the process of long-term settlement has begun (see Tsuda 1999b). Most immigrant *Nikkeijin* are second and third generation (*nisei* and *sansei*) in Brazil, do not speak Japanese very well, and are culturally "Brazilianized."

At first glance, the "ethnically Japanese" Brazilian *Nikkeijin* might not seem to be the most appropriate immigrant group with which to assess future Japanese response to foreigners. Assuming their Japanese ethnic affinity would make them easier to incorporate into Japanese society, their reception might be an early indication of how well Japan will be able to "internationalize" and accommodate other foreign immigrant groups. Also, the broad presence of the culturally Brazilianized *Nikkeijin* challenges restrictive definitions of Japaneseness by causing the Japanese to realize that cultural diversity exists among Japanese descendants. In contrast, culturally and racially different non-*Nikkeijin* foreigners, having no personal ethnic relevance to the Japanese, are therefore less capable of forcing the Japanese to loosen rigid ethnic boundaries and ethnonational identities. If the Japanese Brazilians cannot be ethnically accepted in Japan, it is unlikely that other types of foreign workers would be welcomed.

Judging from the current ethnic status of *Nikkeijin* migrants in Japan the prospects for the domestic internationalization of Japan seem rather bleak. Although labor-deficient Japanese businesses and some local governments and NGOs in cities with high immigrant concentrations are quite receptive and supportive of the Japanese Brazilians, most Japanese in local communities and factories have not crossed ethnic boundaries by socially accepting the *Nikkeijin*, but have excluded them as foreigners in daily interaction. Thus, Japanese Brazilians have become Japan's newest ethnic minority, joining the ranks of Korean Japanese, Burakumin, Ainu, and Okinawans. In turn, the *Nikkeijin* have responded to their marginalization by asserting their Brazilian national identities and cultural differences as a counter-reaction. This has not caused the Japanese to expand their notions of Japaneseness toward multicultural possibilities to include those who are culturally different. Instead, it has renewed awareness of their own Japanese cultural distinctiveness in opposition to Japanese Brazilians. This resurgence of cultural nationalism and *Nihonjinron* discourses among ordinary Japanese citizens in response to immigrants inadvertently reinforces official government ideologies of ethnic homogeneity, thus enhancing the control of the Japanese nation-state.

The Social Marginalization of Japanese Brazilians in Japan[4]

As Brazil's oldest and largest Asian minority (population over 1.2 million), Japanese Brazilians are socially well integrated in Brazilian society but continue to feel culturally "Japanese" and assert a rather prominent Japanese ethnic identity. In general, they are well regarded by mainstream Brazilians for their positive "Japanese" cultural attributes, their relatively high socioeconomic and educational status, and their affiliation with the highly respected country of Japan. In turn, the Brazilian *Nikkeijin* take pride in their Japanese descent and cultural heritage and identify rather strongly with positive images of Japaneseness, actively "reinvent" traditional Japanese cultural activities within their ethnic communities, and generally distance themselves from what they perceive negatively as "Brazilian." So, their Japanese ethnic consciousness remains stronger than their national Brazilian identity (Tsuda 2003b: chapter 1).

When the Japanese Brazilians migrate back to Japan, they expect to be accepted as ethnic Japanese descendants and that they will have congenial relationships with the Japanese.[5] However, confronted by a narrow Japanese ethnonational identity in which Japaneseness is defined not only by Japanese racial descent, but by complete Japanese linguistic and cultural proficiency, the Brazilian *Nikkeijin* discover that although they felt quite culturally "Japanese" in Brazil, they are not ethnically accepted in Japan because they appear culturally foreign not only for their lack of Japanese language proficiency, but also for their Brazilian attitudes and behavior. One Japanese resident in Oizumi-town (Gunma-prefecture) expressed a typical reaction: "There's a lot of *iwakan* [sense of incongruity] towards those who have a Japanese face but are culturally Brazilian. If they have a Japanese face, we interpret this to mean they are Japanese, so we initially approach the *Nikkeijin* this way. But then when we find they are culturally different, we say they are *gaijin* [foreigners]."

Therefore, although the Japanese Brazilians were always called "*japonês*" in Brazil, in Japan they are suddenly labeled "*gaijin*." At the factory where I conducted participant observation (which I will call Toyama), the Brazilian *Nikkeijin* were often addressed as *gaijin-san* (Mr. or Mrs. Foreigner), although personal names were usually used in more familiar situations. The Japanese Brazilians are also referred to as *gaijin* outside the workplace, especially when they speak Portuguese publicly.

Their outsider status is reinforced by the ethnic marginalization they experience and the tendency of most Japanese to avoid unfamiliar foreigners. At Toyama, *Nikkeijin* and Japanese workers remained apart during break and lunch hours, in separate rooms or at different tables, conversing only amongst themselves. Brief smiles or morning greetings and short exchanges of a few words or simple questions constituted their interethnic interaction. Although they worked together on the assembly lines, general conversation between the two groups was usually limited to work instructions. I often witnessed Brazilian *Nikkeijin* and Japanese workers working together on the same machines for hours without exchanging a word.

Outside the workplace, the social alienation of Japanese Brazilians is also quite notable. Few have outside social relationships with their Japanese coworkers. Although some Japanese companies invite their *Nikkeijin* workers to company parties and outings, most Japanese and Japanese Brazilian informants reported that socializing outside such formal occasions was very rare. Even though the Japanese Brazilians do not live in geographically segregated immigrant enclaves, there is some residential segregation—a good number live in apartments where a notable proportion of the residents are other *Nikkeijin*.[6] Interactions between Brazilian *Nikkeijin* and Japanese outside the factory are generally limited to workers at local stores, banks, and municipal offices. Kitagawa (1996) found that 44.3 percent of the Japanese Brazilians reported they had almost no social contact with the Japanese and 15.8 percent had only minimal contact. The only Japanese Brazilians who seem to interact with the Japanese to any notable degree are bilingual interpreters in local government offices or in companies and firms that employ *Nikkeijin* workers. Despite their large numbers and ethnic affinity, *Nikkeijin*-Japanese marriage remains very rare, lower than those between Japanese and Americans.[7]

However, some Japanese attempt to establish closer relationships with Brazilian *Nikkeijin* immigrants and incorporate them socially. Small and medium-sized manufacturers (where most are employed) openly welcome *Nikkeijin* workers (few could stay in business without them). The Japanese employers I interviewed advocated more open immigration policies and even favored granting them permanent residence. Some worked to promote smooth relationships between their Japanese and *Nikkeijin* employees and encouraged them to socialize outside work.

City governments with large *Nikkeijin* populations have generally been receptive, providing foreign workers with language classes and translation services, information handbooks and pamphlets, consultation services (for personal, legal, employment, and social welfare issues), public housing, health insurance and emergency medical coverage, and even limited political representation through foreigner advisory councils. To promote community interethnic interaction and understanding, some have also established international exchange offices that organize special events, festivals, and cultural activities that bring Japanese and foreign residents together (see Tsuda, 2006). They are active in providing basic social services and support for three reasons: they are responsible for the welfare of all local residents (including foreign ones) and wish to avoid conflicts between Japanese and foreigners; Tokyo does little to facilitate the social integration of foreign workers; and immigrants support the municipal economy as workers, consumers, and taxpayers. However, where the number of immigrants is small, local governments have not been active in welcoming and assisting them.

Also, *Nikkeijin* (and other immigrants) with families in Japan have been urged to enroll their children in Japanese schools. Districts with large numbers of *Nikkeijin* students have created special "Japanese classes" with specially trained teachers, developed teaching manuals, hired tutors and assistants, and offered counseling/translation services for foreign students and parents (see Okubo, chapter 9). Japanese Brazilians are welcomed by Japanese Christian churches and many have joined their congregations. In cities with many *Nikkeijin*, Japanese retailers welcome them as customers and even stock Brazilian food and merchandise, post signs in Portuguese, and sometimes hire Portuguese-speaking salesmen.

Also, a few Japanese individuals trying to surmount linguistic and ethnic barriers actively talk with the Japanese Brazilians at work, invite them home to dinner, or go out with them in the evenings. One of my Japanese informants had even learned some Portuguese and socialized with *Nikkeijin* more than with his Japanese friends. A few participated as volunteers in the Japanese Brazilian community. One dated a *Nikkeijin* man for some time.

Nonetheless, most Brazilian *Nikkeijin* informants felt alienated from the Japanese and few felt accepted (Tsuda 2003a). The causes of their marginalization are complex and are not simply the product of a restrictive ethnonational identity that defines them as culturally alien foreigners. Since most Brazilian *Nikkeijin* cannot speak Japanese effectively, language is obviously a barrier. Their segregation also reflects Japanese group dynamics, where sociocultural differences undergird mutually exclusive social groups constituted by insider/outsider distinctions. Japanese ethnic avoidance behavior is sometimes motivated by latent ethnic prejudice toward the *Nikkeijin* based on negative preconceptions of their migration legacy and social status and unfavorable opinions of their "Brazilian" behavior (see Tsuda 2003b: chapter 2).

The social exclusion of the Brazilian *Nikkeijin* also reflects their marginal position in the Japanese labor market. Since most of them are *hiseishain* (informal, temporary contract workers) "borrowed" from outside labor brokers, they do not belong to the companies where they work and therefore remain socially separated from regular Japanese employees. This happens not only in informal interaction, but also during lunch periods (when the *Nikkeijin* eat in separate rooms) and on the assembly line (because the *Nikkeijin* are sometimes placed in segregated work sections). Because they are not company employees, they usually are not invited to company outings and other events. As a casual workforce, they are constantly transferred by their broker between companies depending on production needs. Most Japanese Brazilians at Toyama only worked in the factory for a few months, so few Japanese workers bother to associate with such transients.

The Brazilian *Nikkeijin* also respond to their ethnic rejection by actively withdrawing in an act of ethnic self-segregation. Most do not actively seek out relationships with the Japanese, mainly because the Japanese do not want relationships with them. Although the Japanese Brazilians are beginning to settle long-term (see Tsuda 1999b), many view themselves as sojourners who will return to Brazil in a few years after accumulating sufficient savings. Therefore, they have little incentive to integrate into Japanese society and establish long-term, meaningful relationships with Japanese. Despite their self-perceived temporary status, Brazilian *Nikkeijin* have already created extensive self-contained immigrant communities in parts of Japan (such as Oizumi-town, Gunma-ken, and Hamamatsu and Toyohashi cities in Aichi-ken), supported by an array of Brazilian restaurants, food stores, discos, barbers, entertainment centers, clothing stores, and *Nikkeijin* churches. Large labor brokers are especially active in such communities, providing extensive employment, housing, transportation, and other services mainly in Portuguese. *Nikkeijin* assistance centers offer everything from information and translation to counseling, and local government offices have bilingual *Nikkeijin* liaisons that take care of alien registration and other administrative needs. Although the *Nikkeijin* remain only a minority residentially scattered among the Japanese, such cohesive immigrant communities enable them to live exclusively within their own extensive networks.

The Performance of Brazilian Nationalist Identities

Not only do Japanese Brazilians feel excluded as foreigners in Japan, they become acutely aware of their Brazilian cultural differences, experience ethnic discrimination, and recognize many negative aspects of Japanese cultural behavior (see Tsuda 2003b: chapter 3). In response, many of them feel a resurgence of Brazilian national sentiment and distance themselves by asserting their Brazilian cultural differences.

One way the *Nikkeijin* display their Brazilianness is through dress, a frequent emblem of ethnic difference. Some deliberately wear distinctive Brazilian clothes to catch the attention of the Japanese. Of course, some wear Brazilian clothes in Japan out of comfort or habit, but for others it is a display of cultural defiance. One Brazilian clothing store manager explained that the clothes she sells have distinctive designs, fashions, and colors not found in Japanese department stores. Jeans have colorful ornamental features and women's are tighter around the hips. Shirts have strong (even loud) colors or mosaic patterns, while t-shirts with the Brazilian flag, national colors, or the country's name are also popular.

The performance of Brazilian identities also involves the use of language and greetings. Although Martina, a *sansei* (third-generation) woman, speaks Japanese well, whenever she enters a store she makes a point of speaking Portuguese loud enough so that the Japanese will notice. "I don't want to be confused as Japanese," she said. "So I always show them I am Brazilian." Likewise, some *Nikkeijin* greet each other by publicly embracing or kissing to display Brazilian behavior that is completely incongruous with "Japanese culture" and serves as means of ethnic differentiation.

Some individuals exaggerate their Brazilian behavior in a rebellious, exhibitionist manner. One informant observed cynically, "Some of these Brazilian youth have this attitude toward the Japanese: 'Hey, I'm Brazilian and I am going to act Brazilian in Japan. And if you don't like it, screw you.' As a result, they are seen less favorably by the Japanese. However, in Brazil, they would never have acted like this and do it only in Japan."

Others are more subdued, especially the more acculturated *Nikkeijin*, who feel more pressure to follow Japanese norms. For them, the assertion of their Brazilianness is less ostentatious and is usually limited to introducing themselves as Brazilian to avoid being mistaken as Japanese, relieving themselves of Japanese cultural expectations. Some *Nikkeijin* office workers or students speak fluent Japanese but subtly differentiate themselves as Brazilians by writing their Japanese surnames in *katakana* (a phonetic syllabary used for foreign names) instead of *kanji*. Those with both Brazilian and Japanese first names may use their Brazilian name in Japan, although they may use their Japanese name in Brazil. Others use personal symbols for differentiation: Marcos, a Japanese Brazilian journalist in Japan, wears a goatee as his "little rebellion against the Japanese," an emblem of his ethnic differences from Japanese men, whom he believes do not like facial hair.

The enactment of Brazilian nationalist identities in Japan occurs in collective ritual performances as well. Important examples include Brazilian *Nikkeijin*-organized samba parades in some local communities. Although most never participated in samba in Brazil or scorned it as a lowly Brazilian activity, they find themselves dancing samba for the first time, finding it a lot of fun. However, since they are unfamiliar with this national Brazilian ritual, their performance in Japan does not follow preordained cultural models of samba, but is a spontaneous cultural form generated in the context of enactment. The samba parade I observed in Oizumi-town was improvised, haphazard, and somewhat casual. They wore randomly chosen "samba costumes," ranging from simple bathing suits, clown outfits, or festival clothes with Brazilian national colors (yellow and green), to T-shirts and shorts. Most did not seem to know how to properly dance samba and, even with some familiarity, almost no one could execute it properly. Most participants seemed to be moving and shaking their bodies randomly, some in a lackadaisical manner. The result was a potpourri of costumes and individuals moving their bodies randomly without any pattern or precise rhythm resembling Brazilian samba. The only parts requiring explicit cultural knowledge were the singer of the samba theme and the *bateria* (the drum section that beats out the samba rhythm), comprised almost exclusively of non-*Nikkeijin* Brazilians.

The overall cultural product shared little with Brazilian samba and would have been barely recognizable back home, but in Japan its cultural distinctiveness made it seem very "Brazilian." The performance served as a collective assertion of Brazilian ethnic identity. This cultural authentification is also unintentionally supported by the Japanese spectators, who showed an active interest in these foreign festivities. Since they know less about samba than the Japanese Brazilians, they are unable to critique the performance as "inauthentic." Therefore, the implicit collusion between participant and observer in a foreign context authenticates the spontaneously generated performance as a true display of a distinctive Brazilian culture.

Nikkeijin Return Migrants and Japanese Ethnonational Identity

How do Japanese respond to these *Nikkeijin* and does it influence their ethnonational identity? Does the nationalist assertion of Brazilian culture by *Nikkeijin* cause the Japanese to recognize the ethnic diversity among Japanese descendants and therefore broaden currently exclusionary notions of Japaneseness in ways congenial to multi-ethnic accommodation? Of course, the Japanese Brazilians don't have much impact on Japanese identity because they remain only a minute fraction of the country's population. However, Japanese national identity has been constantly articulated and redefined by encounters with foreign peoples (first China and then "the West") (Befu 1993: 121–125; Ohnuki-Tierney 1990).[8] Undoubtedly, the recent arrival of foreign labor migrants is another historical moment causing many Japanese to reconsider what it means to be Japanese.

The presence of a new *Nikkeijin* immigrant minority could challenge essentialist notions of Japanese ethnic identity, in which the "racially" Japanese (of Japanese descent, having a "Japanese face") are assumed to be "culturally" Japanese too (Kondo 1986). This assumed correspondence between race and culture is the result of Japan's ideology of ethnic homogeneity in which all Japanese are seen as the same race and are perceived as culturally similar (Yoshino 1992: 120).[9] Because the Japanese Brazilians are "racially" Japanese but "culturally" Brazilian, they are ethnic anomalies (Kondo 1986) who defy classification by transgressing the boundaries between "Japanese" and "foreigner." Japanese informants specifically described their disorientation when they first encountered *Nikkeijin*. A freelance journalist spoke of this ethnic incongruity:

> When we first set eyes on the *Nikkeijin*, our spontaneous reaction is one of confusion and shock. We think they are really strange. We assume they are Japanese, so we talk to them, and then wonder why they don't understand us and cannot communicate in Japanese. They look Japanese, but speak in a strange tongue. Most Japanese do not have a concept of a *Nikkeijin*. So we say, 'who are these guys?' We always expected those with a Japanese face to have a certain level of Japanese culture. But the Japanese are now changing this attitude as we realize that the *Nikkeijin* are different.

Therefore, the assertion of cultural difference among *Nikkei* immigrants disrupts the correlation between race and culture, the foundation of Japanese ethnonational identity, potentially leading to new ethnic attitudes (Murphy-Shigematsu 2000: 211). Thus, the socially marginal reveal the basic assumptions and categories by which a society operates (Valentine 1990: 50) and frequently have more of a transformative impact on collective identity than complete insiders or outsiders.[10]

The transformative potential of the Japanese Brazilians does not cause the Japanese to gradually expand their exclusive definition of Japaneseness to include the culturally different but racially similar *Nikkeijin*. Since the *Nikkeijin* are ethnically marginalized as culturally alien "foreigners," most informants claimed that the Japanese Brazilians would never be ethnically accepted as Japanese unless they assimilated completely.

However, the main reason Japanese do not accept the Brazilian *Nikkeijin* is because they perceive the cultural differences of the *Nikkeijin* quite negatively. Most Japanese interviewed were quite disappointed by how culturally Brazilian the *Nikkeijin* have become (Yamanaka 1996: 84). Although some felt this loss of Japanese culture was "natural," many had expected the *Nikkeijin* to have retained more of the Japanese language and culture and expressed their reactions as *gakkari* (disappointment), *kitai hazure* (did not live up to expectations), and *shitsubô* (disappointing, disillusioning). A young Japanese woman in Oizumi remarked: "The *nisei* and *sansei* are disappointing. Because they are the children of Japanese, we want them to maintain Japanese culture, although we feel that it's also natural that it weakens. It all depends on appearance—if they were mixed-blood, we don't expect this, but if they look Japanese, we think that the ability to communicate in Japanese is obvious. Therefore, we feel betrayed when the *Nikkeijin* disappoint us."

This unfavorable perception of Japanese Brazilian behavior is most evident in the workplace. The Japanese assembly line employees generally gave the Brazilian *Nikkeijin* low marks for their work ethic and ability and saw them as lazy, slow, irresponsible, and careless on the job (Yamanaka 1996: 84). Although employers generally had favorable impressions of *Nikkei* workers, a good number looked unfavorably at aspects of their work behavior. The Brazilian *Nikkeijin* are sometimes seen as excessively individualistic, conflictual, uncooperative, and lacking harmonious group coordination. Some Japanese managers claim that the *Nikkeijin* do not help each other out, create conflicts among themselves, have no group spirit, and will not cooperate with each other to raise production levels, obeying only the orders of superiors. The Brazilian *Nikkeijin* are also seen as completely lacking in company loyalty because they frequently quit their jobs (sometimes without properly informing the management) and move to firms offering higher wages and more overtime.

Japanese negative assessments of *Nikkeijin* cultural attributes also occur outside the factory. Some Japanese have unfavorable opinions of the Japanese Brazilians in their neighborhoods. The most frequent complaint from locals is that the Japanese Brazilians are a disturbance (*meiwaku*) because they make excessive noise in their apartments, turn up their stereos, and party until late at night on weekends (see Japan Institute of Labor, 1995, 2003). A Japanese Toyama worker in his thirties who had lived in an apartment with *Nikkeijin* described the disturbance: "In my last apartment, I had *Nikkei* neighbors on both sides and had plenty of experiences with the 'cheerfulness' [*akarusa*] of South America. The neighbors on the right were quiet, but those on the left were the happy type. They would party, talk loud, sing in the bathtub, and play the guitar until late at night without any consciousness that they are in Japan and disturbing others. It wasn't that they were always noisy, but sometimes they seemed to have ten or twenty people in a room."

The street behavior of *Nikkeijin* also creates some negative cultural impressions. Even in Oizumi, where the residents have become used to foreigners in the streets, some still do not like to see *Nikkeijin* walking around in groups, dressed in a strange manner, speaking loudly in Portuguese, and otherwise behaving in ways that seem alien. Although only some *Nikkeijin* behave in ways that call attention to themselves in the streets, this makes them quite conspicuous.

In general, Japanese expressed considerable discomfort toward groups of Japanese Brazilians in public. In fact, when groups cluster in the streets, especially at night, they are seen suspiciously, mistrusted, and actively avoided by some Japanese. "There's an image of crime associated with all foreign workers," an Oizumi resident remarked. "So we are scared when we see the *Nikkeijin* cluster at night ... we don't cross the park at night if we see them hanging around." A similar reaction was shared by Japanese residents in Machida-city (near Tokyo) toward Peruvian *Nikkeijin* who played soccer matches at a local university playing field. Because they danced, drank, made noise, and played Latin music on the radio after the matches until ten at night, complaints were received from local residents who saw the *Nikkeijin* as "too frightening to pass by." Consequently the university stopped renting the field to the *Nikkeijin* (*Nihon Keizai Shimbun*, 14 October 1992).

Because the *Nikkeijin* are ethnically excluded as culturally alien foreigners, most Japanese informants seemed to experience a greater awareness and appreciation of the distinctive national cultural qualities that make them Japanese by contrasting themselves with the culturally different Japanese Brazilians, thus causing a narrowing of ethnonational identity. When they were confronted with people of Japanese descent who are culturally Brazilian, they seemed to realize the importance of the cultural aspects of being Japanese to a much greater extent, which they previously took for granted as a natural consequence of being "racially" Japanese. Thus, although the ethnic encounter with the *Nikkeijin* de-essentializes Japanese ethnic identity by problematizing the assumption that shared racial descent is the fundamental determinant of who is Japanese, it may produce a more restrictive cultural definition of Japanese identity based on an increased cultural nationalism. One Japanese worker spoke about such ethnic reactions most clearly: "After encountering the Brazilian *Nikkeijin*, I have become more conscious of my Japaneseness. This is something you ordinarily don't think about when you are just with other Japanese, but when I am with *Nikkeijin*, although we are of the same blood, I see how different they are from us—in thinking, attitudes, the way they talk and dress—and I recognize what is Japanese about myself, my special Japanese cultural traits. I realize that I am real Japanese, whereas they are not."

Indeed, a majority of my Japanese informants engaged in homogenizing discourses of Japaneseness when reflecting upon the negative ethnic differences of the Japanese Brazilians, characterizing the Japanese as more diligent, formal, quiet, and polite. Only a few of my informants did not have such reactions, mainly those who had insufficient contact with the Brazilian *Nikkeijin* to become really aware of their cultural differences.

Of course, not all of the Japanese I interviewed reacted negatively to the Japanese Brazilians nor engaged in the same discourse of Japanese national uniqueness. It is also important to note that those who did tended to be from the working class and lived in rural industrial cities and therefore were probably not as ethnically receptive and open-minded as more cosmopolitan and better educated middle-class Japanese in large metropolitan areas. Even among the Japanese working class however, there are rare individuals who are ethnically receptive and actively socialize with *Nikkeijin* immigrants.[11]

A few Japanese informants of middle-class background (two of whom lived in the Tokyo area) had positive impressions of the Brazilian *Nikkeijin*, admiring their friendly openness, lightheartedness, and casualness. For instance, one young Japanese woman, who had joined a *Nikkeijin* assistance organization, remarked: "I prefer being with the *Nikkeijin* more than Japanese because they are so different. They are cheerful, lighthearted, and laid-back, unlike the Japanese who are too serious and gloomy. The Japanese are too sensitive and formal, but with *Nikkeijin*, I don't have to use my nerves—I feel more open and less inhibited with them." Another stressed how he likes the *Nikkeijin* because they are openly friendly even to strangers, whereas Japanese keep to themselves and do not talk with people they don't know and are simply bad at relating to outsiders.

Since these Japanese have positive perceptions of the *Nikkeijin*, they are willing to interact and socialize with them unlike those who had negative reactions. However, although they are crossing ethnic boundaries, it is important to note that they are not collapsing the ethnonational boundaries between themselves and the *Nikkeijin* and accepting the *Nikkeijin* as ethnically one of them. Instead, they like the *Nikkeijin* precisely because they are foreign, and therefore, culturally different from the Japanese. And like their more close-minded compatriots, they too experience an increased sense of Japanese national cultural difference vis-à-vis the *Nikkeijin*, as they also engage in a discourse of Japaneseness by homogeneously characterizing themselves as unfriendly and gloomy as well as overly formal, polite, and sensitive. The only difference is that they portray Japanese national character negatively instead of positively.

The one Japanese informant who came closest to identifying with the *Nikkeijin* was a freelance journalist with previous international experience who was dating a Japanese Brazilian. Yet, despite her desire to break free of her ethnic constraints, even she could not completely overcome the cultural barriers that separated her as Japanese from the *Nikkeijin:*

> As Japanese, I feel really constrained and limited by the social system here. But the *Nikkeijin* have more freedom in thought and imagination. I'm impressed by the resilience of their spirit—they don't give up and get depressed like the Japanese. They really have a positive outlook and optimism. Even if they fail economically, they keep coming to Japan and trying again. I see this and realize our restricted character—how rigid and timid we Japanese are. So when I meet *Nikkeijin,* I feel that I am Japanese, but I also feel I do not need to worry about ethnic differences, my Japaneseness, and can relate to them without an ethnic consciousness. But I still see differences that simply won't give way. They remain, and I feel them strongly.

In this manner, even such socially receptive Japanese do not necessarily broaden their ethnonational identities to incorporate the *Nikkeijin.*

Therefore, just as the Japanese Brazilians increase the consciousness of their Brazilian national differences when they encounter the culturally different Japanese, most Japanese also experience an increased awareness of their distinctive Japanese national characteristics and identity when confronted by the cultural differences of the *Nikkeijin.* Instead of identifying with each other across the borders of cultural difference, both migrants and their hosts seem to be hardening mutually exclusive ethnic boundaries.

When asked about the future prospect of increased immigration to Japan, virtually all of my Japanese informants stressed the importance of Japan as an ethnically homogeneous, island nation and felt that the disruption of this mono-ethnicity through immigration would have negative consequences because the ethnically restrictive nature of Japanese society makes it difficult to incorporate large numbers of foreigners. For instance, the reflections of Sasaki-san, a local storeowner, were quite typical: "Ethnic homogeneity is very important for the social framework of Japan. Japan has been this way for centuries and it has contributed to the nation's social stability and prosperity. It is in our national character—we all think similarly and can relate to each other, creating stability and harmony. If we let a bunch of foreign workers with different cultures into Japan, it will destroy this ethnic unity. Japan has always had an island mentality and has been closed and unreceptive to foreigners for this reason." Not only did the presence of the Japanese Brazilians and other immigrant foreigners cause most of my informants to increasingly value the perceived ethnic homogeneity of their nation, they predicted dire future consequences for Japan if the country was forced to accept massive numbers of immigrants, including ethnic discrimination, serious antiforeigner backlashes, increased crime, and ethnically segregated immigrant ghettos.[12]

The Nationalist Consequences of Transnational Migration

The return migration of the Japanese Brazilians and the possible resurgence of national identity among their Japanese hosts have important implications for the study of transnationalism and for the continued salience of the nation-state in the global ecumene. By asserting a Brazilian nationalist identity through actively displaying their Brazilianness in Japan, *Nikkeijin* immigrants seemingly resist Japanese ethnic hegemony by challenging Japan's nationalist project of assimilating culturally incongruous minorities under an ideology of national homogeneity. A number of scholars have claimed that transnational migrants subvert and undermine the power of nation-states by maintaining strong transnational ties to their homeland and not developing any allegiance to their host country. In other words, through a type of "antinationalist nationalism" (Clifford 1994: 307) and a refusal to assimilate to the dominant culture of the host country, they escape the nation-state's hegemonic agenda. Basch, Schiller, and Blanc (1994: 290) interpret global migration as an act of resistance and opposition by individuals to the state, while Arjun Appadurai (1996) associates it with the emergence of "postnational imaginaries" that produce new forms of transnational allegiance that hasten the decline of the nation-state.

Undoubtedly, this is one reason (among others) why countries that value ethnic homogeneity discourage, if not prohibit large-scale immigration. Indeed, the massive influx of ethnically different foreigners has been strongly perceived by the Japanese government as a threat to social stability and national integrity (Lie 2001: 49). In fact, one of the most prominently cited reasons among Japanese immigration policy makers for why Japan should not accept unskilled foreign workers has been the fear that public order will be disrupted by increased ethnic conflict and discrimination caused by ethnic diversity (Liberal Democratic Party 1992; Ministry of Justice 1994; Ministry of Labor 1991, 1992; Nojima 1989). Although the migration of the "ethnic Japanese" *Nikkeijin* was initially seen as an exception, the government's opinion seems to have changed recently. Since Japanese immigration policy makers expected to receive only a small number of *Nikkeijin* sojourners, they were unprepared for the explosive influx that resulted and did not realize that so many Japanese Brazilians would bring their families and settle in Japan (Kajita 1994: 168). In addition, the *Nikkeijin* were more culturally Brazilian than expected and have not smoothly assimilated to Japanese society. As a result, certain government officials seem to regret their decision to openly admit the *Nikkeijin*. A former Ministry of Labor official stated: "The *Nikkeijin* that the Immigration Bureau [of the Ministry of Justice] intended to accept were different. We were expecting that they would be more culturally Japanese and speak Japanese more. But those who actually came were not the type we expected. Sometimes, we look at some of these people and say, is this really a *Nikkeijin*? I mean, they have no inkling about Japanese culture, and don't speak Japanese.... If we had known so many *Nikkeijin* would come, we would not have allowed them to freely enter Japan."

However, I have suggested here that transnational migration has various unintended consequences and may not be as serious a challenge to the Japanese government's attempt to promote national unity through an ideology of ethnic homogeneity. Indeed, my analysis indicates that the massive influx of *Nikkeijin* immigrants, by shifting the definition of Japaneseness from race to culture, may intensify cultural nationalism and create a greater awareness among Japanese of their distinctive cultural homogeneity (Douglass and Roberts 2000: 26, 30), thus implicitly revitalizing their sense of national allegiance. In fact, as discussed above, my Japanese informants responded to the presence of culturally alien Japanese Brazilian immigrants by advocating the same ideology of ethnic homogeneity and national unity that the Japanese government has been propagating, thus enhancing the ethnic control of the nation-state. In fact, although repeated past intrusions of the foreign have introduced considerable internal heterogeneity to Japanese society, the discourse of Japanese ethnic homogeneity has been remarkably resilient (Ivy 1995: 9, Lie 2001: 50–51) and will continue to remain effective despite the influx of foreign workers into Japan. Therefore, the presence of immigrants with transnational loyalties that resist assimilation pressures in Japan reinforces, more than challenges and transforms the nationalist ideologies that support the hegemony of the Japanese state.

Conclusion: The Future of Japan as a Country of Immigration

How the Japanese will react to *non-Nikkeijin* foreign workers in the future is still an open question.[13] Will they be even less tolerant and accepting of immigrants who are *both* culturally and racially foreign? Do some Japanese find non-*Nikkeijin* immigrants more socially acceptable and are they therefore more likely to reconsider and reduce the country's restrictive ethnic barriers in response to them? Or do the Japanese react in a more negative and ethnically exclusionary manner to the foreignness of the *Nikkeijin* precisely because they are Japanese descendants and were thus expected to be more culturally similar?

My interviews with Japanese informants seemed to indicate that this was not the case. Although many Japanese react negatively to the Japanese

Brazilians, most of my informants felt a certain amount of ethnic affinity to them because of their Japanese descent and clearly preferred them to foreigners of non-Japanese descent, who are completely alien. Of course, this is especially true toward Japanese Brazilians who could speak some Japanese. However, even toward the *Nikkeijin* who had become culturally foreign, there was a strong sense among my informants that they could somehow be culturally comprehended because of their shared descent. As a result, many of the Japanese I spoke with mentioned how they felt *shitashimi* (familiarity and affinity) toward the Brazilian *Nikkeijin* and sometimes even referred to them as *doho* (brethren) or *miuchi* (companions of the inner circle). For example, this type of general sentiment was expressed by a Japanese factory worker in Oizumi: "Discrimination and disparagement is less toward the Brazilian *Nikkeijin* because they have a Japanese face. This creates a feeling of commonality with them as our brethren. Since we see them as people who were originally Japanese, we feel closer to them than other foreigners. There is much more discrimination toward the Korean Japanese."

Therefore, some of my informants felt safer and more at ease with the Japanese Brazilians than with other foreign workers. According to one local Japanese business owner: "At least with the *Nikkeijin*, we feel their blood ties as part of the Japanese group and a sense of commonality and security, in contrast to other foreign workers whom we approach with caution because some of them look scary and are a source of fear. I tend to relax more and feel safer with *Nikkeijin* because of this sense of affinity."

A number of my Japanese informants also noted that they held less prejudice toward the Brazilian *Nikkeijin* because they had very little knowledge of Brazil and thus had no reason to actively dislike the country, given its lack of historical contact or conflict with Japan. Because of such reasons, those Japanese who had negative attitudes about foreign workers in general and wished they would promptly leave Japan mentioned that they could at least tolerate the presence of *Nikkeijin* immigrants and learn to live with them if necessary.

However, even with the *Nikkeijin*, serious conflicts with Japanese are not unknown. Several years ago, complaints from local Japanese residents about Japanese Brazilian residents in the Homi public housing complex of Toyota City (Aichi Prefecture) over improper garbage disposal, noise, theft, and vandalism triggered a campaign by a right-wing group to expel the *Nikkeijin* from the neighborhood, resulting in a campaign vehicle being set on fire. The tension between the Japanese and *Nikkeijin* threatened to escalate into violence and retaliation before the situation was defused partly with the deployment of police officers (Sellek 2001: 215–216).

Nonetheless, there was general consensus among those Japanese I interviewed that there is much more prejudice and discrimination toward Korean Japanese because they are not of Japanese descent (see Hester, chapter 7), even though most of them have been born and raised in Japan and are culturally assimilated. Others cited previously low images Japan had of Korea and Koreans, as well as the historical antagonism between the two countries caused by Japan's colonial past and wartime atrocities. My informants also claimed that discrimination was greater toward mixed-descent *Nikkeijin* (*konketsu*), who were seen as more foreign in contrast to *Nikkeijin* of pure Japanese descent. In this manner, my informants' ethnic preferences were based on perceived degrees of racial closeness. Indeed, a number of them indicated that they are very wary of racially different foreigners (especially those who are non-White). Even in a place like Oizumi where foreigners of all types have become a common sight in the streets, Japanese residents still actively avoid approaching or talking with them or sitting near them on trains, especially at night and especially if the foreigner is dark-skinned. Non-*Nikkeijin* Brazilians of darker complexion in Japan report that they experience more discrimination and are sometimes mistaken for Pakistanis (called "Pakis") or Iranians. It is also quite apparent that the level of socioeconomic marginalization of foreign workers in the Japanese labor market also closely follows this racialized hierarchy of ethnic preference (Mori 1994). The comments of one Japanese employer were quite illustrative:

> When it comes to hiring foreigners, there are clearly several levels based on like and dislike. We feel [ethnically] the closest to the *Nikkeijin,* so they work at the best firms with the best wages. Then come Chinese and Koreans, whom we find less preferable and therefore, they work in less desirable jobs. At the bottom are Bangladeshis and Iranians, who work in the smallest companies that pay the lowest wages. We avoid interacting with Middle Easterners the most, so they get the worst jobs. It really shouldn't be this way, but it just is.

Therefore, if Japan is currently having trouble ethnically accepting and socially integrating its own *Nikkeijin* descendants, its ability to do so for other, more alien immigrants in the future is seriously in doubt. Not only are such immigrants likely to remain both ethnically and socioeconomically segregated, they may become targets of anti-immigrant, nationalist sentiment if there is a massive expansion of the foreign population, as has happened in other immigrant societies. Are my Japanese informants correct in predicting nativist backlashes and public protests, and even violence against foreigners? Indeed, in the late 1980s and early 1990s, when immigration was a contentious social issue in Japan, there were already demonstrations and propaganda by Japanese right-wing groups against immigrants and a large number of neo-Nazi flyers were posted and distributed, urging Japan to expel immigrant foreigners (*Asahi Shimbun*, 7 April 1993; *Japan Times*, 16 October 1989). This is troublesome especially because the immigrant population in Japan is still much smaller than that of European and American countries. However, Japan has always had vocal and prominent right-wing extremist groups that have sometimes resorted to violence to promote their ends. As in the case of Germany, even if the general public remains tolerant and restrained, violent reactions from a small minority of extremists are enough to create a general social crisis. Although concern about the "foreign worker problem" has abated at all levels in Japanese society because of the decade-long recession and stabilization of the immigrant population, the Japanese media has continued to publish prominent articles about alleged increases in foreigner crime, fueling public fears that immigration (especially illegal immigration) is leading to a deterioration in public safety. In fact, 49.2 percent of the Japanese public already feel that illegal immigrants have had a bad impact on Japanese society and close to 50 percent want the government to deport them (up significantly from 32.1 and 33.6 percent respectively ten years ago) (Prime Minister's Office 2000). In response to such public concerns, the Japanese government decided to halve the number of illegal immigrants by mobilizing immigration officers and police as part of a plan (backed by the prime minister and the Cabinet) to reduce the rising crime rate. A government Web site has also been set up to allow Japanese residents to report to immigration officials foreigners that they suspect may be illegal immigrants. If such signs are any indication, Japan's eventual transition to a tolerant and inclusive multiethnic society will indeed be quite difficult.

Notes

1. Only a little over 1 percent of Japan's population is foreign born, in contrast to most European and American countries where the percentage ranges from 3 to over 10 percent.
2. Because Japan's fertility rate—one of the lowest in the world—continues to decline (it fell almost 32 percent since 1965 to 1.3 children per woman in 1999), the United Nations recently estimated that its entire population will contract by 21.6 million by 2050, forcing the country to import over 640,000 immigrants *per year* just to maintain its present work force or face a 6.7 percent annual drop in GDP (United Nations 2000).
3. For an analysis of the causes of Japanese Brazilian return migration, see Tsuda (1999a).
4. This chapter is based on over twenty months of intensive fieldwork and participant observation in Japan and Brazil. Nine months were spent in Brazil (1993–1994) among two separate Japanese Brazilian communities in Porto Alegre (Rio Grande do Sul) and Ribeirão Preto (São Paulo). During my stay in Japan (1994–1995), I conducted fieldwork in Kawasaki (Kanagawa-prefecture) and Oizumi Town and Ota City (in Gunma-prefecture), where I worked for four intensive months as a participant observer in a large electrical appliance factory with about ten thousand workers, of which one thousand were Japanese Brazilians. Close to one hundred in-depth interviews (in Portuguese and Japanese) were conducted with Japanese Brazilians and Japanese workers, residents, employers, and officials (Tsuda 2003b: 1–44).

5. The intermarriage rate in Brazil is reported to be around 45.9 percent (Yamanaka 1997: 20), and as a result, 6 percent of the *Nisei* and 42 percent of the *sansei* are of mixed descent. However, there are fewer mixed-descent *Nikkeijin* in Japan, partly because they have greater difficulty obtaining a visa for Japan.

6. Only 12.7 percent of the *Nikkeijin* live in apartments with only Japanese residents; 33.6 percent live in apartments where over 25 percent of the residents are other *Nikkeijin* (Kitagawa 1997). The proportion is higher in communities where they are highly concentrated. Although the reasons for this residential segregation are complex (Tsuda 2003a, 2003b: chapters 2–3), there is a tendency for Japanese residents to move out of apartments when *Nikkeijin* move in.

7. In 1993, there were only 771 marriages between Japanese and Brazilian nationals (almost all are *Nikkeijin*) compared with 1,625 intermarriages between Japanese and Americans. This is especially notable because the population of Americans in Japan was only one-fourth of the Brazilian population at that time and linguistic/racial/cultural barriers are much greater between Japanese and Americans compared with Japanese and Brazilian *Nikkeijin*.

8. Likewise, Harootunian (1988) analyzes how Japanese nativist discourse and the construction of a distinctive Japanese national identity was a critical and oppositional reaction to the influence of Chinese thought and culture in early modern Japanese history.

9. In this manner, when race and culture are seen as correlated, they tend to be conflated (Medina 1997).

10. Rosaldo claims that those who live in the "border zones" of gender, race, ethnicity, or nationality are frequently most capable of creativity and change through transcultural blending (Rosaldo 1989: 207–209, 215–217). According to Rutherford, the margin is a place of resistance that threatens to deconstruct dominant and hegemonic forms of knowledge (Rutherford1990: 22). Marginal figures in Japanese history have served as metaphors for symbolic transformations in collective self-representations (Ohnuki-Tierney 1987).

11. However, I was somewhat surprised that the three Japanese factory workers in Oizumi I knew who socialized with the Japanese Brazilians (either currently or in the past) still had rather strong ethnic prejudices about them.

12. The most serious incident between *Nikkeijin* residents and Japanese occurred in 1997, when a gang of Japanese youth randomly assaulted more than ten Japanese Brazilian youth in a park near Komaki station (Aichi Prefecture) as an act of revenge. A fourteen-year-old *Nikkeijin* youth was kicked, beaten, and stabbed, dying three days later at a hospital.

13. See Tsuda and Cornelius (2004) for a more detailed analysis of Japanese public opinion toward immigrants.

References

Appadurai, Arjun. 1996. *Modernity at Large: Cultural Dimensions of Globalization.* Minneapolis: University of Minnesota.

Basch, Linda, Nina Glick Schiller, and Cristina Szanton Blanc. 1994. *Nations Unbound: Transnational Projects, Postcolonial Predicaments, and Deterritorialized Nation-States.* Amsterdam: Gordon and Breach Publishers.

Befu, Harumi. 1993. "Internationalization of Japan and Nihon Bunkaron." In *The Challenge of Japan's Internationalization: Organization and Cul-*

ture, ed. Hiroshi Mannari and Harumi Befu. Nishinomiya: Kwansei Gakuin University.

Clifford, James. 1994. "Diasporas." *Cultural Anthropology* 9 (3): 302–338.

Douglass, Mike, and Glenda S. Roberts. 2000. "Japan in a Global Age of Migration." In *Japan and Global Migration: Foreign Workers and the Advent of a Multicultural Society*, ed. Mike Douglass and Glenda S. Roberts, 3–37. London: Routledge.

Harootunian, Harry D. 1988. *Things Seen and Unseen: Discourse and Ideology in Tokugawa Nativism*. Chicago: University of Chicago Press.

Ivy, Marilyn. 1995. *Discourses of the Vanishing: Modernity, Phantasm, Japan.* Chicago: University of Chicago Press.

Japan Institute of Labor. 1995. *Nikkeijin Rôdôsha no Jukyû Shisutemu to Shûrô Keiken* (The Demand/Supply System and Employment Experiences of Nikkeiin Workers). Tokyo: Japan Institute of Labor.

Kajita, Takamichi. 1994. *Gaikokujin Rôdôsha to Nihon* [Foreign laborers and Japan]. Tokyo.

Kitagawa, Toyoie. 1996. "Hamamatsushi ni Okeru Nikkei Burajirujin no Seikatsu Kôzô to Ishiki: Nippaku Ryôkoku Chôsa wo Fumaete [The lives and consciousness of the Brazilian Nikkeijin in Hamamatsu City: Based on surveys in both Japan and Brazil]." *Toyo Daigaku Shakai Gakubu Kiyo* [Bulletin of the Department of Sociology at Toyo University] 34 (1): 109–196.

———. 1997. "Burajiru-taun no Keisei to Deasupora: Nikkei Burajirujin no Teijyûka ni Kansuru Nananen Keizoku Ôizumi-machi Chôsa [Diaspora and the formation of Brazil-town: A continuing seven-year Oizumi-town survey about the settlement of Brazilian Nikkeijin]." *Tôyô Daigaku Shakai Gakubu Kiyo* [Bulletin of the Department of Sociology at Tôyô University] 34 (3): 66–173.

Kondo, Dorinne K. 1986. "Dissolution and Reconstitution of Self: Implications for Anthropological Epistemology." *Cultural Anthropology* 1 (1): 74–88.

Liberal Democratic Party. 1992. *Kokusaika Jidai ni Taiô Shite: Omo to Shite Gaikokujin Mondai ni Kansuru Teigen* [In response to the age of internationalization: A proposal about the foreign labor problem]. Tokyo.

Lie, John. 2001. *Multiethnic Japan.* Cambridge: Harvard University Press.

Medina, Laurie Kroshus. 1997. "Defining Difference, Forging Unity: The Co-construction of Race, Ethnicity, and Nation in Belize." *Ethnic and Racial Studies* 20 (4): 757–780.

Ministry of Justice. 1994. *Shutsunyûkoku Kanri Gyôsei no Genjyô to Tômen no Kadai* [Administration of immigration control and current topics]. Tokyo.

Ministry of Labor. 1991. *Gaikokujin Rôdôsha ga Rôdômento ni Oyobosu Eikyôto ni Kansuru Kenkyûkai* [Research group study on the impact of foreign laborers]. Tokyo.

———. 1992. *Gaikokujin Rôdôsha ga Rodomento ni Oyobosu Eikyôto ni Kansuru Kenkyukai Senmonbukai* [Expert research group study on the impact of foreign laborers]. Tokyo.

Mori, Hiromi. 1994. "Nikkei Shûdanshi ni totte no 'Dekasegi' no Motsu Imi: San Nikei Shûdanchi no Dekasegi Keitai to Eikyô no Taihi wo Tôshite [The meaning of 'Dekasegi' for areas of Nikkeijin noncentration: A comparison of the composition and influence of Dekasegi in three Nikkei communities]." *Ijyû Kenkyû* 31: 40–57.

Murphy-Shigematsu, Stephen. 2000. "Identities of Multiethnic People in Japan." In *Japan and Global Migration: Foreign Workers and the Advent of a Multicultural Society,* ed. Mike Douglass and Glenda S. Roberts, 196–216. London: Routledge.

Nojima, Toshihiko. 1989. "Susumetai Nikkeijin no Tokubetsu Ukeire [Proposal for the special admission of the Nikkeijin]." *Gekkan Jiyû Minsu,* November: 92–99.

Ohnuki-Tierney, Emiko. 1987. *The Monkey as Mirror: Symbolic Transformations in Japanese History.* Princeton, NJ: Princeton University Press.

———. 1990. "The Ambivalent Self of the Contemporary Japanese." *Cultural Anthropology* 5: 197–210.

Prime Minister's Office. 2000. *Gaikokujin Rôdôsha Mondai ni Kansuru Seron Chôsa* (Public Opinion Survey about the Foreign Worker Problem). Tokyo: Prime Minister's Office.

Rosaldo, Renato. 1989. *Culture and Truth: The Remaking of Social Analysis.* Boston: Beacon Press.

Rutherford, Jonathan. 1990. "A Place Called Home." In *Identity: Community, Culture, Difference,* ed. Jonathan Rutherford, 9–27. London: Lawrence and Wishart.

Sellek, Yoko. 2001. *Migrant Labour in Japan.* New York: Palgrave.

Tsuda, Takeyuki. 1999a. "The Motivation to Migrate: The Ethnic and Sociocultural Constitution of the Japanese-Brazilian Return Migration System." *Economic Development and Cultural Change* 48 (1): 1–31.

———. 1999b. "The Permanence of 'Temporary' Migration: The 'Structural Embeddedness' of Japanese-Brazilian Migrant Workers in Japan." *Journal of Asian Studies* 58 (3): 687–722.

———. 2003a. "Homeland-less Abroad: Transnational Liminality, Social Alienation, and Personal Malaise." In *Searching for Home Abroad: Japanese Brazilians and the Transnational Moment,* ed. Jeffrey Lesser. Durham, NC: Duke University Press.

————. 2003b. *Strangers in Their Ethnic Homeland: Japanese Brazilian Return Migration in Transnational Perspective.* New York: Columbia University Press.

————. 2006. "Localities and the Struggle for Immigrant Rights: The Significance of Local Citizenship in Recent Countries of Immigration." In *Local Citizenship in Recent Countries of Immigration: Japan in Comparative Perspective,* ed. Takeyuki Tsuda, 3–36. La Jolla, CA.

Tsuda, Takeyuki, and W. A. Cornelius. 2004. "Japan: Government Policy and Immigrant Reality." In *Controlling Immigration: A Global Perspective,* 2nd ed., eds. W. A. Cornelius, T. Tsuda, P. L. Martin, and J. F. Hollifield, 439–476. Stanford, CA: Stanford University Press.

United Nations. 2000. *Replacement Migration: Is It a Solution to Declining and Aging Populations?* New York: United Nations.

Valentine, James. 1990. "On the Borderline: The Significance of Marginality in Japanese Society." In *Unwrapping Japan: Society and Culture in Anthropological Perspective,* ed. Eyal Ben-Ari, 36–57. Manchester: Manchester University Press.

Yamanaka, Keiko. 1996. "Return Migration of Japanese-Brazilians to Japan: the Nikkeijin as Ethnic Minority and Political Construct." *Diaspora* 5 (1): 65–97.

————. 1997. "Return Migration of Japanese Brazilian Women: Household Strategies and Search for the "Homeland."' In *Beyond Boundaries: Selected Papers on Refugees and Immigrants,* Vol. 5, eds. R. Krulfeld and D. Baxter, 11–34. Arlington, VA: American Anthropological Association.

Yoshino, Kosaku. 1992. *Cultural Nationalism in Contemporary Japan: A Sociological Enquiry.* London: Routledge.

7

DATSU ZAINICHI-RON:
AN EMERGING DISCOURSE ON BELONGING
AMONG ETHNIC KOREANS IN JAPAN

Jeffry T. Hester

IN THIS CHAPTER, I DESCRIBE an emerging discourse in the debate among Koreans in Japan concerning identity and belonging within Japanese society. Within this discourse, there is recognition of the instability of living as *"Zainichi,"* or as foreign residents in Japan, and a willingness to consider the acquisition of Japanese nationality as a step toward resolving this instability.

What is most noteworthy here is the breaking of a long-standing taboo among Koreans in Japan against public advocacy of naturalization. In the context of the modern historical relationship between Korea and Japan, and given the prevailing concept of belonging inherent in the nationality concept prevailing in postwar Japan, that is, one based on descent, acquiring Japanese nationality has been understood to equal a rejection of ethnic identity, pride, and affiliation. For many individuals, naturalization has often brought criticism from co-ethnics and isolation from the Korean community. Among Koreans, the naturalization option is now less stigmatized and has even begun to be promoted in some quarters. On the Japanese side, an emergent ideology and sentiment of *kyôsei*, (living together [with difference]), has reduced the risk of expressing or displaying elements of difference in heritage or ethnic background. These two mutually informing trends attest to recent changes in the quality of the ethnonational boundaries between "Korean" and "Japanese." They are creating the space for the emergence of hyphenated "Korean-Japanese," a new type of Japanese, a Japanese who can trace their recent ancestral roots to the Korean

---

Endnotes for this chapter begin on page 148.

peninsula. These new Japanese, in turn, bear the potential for redefining the boundaries of "Japaneseness."

I must emphasize at the outset that first, the shifts in discourse I am suggesting are part of a dialectical process that has been unfolding over the decades since the end of the Pacific War, and that the position in the debate I am highlighting does not go uncontested. As evidence for the changes I am referring to, I focus on a few recently published books that address these issues. To place this emerging discourse in context, I begin with a brief historical sketch of the shifting conditions of Korean belonging in Japanese society and perspectives on the issue among resident Koreans in Japan.

From Diasporic Community to Settled Foreigners

Postwar shifts in Japanese immigration and nationality law, in social attitudes within Japan, in Japanese relations with the states on the Korean peninsula, and in generational and political dynamics within the resident Korean community itself have wrought substantial changes in the social and legal positions, as well as subjectivities, of Koreans in Japan. A rough-and-ready periodization of these changes might look as follows:

1) From the end of the Pacific War through 1965, with the signing of the Japan-Republic of Korea normalization treaty;

2) From that point through 1991, when the immigrant status of "special permanent residence" (*tokubetsu eijū*) was established, equalizing conditions of residence for all former colonial subjects still resident in Japan, and their descendants;

3) From 1991 to the present, a period of increasing levels of naturalization, a growing movement for local suffrage, increasing proportions of marriages to Japanese nationals, and growing numbers of offspring who can trace a double Japanese and Korean lineage.

As labels of convenience, I call the first period that of "repatriatism," the second period the period of "stabilization" of conditions of residence, and the third period that of "approaching denizenship."

Repatriation Period

The majority of the more than 2 million Koreans resident in Japan at the end of the Pacific War returned to the peninsula over several months after August 1945.[1] Still, with the severe restrictions on the volume of goods and amount of valuables allowed to be carried back to Korea, and given the conditions prevailing there after the war (Lee and DeVos 1981: 59–60), more than 600,000 remained, primarily being those who had established some base of livelihood in Japan before the war (Kim 2004: 103–106).

Those who deferred or declined repatriation were left in an ambiguous and unstable status. While formally Japanese nationals, with family registers (*koseki*) on the Korean peninsula, they were stripped of suffrage in December 1945, and made subject to the alien registration law in 1947. In 1952, when the US-Japan peace treaty came into effect, Koreans and other former colonial nationals were formally stripped of their Japanese nationality. As Japan nationality law reckons nationality on the basis of descent (*jus sanguinis*) rather than place of birth, children born of Korean nationals in Japan inherit their parents' foreign nationality.

What one might call an autonomous Korean identity movement in Japan was launched immediately after the war's end by, and for, resident Koreans. This involved the construction of a nationwide system of ethnic schools designed to help "de-Japanize" Koreans (Lee and DeVos 1981: 63), especially Japan-born Korean youth, following decades of state-led assimilation as imperial subjects (Hester 2000; Inokuchi 2000). This movement was broadly conceived of as a recovery of both national identity and cultural competence to smooth the way for eventual return to the homeland, when conditions permitted. In fact, a second round of repatriation did take place, primarily in the late 1950s and early 1960s, this time to North Korea.[2] A total of some ninety-three thousand people in total—the greatest number Koreans but including over six thousand Japanese nationals (mostly Japanese spouses)—made the move to the North (Ryang 1997: 113–115; Yang 1996: 100–101). During this period, with first-generation Koreans still dominant, and with harsh discrimination and poverty an ever-present reality, the homeland was a constant reference point, and North-South politics, within the context of the international Cold War struggle, was an inescapable framework in the lives of Koreans in Japan.

From 1952 through 1965, Koreans lived in Japan under a legal framework that exposed them to deportation for a wide variety of offenses and that greatly restricted their access to state-provided social services. Those born after 1952 were required to renew their residence permit every three years. The clear intention of the immigration control and alien registration provisions was to maintain the subordinate status of Koreans within Japanese society, subject them to rigorous surveillance and control, and urge their assimilation and naturalization under the strict terms set by the Japanese state. Alternatively, as Morris-Suzuki has recently suggested, measures were also taken to encourage the departure from Japan of pro-Pyongyang Koreans through the repatriation program mentioned above.[3]

Stabilization

A major shift in this situation was prompted by the signing of the Republic of Korea-Japan Normalization Treaty in 1965, which included among its subsidiary agreements one covering the legal status and treatment of nationals of the ROK (Republic of Korea) residing in Japan. This would provide a more secure status of permanent residence for those qualifying, designated "permanent residency under agreement" (*kyôtei eijû*). The actions punishable by deportation were greatly reduced (but not eliminated), while a degree of access to social welfare benefits was introduced.[4] The agreement, however, conditioned such status on possession of ROK nationality, requiring those seeking the new status to register within five years of the treaty coming into effect in January 1966. Residency under the provisions of the Normalization Treaty applied only to those registering as ROK nationals and their children. The status of future generations was left for future negotiations slated for twenty-five years later, giving rise to the so-called 1991 problem.

In 1982, a revision of the immigration law applying to non-ROK nationals finally allowed them permanent residency, but still not equality with ROK nationals in terms of residence stability (range of crimes exposing one to deportation) and access to social services.

Approaching "Denizenship"

Full equality among former colonial subjects and their foreign-national descendants, and an immigration regime that guaranteed permanent residency through the generations, was established only in 1991, following Japan-ROK negotiations, with the creation of the "special permanent residency" (*tokubetsu eijû*) category, applying to all those had been "divested of Japanese nationality" in 1952.

The early 1990s also witnessed a rise in rates of naturalization among foreign national Koreans in Japan. Generally hovering between four and six thousand annually over the two decades from 1970, the number topped seven thousand for the first time in 1992, surpassed ten thousand in 1995, and has been maintained at around ten thousand since. The rate of naturalization doubled during the decade of the 1990s. Since 1952, nearly a quarter of a million Koreans in Japan have taken Japanese nationality. The year 1991 also witnessed the peak population of foreign national Koreans resident in Japan, at just under 700,000. The figure has fallen every year since, owing primarily to the large proportion of Korean-Japanese "international marriages," the offspring of which tend to be Japanese,[5] and to naturalization.

In 1993, the alien registration law was amended to eliminate the provision for fingerprinting permanent residents in Japan, as the culmination of a nearly decade-long movement among Koreans and others in Japan. The mid 1990s also witnessed the launching of a prominent debate over, and full-fledged national political movement aiming at, local suffrage for permanent residents in Japan.

Zainichi and Beyond: The Internal Debate over Belonging

By the 1970s, as Japan-born second-generation Koreans became the moving force of the community,[6] realistic prospects of return had become more distant. A turning point in discussions among Koreans concerning their belonging in Japan occurred with the Hitachi employment discrimination case (Park 1999: 39–53). Here, a young Korean high school graduate named Pak Jong-shik had applied to the company under his Japanese name "Arai," passed the company recruitment process and received an offer of employment. When the company discovered that Pak was actually of Korean nationality, they withdrew their offer. The man sued Hitachi in an effort to force the company to overturn its refusal of employment (Lee and DeVos 1981: 277–278). A support network comprising both Japanese and Koreans grew up around the case, providing an organization base and political spark for further activism to promote social and civil equality for resident Koreans. Many ethnic organizations, however, distanced themselves from Pak's movement, on the grounds that, to the extent that it was a demand for integration into Japanese society, it promoted the assimilation of Koreans. There has ever since been a tension between a civil rights movement among Koreans and streams of thought centered on promoting ethnic consciousness and ethnic solidarity that emphasize the importance of the homeland and the Korean nation in the lives of Korean residents in Japan.

The 1970s and 1980s witnessed important debates regarding how Koreans should position themselves between Japan, where their daily lives unfold, and Korea, where their roots lie. Helping to frame the debate among Koreans was an intervention from the Japanese side from an official of the Immigration Bureau, by the name of Sakanaka Hidenori. In 1977, in the pages of a journal issued by the Ministry of Justice, Sakanaka made the case that naturalization was the best route both for Koreans themselves and for Japanese society, in order the solve the contradiction between Koreans being, in fact, culturally "quasi-Japanese" (*jun-Nihonjin*) while belonging to the legal category of "foreigner." Engaged in an internal debate within Japanese political circles about how to treat resident Koreans in the context of state security, Sakanaka was urging that the position of Koreans be stabilized as much as possible, and that the choice of naturalization be made easier, to encourage their assimilation and integration within Japanese society. This was against a position that advocated leaving Koreans in an unstable position, as discussed above, in order to encourage them to repatriate or naturalize (Sakanaka 1999: 8–9). Korean intellectuals responded to Sakanaka's reasoning only with criticism, equating naturalization with an assimilation policy that encouraged the loss of a Korean identity (Sakanaka 1999: 12–14).

It was in this context that Kim Tong-myung proposed a "third way" for Koreans in an essay titled "Zainichi Chôsenjin no 'daisan no michi'" (The third path for Koreans in Japan) (1979).[7] As an alternative to both "repatriatism," that is, living with primary reference to the homeland, and naturalization, that is, abandoning the homeland and the Korean community for what was widely regarded as rejection of Koreanness, Kim advocated "living as *Zainichi*," that is, working to create a life based in Japan while maintaining foreign nationality and Korean identity (Park 1999: 76–78). As Park Il points out (77), Kim rejected both Sakanaka's suggestion of the naturalization option as well as the position of individuals and ethnic organizations that the fate of Koreans in Japan was integrally bound up with the fate of the homeland, which should in turn be an integral part of the consciousness of Koreans in Japan.

Another series of debates erupted in the mid 1980s, most prominently between Yang Tae-ho and Kang Sang-jun. The former emphasized the dangers inherent in the anti-discrimination and civil rights movements based on the assumption of settlement in Japan as long as the concept of "difference" that these movements were supposed to protect was unstable and vague. Raising the specter of assimilation (*naikokuminka*), Kang argued that a stable ethnonational consciousness, referencing the homeland, was essential to maintaining an autonomous Korean subjectivity (*shutaisei*). He advocated an approach that would anchor a Korean subjectivity within the historical experience of the movement from Korea to Japan (Park 1999: 79) and would thus maintain an element of homeland orientation.

The position of antidiscrimination activist Yang Tae-ho is suggested in the title of his major work, the book *You Can't Return to Pusan (Pusan ni kaerenai)* (Yang 1984). Yang accused Kang of placing too much emphasis on the homeland as a constant reference point for Koreans in Japan, arguing that an ethnic consciousness of Koreans should be based on the objective fact of Korean settlement in Japan. The fate of Koreans in Japan, he argued, should not be left in the hands of the political forces in the homeland. Rather, urging that Koreans in Japan maintain a critical stance toward both regimes on the peninsula, Yang advocated a particular, autonomous subjectivity for Koreans resident in Japan (Park 1999: 80–81).

Datsu Zainichi-ron

What I call *"datsu Zainichi-ron"* (or "the discourse of abandoning *Zainichi*") refers to a discourse that critiques and/or works toward overcoming the instability or other limits perceived in the *"Zainichi"* position. The term *Zainichi* means literally "present in Japan," and is used in the phrase *"Zainichi Kankoku-Chôsenjin,"* and the increasingly common *"Zainichi Korian,"* with Korean rendered in the *katakana* phonetic script in a move to avoid the political division embedded in the *"Kankoku-Chôsen"* phrase. As I have suggested, since the 1970s there have been a number of works in a genre one might call "*Zainichi-ron*" that attempt to provide a kind of guide to positioning Koreans in Japan between Japanese residence and progressive "Japanization" on the one hand, and the peninsular roots that have marked them as Other in Japan. "*Zainichi*" has become an identity category, even as it is contested and unstable.

The colonial experience is sedimented in the usage of the term. Thus, the term unambiguously distinguishes between Koreans who trace their roots in Japan to the colonial period and "newcomer" Koreans who have come to reside in Japan mostly since the mid 1980s, even though the latter are just as much "present in Japan." On the other hand, those of Korean background who trace their roots in Japan to the colonial period but who have acquired Japanese nationality are sometimes included within the "*Zainichi*" category.

There is also a degree of tenuousness embedded in "*Zainichi*" reflecting its roots as a term used to describe a diasporic population. Reflecting the boundary shifts I refer to in this chapter, one now often comes upon the phrase, "*teijû Korian*," as well as "*teijû gaikokujin*," that is, Koreans, or foreigners, respectively, "settled in Japan." This newer usage is meant to reflect the reality of "non-ethnic Japanese" sharing the fate of ethnic Japanese as constituents of Japanese society. The term may include Japanese nationals of Korean heritage, that is, those who have naturalized, and children of "international marriages."[8]

Toward "Korean-Japanese"

There has recently appeared within Korean circles in Japan a discourse that asserts the limits of the "third way" of "*Zainichi*" and advocates what is presented as a more stable position as "Korean-Japanese" (*Kankoku-kei Nihonjin, Chôsen-kei Nihonjin, Korian-kei Nihonjin, Korian-japaniizu*) through the acquisition of Japanese nationality. Solutions to the experienced contradictions of "*Zainichi*" have been proposed in a handful of books and essays under such titles as:

(1) *Dare no tame demo naku: "Kankoku-kei Nihonjin" toshite ikiru* (For nobody but myself: Living as a Korean-Japanese) (1996), by the naturalized Japan-born ethnic Korean Kaneko Hiroshi

(2) *Nihonjin ni naritai Zainichi Kankokujin* (Resident Koreans who want to become Japanese) (2000), by Iwamoto Mitsuo, also known by his Korean name, I In-shik

(3) *Dai-yon no sentaku: Kankokukei Nihonjin—Sekai roppyakuman Kanminzoku no ikizama to kokuseki* (The Fourth Choice: Korean-Japanese—The Lifestyle and Nationality of the Six Million Ethnic Koreans around the World) (2001), by Kawa Heigyoku

(4) *ZaiNichi Kankokujin no shûen* (The Final Chapter of "Zainichi") (2001), by Tei Tai-kin, whose name is read in Korean as Chung Daekyung

(5) And for good measure, a work by Korean-born and Korea-based journalist Chi Tong-wook, entitled *Zainichi wo yamenasai: Nanajûman-nin no yûshû na mainoriti ni tsugu* (Quit Being Zainichi) (1997).

Noteworthy, to begin with, is the use of the term, *Kankoku-kei Nihonjin*, or "Korean-Japanese" ("Japanese of Korean descent"). What until recently would have been understood as an oxymoron, and very likely still is by most, the term itself is a recent coinage and does some rather powerful conceptual work. The term "Japanese" or "*Nihonjin*" is widely understood as a descent-based ethnic category.[9] To modify it with another descent-based ethnic qualifier (as "Korean" is also widely understood to be) is, in common-sense terms, to create an oxymoron. Going against the grain of this common sense, the term "*Kankoku-kei Nihonjin*" displaces the descent-based ethnic signification rooted in the term "Nihonjin/Japanese." In doing so, it insists on the usually semantically weak civil-political sense of "Japanese," with which is paired Korean ethnicity or descent. "Japanese" is thus rendered as a civil-political category, with its usually strong association with "race," language, or culture greatly weakened.

This stands in contrast to another way of formulating the mix of Korean heritage and Japanese nationality as presented in the term "*Nihonseki Chôsenjin*," or "Korean with Japanese nationality." This is one of the terms used more commonly to date. It has been used, for example, in the movement among those naturalized Koreans who wish to regain the use of their ethnic Korean names as official names. This term also separates the concepts of descent-based ethnicity and politico-legal affiliation, but leaves the concept of "Japanese" intact as an alloy of descent-based and political belonging.

And this distinction of the ethnicity and civic affiliation is what is at the core of the argument in some of these books: that the acquisition of Japanese nationality need not necessarily mean the abandonment of a sense of Koreanness, of pride in Korean heritage, of "being" Korean. This is what Kawa deems "the fourth way:" not repatriatism, not living as a foreign resident, not rejecting ethnic heritage through a naturalization involving complete absorption in a "monoethnic Japan," but an acquisition of full civic-political membership in the Japanese polity, while maintaining a pride in Korean heritage, including the display of one's Korean heritage through the regular use of ethnic names.

Two of the books share an interesting argument to urge *Zainichi* to stabilize their position in Japan: Kawa (2001) devotes a major portion of his book, and Chi part of a chapter (1997: 148–170), to presenting what Koreans residing outside of Korea are doing. In overwhelming numbers, what they are doing is taking up the nationality of the country in which they reside. *Zainichi* are depicted as the exception within the normative behavior of ethnic Koreans abroad (Chi 1997: 170–172; Kawa 2001: 45–48). Therefore, they suggest, there is nothing "un-Korean" about taking up a non-Korean, host-country nationality. In fact, Kawa explains, in a law passed in the Republic of Korea in 1999 concerning the treatment of overseas Koreans, ethnic Koreans who take up other nationalities are fully recognized as Koreans

(2001: 49–50). Naturalization is thus presented as a legitimate, logical, even "natural" choice for Koreans pursuing their lives outside of Korea.

Tei, the author of *The Final Chapter of Zainichi* [*Zainichi Kankokujin no Shûen*], both predicts and advocates an end to "*Zainichi*" as a kind of liminal, unstable category embodying a contradiction between formal national affiliation with the Republic of Korea and emotional attachments and identifications defined by their residence in Japan. This contradiction, Tei asserts, renders *Zainichi* into a kind of existence "which they cannot explain to themselves" (Tei 2001: 8). Their sense of themselves as Koreans or as foreigners is weak, leaving them as "Koreans on paper" only (15). Echoing Kawa and Chi, Tei argues that the only solution to these contradictions is to adjust formal affiliation to the facts of residence and emotional attachment, that is, to take Japanese nationality (56–58).

In advocating this kind of adjustment, all three of these authors rebut the argument that acquiring Japanese nationality is tantamount to abandonment of ethnic sentiments and absorption into a monoethnic Japan. To the contrary, Tei, for instance, asserts that "the birth of Korean-Japanese" (*Korian-kei Nihonjin*) will be a "turning point" in the development of a "multidimensional Japanese society" (*Nihon shakai no tagenka*) (Tei 2001: 5). Kawa holds that Koreans acquiring Japanese nationality while maintaining pride in their Korean heritage, including the use of ethnic names, will be part of Japan's transition to a "multiethnic society of living together" (*taminzoku kyôsei shakai*) (Kawa 2001: 329–330). Chi is rooting for *Zainichi* Koreans to give up their *Zainichi* position to become "Korean-Japanese" (*Korian-Japaniizu*) and to be the "most cosmopolitan" (*mottomo kosumoporitan*) of Japanese, to be the supreme Japanese "internationalists" (*kokusaijin*) (Chi 1997: 210–211).

What each of these authors are attempting to do is to pry apart the descent-based notions of ethnonational affiliation and the civil-political aspects of nationality that have heretofore adhered in the definition of "Japanese." It is this move that creates the possibility of acquiring Japanese nationality while maintaining a positive link to one's heritage and one's co-ethnics. Rejecting the coerced assimilation rooted in the colonial experience and in the postwar legal and social regime in which Koreans have been bound, it also permits a positioning of ethnic Koreans as equal members of Japanese society.

Conclusions

As recent works by Morris-Suzuki (1998), Oguma (1998, 2002), Lie (2001), and others have pointed out, the boundaries of "the Japanese," the ways of conceptualizing Japaneseness and criteria for belonging in Japanese society, are not fixed and stable, but respond to internal and external dynamics. It would be wise to assume that they will continue to change.

There has been an informing reciprocity between changes within the Korean community in Japan and changes within Japanese society as a whole. As Japanese society begins to offer a "third way" of dealing with difference, that is, not exclusion, not erasure through assimilation, but positive recognition, those of Korean background are more able to carry the Korean elements of their identity, and to express them, as they move across boundaries of formal political affiliation. One can be *"Nihonjin,"* the authors discussed above assert, without abandoning a sense of a heritage rooted in Korea. Minimally, these works suggest, a conceptual barrier—and something of a taboo—has been broken in the discourse of belonging among Koreans.

What is less noticeable are any signs that ethnic Japanese have altered their sense of *"Nihonjin"* as an exclusive, descent-based category. While the notion of "living together (with difference)" makes explicit a new sense that Japanese share their society with non-Japanese, it does little to challenge the ethnic Japanese understanding of what constitutes the category of *"Nihonjin"* or the common sense of the privilege that accompanies membership in that category. Perhaps people who call themselves "Korean-Japanese" will contribute to expanding the limits and character of inclusion in Japan.

Notes

1. An estimated 1.3 million Koreans had returned to the Korean peninsula from Japan by the end of March 1946 (So 1999: 95).
2. Movement continued intermittently until 1984 (Yang 1996: 100–101).
3. Tessa Morris-Suzuki (2005) has recently argued, based on materials declassified in 2004, that the program of repatriation to North Korea was secretly promoted by the Japanese government, by lobbying the International Committee of the Red Cross to undertake a role, and by cutting or eliminating social welfare payments to resident Koreans.
4. Changsoo Lee minimizes the significance of the changes in treatment that the ROK-Japan agreement conferred in practice, since the benefits explicitly enumerated in the agreement Koreans were already receiving to a minimal extent, while most social welfare benefits (e.g., child welfare, old age stipends, assistance for handicapped children) were not guaranteed by the agreement (Lee and DeVos 1981: 150–151).
5. This trend was partially enabled by the change in the Japanese nationality law, in effect from 1985, from a patrilineal to a bilineal reckoning of the nationality of offspring in cases of a Japanese and non-Japanese couple as parents. Japan-born offspring of such "international marriages" are permitted to choose nationality up to the age of 22. Until that time, unless they choose a non-Japanese nationality, they are recorded as Japanese. Over 80 percent of Korean marriages in Japan are to Japanese nationals.
6. Japan-born Koreans in fact constituted 64 percent of resident Koreans in Japan as early as 1959 (Yang 1984: 11).
7. Chapman (2004) has written insightfully on this essay and subsequent developments in the discourse of identity among Koreans in Japan.
8. Harajiri (1997) gives notable example of such usage.

9. As Morris-Suzuki explains, "By the beginning of the twentieth century, Japanese nationality was increasingly being linked to the idea of an organically united Japanese 'Volk' (*minzoku*). The concept of *minzoku* ... allowed a convenient blurring between the cultural and genetic aspects of ethnicity, while emphasizing the organic unity of the Japanese people. In this process, the word 'Japan' (*Nihon*) itself played a central and problematic role. On the one hand, the Japanese state was defined as the bearer of progress in the archipelago's history; on the other, the name of the state itself was transformed into an ethnonym, so that 'Japanese' (*Nihonjin*) was seen as a racial designation" (1998: 32).

References

Chapman, David. 2004. "The Third Way and Beyond: Zainichi Korean Identity and the Politics of Belonging." *Japanese Studies* 24 (1): 29–44.

Chi, Tong-wook.. 1997. *Zainichi wo yamenasai: Nanajûman-nin no yûshû na mainoriti ni tsugu* [Quit being Zainichi: Proclaiming to an excellent minority group of 700,000]. Tokyo: The Massada.

Harajiri, Hideki. 1997. *Nihon teijû Korian no nichijô to seikatsu—bunkajin-ruigakuteki apurôchi* [The daily life and lifestyle of Koreans settled in Japan: An anthropological approach]. Tokyo: Akashi Shoten.

Hester, Jeffry. 2000. "Kids between Nations: Ethnic Classes in the Construction of Korean Identities in Japanese Public Schools." In *Koreans in Japan: Critical Voices from the Margin*, ed. Sonia Ryang, 175–196. New York: Routledge.

Inokuchi, Hiromitsu. 2000. "Korean Ethnic Schools in Occupied Japan, 1945–52." In *Koreans in Japan: Critical Voices from the Margin*, ed. Sonia Ryang, 140–156. New York: Routledge.

Iwamoto, Mitsuo (I In-shik). 2000. *Nihonjin ni naritai Zainichi Kankokujin* [A resident Korean who wants to become Japanese]. Tokyo: Asahi Sonorama.

Kaneko, Hiroshi. 1996. *Dare no tame demo naku: "Kankoku-kei Nihonjin" toshite ikiru* [For nobody but myself: Living as a Korean-Japanese]. Tokyo: San'ichi Shobô.

Kawa, Heigyoku. 2001. *Dai-yon no sentaku: Kankokukei Nihonjin—Sekai roppyakuman Kanminzoku no ikizama to kokuseki* [The fourth choice: Korean-Japanese—The lifestyle and nationality of the six million ethnic Koreans around the world]. Tokyo: Bungeisha.

Kim, Chan-jong. 2004. Zainichi, gekidô no hyaku nen. [Koreans in Japan, one hundred turbulent years]. Tokyo: Asahi Shinbunsha.

Kim, Tong-myung. 1979. "ZaiNichi Chôsenjin no 'daisan no michi'." [The third path for Koreans in Japan]. *Chôsenjin* 17.

Lee, Chang-soo, and George DeVos. 1981. *Koreans in Japan: Ethnic Conflict and Accommodation*. Berkeley: University of California Press.

Lie, John. 2001. *Multicultural Japan*. Cambridge: Harvard University Press.

Morris-Suzuki, Tessa. 1998. *Re-inventing Japan: Time, Space, Nation*. Armonk, NY: M. E. Sharpe.

————. 2005. "Japan's Hidden Role in the 'Return' of Zainichi Koreans to North Korea." 7 Feburary 2005. *ZNet*. http://www.zmag.org/content/showarticle.cfm?ItemID=7194 (13 March 2005).

Oguma, Eiji. 1998. *"Nihonjin" no kyôkai : Okinawa, Ainu, Taiwan, Chôsen, shokuminchi shihai kara fukki undo made* [The boundaries of "Japanese": Okinawans, Ainu, Taiwan, Korea, from colonial rule to movement for return]. Tokyo: Shinyôsha.

Oguma, Eiji. 2002. *A Genealogy of 'Japanese' Self-images*. Melbourne: Trans Pacific Press.

Park, Il. 1999. *"Zainichi" to iu ikikata* [The way of life of "Zainichi"]. Tokyo: Kodansha.

Ryang, Sonia. 1997. *North Koreans in Japan: Language, Ideology, and Identity*. Boulder, CO: Westview Press.

Sakanaka, Hidenori. 1999. *Zainichi Kankoku-Chôsenjin seisakuron no tenkai* [The development of policy towards resident Koreans in Japan.] Tokyo: Nihon Kajo Shuppan.

So, Kun Shik. 1999. "Zainichi Chôsenjin no rekishiteki keisei (The historical formation of Koreans in Japan)." In Zainichi Chôsenjin: rekishi, genjô, tenbô [Koreans in Japan: History, present situation, prospects], ed. Pak Chon-myon, 75–99. Tokyo: Akashi Shoten.

Tei, Tai-kin (Tei Daekyung). 2001. *ZaiNichi Kankokujin no shûen* [The final chapter of "Zainichi"]. Tokyo: Bunshun Shinsho.

Yang, Tae-ho. 1984. *"Pusan" ni kaerenai: "Kokusaika" no naka no Zainichi Chôsen-Kankokujin* [You can't return to Pusan: Resident Koreans in Japan in the midst of internationalization]. Tokyo: Daisan Shokan.

————. 1996. *Zainichi Kankoku-Chôsenjin Tokuhon* [Reader on Koreans in Japan]. Tokyo: Ryokufû Shuppan.

8

TRANSNATIONAL COMMUNITY ACTIVITIES OF NEPALI VISA-OVERSTAYERS IN JAPAN: GOVERNANCE AND TRANSNATIONALISM FROM BELOW

Keiko Yamanaka

Introduction

NEARLY TWO DECADES AFTER AN INFLUX of immigrant workers in the late 1980s, Japan stands at the crossroads of becoming a multicultural society.[1] Global migration has revealed the glaring inadequacy of the nation's laws and public services in meeting the needs of increasing numbers of noncitizen residents and their families. It has also brought to the fore among Japanese citizens an awareness of the need for a human rights consciousness, which is required to develop universal standards for building a multicultural society (Yamanaka 2003a). In response, a few dedicated Japanese volunteers have organized groups and networks to alleviate problems faced by immigrants and promote public awareness of issues of equal rights and cultural diversity (Shipper 2002). At the same time, immigrant populations have organized mutual-help associations to mobilize their cultural and community resources in defense of their rights. In many cases, these citizens' and immigrants' organizations have collaborated toward common goals.

This article presents some examples of such immigrant-citizen coalitions to enhance democratic governance at the grassroots level, drawing from my study of a small community of Nepali visa-overstayers in Tokai, central Japan. The research population, estimated at five hundred, comprises primarily working-age males of Tibeto-Burman language-speaking Buddhist groups from western and eastern Nepal, commonly referred to as "Mongols" by anthropologists as well as by themselves. Most of these

---

Endnotes for this chapter begin on page 167.

migrants entered Japan with valid tourist visas and overstayed after their three-month expiration date, while working illegally in small-scale manufacturing and construction industries. They have willingly endured the hardships inflicted upon them as unauthorized workers in jobs shunned by Japanese in exchange for wages that far exceed those in Nepal. In their scarce free time, they have established a variety of organizations and community activities in which Japanese citizens often participate as friends, guests, and advocates of their rights.

These vibrant community activities by unauthorized workers raise intriguing questions about their agency and self-governance, and about Japanese immigration policies, public reception, and civic activism affecting the life spaces of these foreigners. Japan's 1990 Revised Immigration Law rules that foreign labor is limited to skilled occupations, while prohibiting hiring unskilled foreigners (Cornelius 1994; Tsuda and Cornelius 2004; Yamanaka 1993). Consequently, unauthorized immigrants are subject to high levels of prejudice, discrimination, and exploitation by the bureaucracy, employers, and the public. Despite all this, Tokai Nepalis are able to carry out a variety of transnationally organized projects and activities, frequently in collaboration with Japanese citizens. How can this be explained?

This chapter focuses on three topics that shed light on the social-political contexts in which Nepali transnational community activities take place, supported by small but committed numbers of Japanese citizens and activists: Nepali migration history, social capital, and increasing political activism; growing contradictions in Japan's restrictive immigration policy; and emerging global civil society movements that bridge civic activism across national and cultural boundaries. The analysis begins with a brief theoretical discussion, followed by a detailed description of the Nepali immigrant community and examples of its transnational community projects and activities, in which I participated between 1998 and 2000.

Transnationalism from Below

The recent flurry of literature on "transnationalism from below" emphasizes the importance of agency that has been generated among immigrant populations of humble origin as a result of transnational activities (Guarnizo and Smith 1998). Until the 1970s, elite groups with national and corporate interests had monopolized international space and cross-border activities. With the recent upsurge of global migration in the 1980s, "ordinary people" have comprised the majority of immigration flows, engaging in various kinds of trans-border activities, both economic and non-economic (Portes et al. 1999). By "non-elite immigrants," I mean those immigrants at the destination and their counterparts at the place of origin whose interests are grounded in their families and communities, rather than in the state, corporations, or markets. As noncitizens belonging to marginalized classes and ethnicities, these immigrants routinely encounter market exploitation and everyday racism in the host societies.

Transnational activities, be they cultural, entrepreneurial, or political, provide the immigrants with means of overcoming such adverse forces. By linking their interests and activities with those of counterparts in their countries of origin, the immigrants are able to draw upon resources and ideas grounded in everyday practices and social relationships in their native lands. Here I refer to "transnational community activities" as cultural, social, and political activities of non-elite immigrants for common goals that take place across borders on a regular basis. Such grassroots activities allow immigrants to affirm their cultural identities, while enabling them to expand collective interests by demanding equal rights and social justice. Transnationalism from below thus produces counter-hegemonic power to resist the global and institutional inequality to which immigrants and their families are continuously subjected (Mahler 1998).

From the 1980s onwards, coeval with global immigration, there has been a rise of transnational civil society movements throughout the world. Combined with human rights conventions sponsored by international organizations, transnational civil activism constitutes a third force in counteracting the power of global capitalism and its collaborating governments in protection of relatively defenseless citizens. "Civil society" refers to voluntary organizations independent of national governments and global markets, formed to enhance citizens' participation in democratic governance (CIVICUS 1994; Janoski 1998; Stienstra 1999). These include nongovernmental organizations (NGOs); nonprofit organizations (NPOs); citizens' groups and networks; educational, religious, and charitable institutions; community organizations; and labor unions. In the face of global corporate power, concerned citizens have formed grassroots organizations in order to take back control of their life spaces on such issues as human rights, migration, environment, inequality, health (particularly HIV/AIDS), and war.

Such civilian mobilization has recently drawn academic interest to forms of "governance from below," wherein ordinary citizens participate in "the exercise of power in a variety of institutional contexts, the object of which is to direct, control, and regulate activities in the interests of people as citizens, voters, and workers" (Robinson 1996: 347). Scholars find such transnationally democratic governance similar to forms of political "transnationalism from below," wherein coalitions of citizens of various nationalities, ethnicities, and classes exercise power transcending national boundaries (Guarnizo and Smith 1998).

The transnational nature of labor migration and the need to protect immigrant workers help establish global civil society institutions through transnational advocacy networking (Piper and Uhlin 2002). Unlike Europe, Asia has no regional organizations that oversee immigration policies and employers' treatment of immigrant workers, making cross-border activism critical in the face of often authoritarian governments.

Since the late 1980s, Japan provides an interesting example of global labor migration, transnational community activities, and transnational civil activism. By then, like all highly industrialized countries, Japan, as an economic giant plagued by low fertility and a rapidly aging population, had received an influx of immigrant workers, not only from nearby Asia but also distant Latin America, as a result of large differentials in wages and living standards between these countries and Japan (Yamanaka 1999). However, Japan is often cited as a country that does not regard labor importation as a viable option for solving an acute labor shortage. The maintenance of ethnic and class homogeneity is said to be the primary reason for the country's exclusion of unskilled foreigners.

Nonetheless, Japan is home to many global immigrants, both authorized and unauthorized, and is becoming increasingly characterized by a multiethnic population, human rights discourse, and transnational civil activism.

A Nepali Immigrant Community in Central Japan

I began research on Nepali labor migration to Japan during a six-month residence in Kathmandu in 1994 (Yamanaka 2000b). Among my informants were two men who had recently returned after several years' sojourn in Japan and who provided me with contacts among workers remaining in Japan. Thus I was able to enter a community of unauthorized workers in Hamamatsu, a city of half a million in western Shizuoka Prefecture, 257 kilometers southwest of Tokyo. Hamamatsu and its satellite cities, Kosai and Iwata, among others, host headquarters for automobile and motorcycle companies, including Suzuki, Yamaha, and Honda, together with thousands of subcontractors who supply the parts. Contiguous and to the west of these cities lies Toyohashi, a city of 350,000, and its neighbors, including Toyokawa and Toyota, in the eastern part of the adjacent Aichi Prefecture. They host another giant car company, Toyota, and its thousands of subcontractors.

Immigrant workers, both documented and undocumented, find this industrial area (referred to hereafter as Tokai) attractive because of its chronic labor shortage among small-scale employers. In March 1998, for example, 10,110 Brazilians of Japanese descent were registered as long-term residents in Hamamatsu alone (Yamanaka 2000a, 2003b). The number of unauthorized workers in Tokai is difficult to estimate, but there are many, mostly from Asia. Nepali informants estimate about five hundred Nepali men and women work in the area,[2] out of an estimated three thousand Nepali visa-overstayers in Japan according to Japanese immigration records from 1986 to 1995 (Yamanaka 2000b: 65). From November 1994 until July 2000, I visited the community, administering questionnaires, observing community affairs, and participating in organized activities. I also revisited Nepal in 1995, 1997, 1998, and 2000, its capital city Kathmandu, and Pokhara, its fourth-largest city, interviewing returnees from Japan and selected citizens who were knowledgeable about migration history, ethnic politics, and current events in Nepal.

Diverse Backgrounds

The research population consists primarily of members of Tibeto-Burman language-speaking Buddhist groups from Nepal's western and eastern middle-hills—groups such as the Gurung and Magar from the west and the Rai and Limbu from the east. Men of these groups, identified by the British as "martial races," were recruited by the British and Indian Armies as "Gurkha" soldiers for some 180 years, serving throughout the world in times of peace and war. Rural Nepalis became increasingly dependent on remittances, while developing a "culture of emigration" with extensive transnational Nepali networks, groups, and organizations throughout the world, particularly in East Asia where Hong Kong has hosted the headquarters of the British Gurkha Brigades since 1970.

Increasing global migration in the late 1980s, coinciding with Britain's preparation for the return of Hong Kong to China, entailed yearly reductions of recruits into the Gurkha Brigades during the mid 1990s. After a short recession in the mid 1980s, the Japanese economy rapidly expanded later in the decade, resulting in serious labor shortages among such labor-intensive industries as manufacturing, construction, and services. Hundreds of thousands of migrant workers, both male and female, arrived mostly from neighboring Asian countries, including Nepal, to supplement Japan's rapidly dwindling and aging labor force (Morita and Sassen 1994; Yamanaka 1999). Japan's official prohibition on unskilled foreign labor was no deterrent to the 300,000 illegal visa-overstayers who had arrived by the early 1990s, engaged in manual labor while remitting savings to their home countries (Cornelius 1994: 384).

After a few adult Tibeto-Burman Nepali males had arrived and established a channel for immigration, their families, including brothers, cousins, uncles, and a trickle of wives and sisters, followed in their footsteps. Recognizing the rewards of labor migration, members of ethnic groups without a history of overseas service soon followed. Included were three groups that have historically constituted Nepal's power brokers, monopolizing major positions in the government, bureaucracy, military, economy, and religion: the Newar (the indigenous population of the Kathmandu Valley), and the two Hindu elite caste categories, Brahman and Chhetri. Thus the small Tokai Nepali community was characterized by men and women of extraordinary diversity in terms of ethnicity, class, region, language, and religion.

However, all these diverse Nepali shared characteristics relevant to emigration. They had been relatively well educated in Nepal, and many had graduated from high school or beyond. Yet the majority were students or in relatively low-prestige occupations, such as self-employed shopkeepers or farmers. Some had previously migrated for work to the Middle East, Europe, and other regions. In the late 1980s and early 1990s, inflation and soaring unemployment in Nepal brought relative poverty, particularly in urban centers such as Kathmandu and Pokhara (Subba 1996). Among the educated who lacked job experience or personal connections, especially those of ethnic minority status such as Tibeto-Burman groups, emigration became an increasingly attractive occupational alternative.

Illegal Employment

After the expiration of their tourist visas, all these diverse Nepali immigrants become categorized by immigration law as "illegal foreign residents," absorbed informally into the workforce as inexpensive, temporary, and tractable laborers working for the weakest, most unstable employers. Although demanding tasks and abusive employers are common, Nepali workers in Tokai generally express considerable satisfaction since they earn wages far higher than in Nepal. My survey of 159 men and 30 women revealed that in the mid 1990s these unauthorized workers earned wages comparable with those of documented workers (such as Japanese Brazilians) and even of Japanese coworkers (Yamanaka 2000b: 84–88; Yamanaka 2003b: 182–186). On the average, Nepali men earned 1,125 yen per hour (then approximately US $11), and women earned 835 yen (US $8). In Kathmandu, a governmental official or university professor earned about 5,000 Nepal rupees (roughly US $100) a month. In Tokai, an illegal, unskilled male made that amount every day.

The data further reveal that, while workers' age, education, and ethnicity have little relationship to their wage levels, the type of industry, the years spent in Japan, and the number of job changes all make small but significant differences to their earnings. Comparisons of manufacturing industry wages among illegal Nepali, legal Japanese Brazilian, and Japanese workers show that differences in national, ethnic, and legal status do not contribute significantly to wage differences. In contrast, gender divides and ranks workers in Japan according to well-established patterns of wage and social discrimination against women (Brinton 1993; Yamanaka 2003b). These data suggest that small-scale Japanese employers value highly unauthorized (in this case Nepali) male workers' willingness and physical capacity for the demanding jobs shunned by Japanese.

Social Marginality

The ultimate goal of foreign workers, particularly unauthorized ones, is to save a large sum of money and return home as soon as possible. Japan is a "heaven" for achieving this goal, according to one Nepali immigrant. But its underground labor markets are far from heavenly in their treatment of illegal workers. Small factories and construction sites are ridden with labor exploitation and occupational hazards. Small-scale employers, lacking capital and credit, frequently ignore safety codes, postpone paying salaries for months, or go out of business without paying their employees. Illegal workers have no recourse but to seek a new employer.

In addition, Nepali illegal workers suffer severe social invisibility and personal isolation. As day laborers, they work in factories or construction sites for ten hours a day, six days a week. Fear of being apprehended inhibits both their public and private social participation. The limited duration, frequent geographical mobility, and clandestine nature of their presence in Japan prevent most of them from making friends beyond the Nepali community.[3] As illegitimate aliens, they lack access to inexpensive medical care, posing a serious threat to those who perform hazardous jobs in workplaces often devoid of adequate safety measures.

Examples of Nepali Community Activities: Sunday Get-Together

Shortly after beginning my research in Hamamatsu, I became familiar with the lively and well-organized community activities of these immigrants. For example, thirty to fifty Nepali men (and a few women) gathered every Sunday afternoon—their only day off—in a small, circular park within the Central Bus Station.[4] There they chatted in their various languages, exchanging information about friends, jobs, and news from home. There they could entrust part of their earnings to a designated agent, who would deposit them in a bank, to be forwarded to their families in Nepal. This kind of meeting is important for all foreign workers, for their social and cultural needs are great in their unfamiliar environments. Having a regular time and place to meet avoids their having to make individual arrangements (cf. Filipina domestic workers in Hong Kong, see Constable 1997).

Organizational and Communal Activities

In addition to Sundays, Nepalis in Tokai meet for more highly structured activities, in which Japanese activists, volunteers, friends, and sometimes employers often assist and participate. Several examples of these from my 1998–2000 research included:

Annual Program of the Nepali Welfare Society of Japan (Toyohashi, February 1998). The Nepali Welfare Society of Japan (NWSJ), established in 1995, sponsored a program in a public hall to celebrate its third anniversary. Immigrant men and women of the Himalayan Club performed Nepali music and dance. About four hundred Nepali attended together with several Japanese friends and volunteer activists.

Opening ceremony of a Nepali store (Toyota, September 1998). The opening of a new store stocking Nepali and other Asian foods, videos, tapes, magazines, and so on, and owned by a Nepali legal resident, was celebrated. A Japanese Buddhist priest conducted a *puja* (Hindi for "ritual") in front of the decorated store, while some two hundred Nepali watched from the parking lot and the street. A popular Nepali actress visiting Japan gave a short speech.

Dashain Festival party (Toyohashi, October 1998). The NWSJ rented a large hall to celebrate the Nepali festival of *Dashain*. This featured Nepali music followed by a catered Japanese buffet. At least two hundred Nepali attended, including a former Nepali government cabinet member. A local Japanese labor union leader was an honored guest.

Wedding reception (Hamamatsu, February 1999). A Nepali couple, recently married in Japan, held a Sunday afternoon reception in an Indian restaurant. About one hundred Nepali and ten Japanese friends and employers celebrated with abundant Indian food and beer.

Summer bowling championship (Toyokawa, July 1999). Tamu Dhii Nagoya, a branch of the Gurung Association-Japan, sponsored a bowling tournament. They reserved half of a large Japanese bowling hall. Sixteen teams competed, some wearing team uniforms or carrying team flags, and trophies were awarded to the winning team and "the most valuable player." Japanese bowlers were apparently oblivious to the lively and conspicuous crowd of Nepalis. Participants and spectators numbered about one hundred, most of whom then moved to a Japanese-owned Asian restaurant to celebrate with South Asian snacks and beer.

Charity show (Hamamatsu, June 2000). To collect money for charitable activities in Nepal, the Mount Everest Club organized a cultural show in a public hall. Six artists were brought from Nepal to provide a program of Nepali music and dance for some three hundred Nepalis. A Japanese activist who helped process the application forms for visas for the Nepali artists also attended.

Publications. A number of subgroups within the Tokai Nepali community published magazines, on their own or in cooperation with Nepali organizations elsewhere in Japan. The articles, mostly in Nepali, were written and edited in Japan by immigrants. They were then sent to Nepal to be printed before being returned to Japan for distribution. The magazines included: *Himali Sandeshi,* published by NWSJ; *Koseli,* published by the Himalayan Club; *Tamu Dhii,* published by the Tamu Dhii, Gurung Association; and *Peace,* published by the Tamang Association.

Mutual assistance. Leaders of the NWSJ and other ethnic associations keep close contact with Japanese NGO volunteers and labor union officials for assistance in negotiating with employers and the Labor Standards Bureau in the frequent instances of labor abuse such as unpaid wages and work-related injuries. Likewise, when a member requires expensive treatment such as hospitalization, surgery, and medication, major regional organizations initiate donation drives among their communication networks of more than two thousand Nepali in the Tokai area and the Tokyo Greater Metropolitan Areas.

Tolerance, Acceptance, and Support

These Nepali community activities suggest that despite Japan's reputed inhospitality to unauthorized workers, there are islands of passive tolerance that afford these visa-overstayers refuge from the sea of suspicion and hostility that surrounds them. The frequent participation of Japanese citizens also suggests not only social acceptance of the unauthorized immigrants by those Japanese who interact with them, but also strong support by committed Japanese activists for their organized activities. The following observations offer further confirmation:

(1) Members of the Nepali community have welcomed me, a Japanese woman (recently back from Nepal), to study their migration experiences and have invited me to participate in many of their organized activities.

(2) The Nepali frequently hold community activities in highly visible public and commercial spaces where Japanese people are present and sometimes participate.

(3) Official visitors from Nepal—politicians, diplomats, performers, and artists—often participate in these events or send congratulatory messages.

Explanations for this state of affairs must be sought in an understanding of the broader historical, social, economic, and political contexts of the two countries.

Nepali Human, Social, and Political Capital

For Nepal, the sending country, the most relevant factors are the immigrants' migration history and the human, social, and political capital that enables them to act in unison on the basis of their shared identity and experience. Specifically, Nepal's sudden 1990 "democracy movement" unleashed unprecedented political energy and unity among Nepali citizens—especially the small but increasingly discontented urban middle class—against the autocratic one-party regime in Nepal at that time. This movement coincided with processes of global migration that brought young, educated men (and women) to Japan to work as immigrants without rights in Asia's wealthiest country.

Migration History and Social Capital

The Gurkhas' role in preserving Britain's colonial power in South and Southeast Asia has been amply documented (Banskota 1994; Caplan 1970; Cross 1985; Des Chene 1991). That 180-year tradition of foreign military service has also shaped the history and cultures of the Tibeto-Burman Buddhist groups. It has provided thousands of Gurkha households with a steady source of cash to supplement the subsistence economies of terrace farming and cattle herding in precipitous Himalayan pastures. Soldiers' remittances and retirees' pensions enabled their households to enjoy living standards higher than those of households without soldiers (Blaikie et al. 1980; Caplan 1970; Hitchcock 1966; Macfarlane 1976; Pignède 1966).

During their fifteen or more years of military service in the British or Indian Army, individual young soldiers were exposed to foreign military organizations, regulations, and technologies, as well as to diverse cultures and ideas throughout the world. Wives and children frequently accompanied them to the military cantonments in stations such as Hong Kong, Singapore, and Dehra Dun. Thus, many Gurkha children grew up in a Nepali diaspora with identities and experiences distinct from those of most Nepali children (Pettigrew 2000). Upon retirement, ex-soldiers returned to their home villages, where they often exercised political leadership and contributed to economic development (Des Chene 1991; Höfer 1978). Foreign military service has also resulted in the formation of many Gurkha mutual benefit organizations in the areas of health, education, political activism, and other common interests.

Dense networks of organized reciprocity and civic solidarity constitute a basis for grassroots democracy and effective governance to develop among a citizenry (Putnam 1995). Drawing the analogy with "human capital" as enhancing individual productivity, Putnam defines "social capital" as "features of social organization such as networks, norms, and social trust that facilitate coordination and cooperation for mutual benefit" (1995: 67). This notion of collective action helps to explain why and how Nepali workers in Japan, often children or other relatives of ex-Gurkha soldiers, have so frequently organized community activities for their mutual interests.

A few active members of such Nepali organizations and activities in Japan were immigrants of Newar, Brahman, or Chhetri origins who lacked any military or other tradition of migration. They were able to unite as a result of strong feelings of national identity rooted in common political awareness drawn from the dramatic changes of the early 1990s that transformed Nepal from an autocracy to a democracy.

Democracy Movement and Political Capital

In April 1990, a massive popular movement resulted in the replacement of Nepal's 29-year-old one-party system with a new multi-party system (Brown 1996; Hoftun et al. 1999). In November 1990, the nation established a constitutional monarchy with sovereignty vested in its citizens. The 1990 constitution guaranteed democratic principles, most notably freedom of speech, assembly, and religion. Until then, following an earlier short-lived attempt at democracy (1951–1960), the authoritarian (Panchayat) regime had suppressed the country's extraordinarily heterogeneous population. Estimated at 18.5 million in 1990, the Nepali population comprised more than sixty ethnic and caste groups, each with its distinctive history and social status, and drawing from a variety of languages and religions (Berreman 1963; Nepalese Central Bureau of Statistics 1996). The majority engaged in subsistence agriculture in the Himalayan middle hills, having survived for decades the poverty and inequality that characterized the Nepali village social order (Caplan 1967; Hitchcock 1966; Pignéde 1966).

The sudden 1990 restoration of multi-party democracy inspired Nepali citizens of diverse ethnicities, religions, regions, languages, classes, and ideologies to assert their rights and participate in national and local politics for the first time in thirty years. Long oppressed under autocracy led by the Hindu elite, many Tibeto-Burman Buddhist minority groups also established political parties and organizations to promote their collective interests and cultural identities (Hoftun et al. 1999: 320–330). It was during these vibrant and volatile moments in Nepal's history in the late 1980s and early 1990s that young, relatively educated Nepali men departed for Japan. Upon arrival, they found themselves surrounded by an unfamiliar culture and a hostile immigration policy that defined them as illegal workers and visa-overstayers.

Japan's "Back Door" Immigration Policy

Nikkeijin and Asians

The influx of 100,000 or more foreign workers in the late 1980s posed a complex dilemma for the Japanese government (Cornelius 1994; Tsuda and Cornelius 2004; Weiner and Hanami 1998; Yamanaka 1993). By relaxing immigration policies, Japan might satisfy its demand for labor from the large pool of unemployed and underemployed in neighboring Asian countries. Yet policy makers saw mounting evidence from Europe and North America that temporary foreign workers could become permanent immigrants who would be a source of political, economic, and social tensions.

The government therefore chose an ad hoc policy that combined the two options—bringing in cheap foreign labor but limiting it to "Japanese" people. The 1989 amendment of the Immigration Control and Refugee Recognition Law (hereafter, the Revised Immigration Law), which took effect in June 1990, permitted descendants of Japanese emigrants (*Nikkeijin*, literally "people of Japanese descent") up to the third generation to enter the country legally, without restriction on their socioeconomic activities. This law also instituted criminal penalties for the recruitment and hiring of illegal foreign workers: three years imprisonment or a maximum fine of two million yen (roughly US $20,000).

The Revised Immigration Law immediately affected inflows of foreign workers and their employment opportunities. Encouraged by their legalized status, *Nikkeijin* began to arrive en masse, mostly from Brazil (and a few from Peru; in this book, see Tsuda, chapter 6). The admission of Brazilians increased fourfold from 19,000 in 1988 to 79,000 in 1990. By 1996 more than 200,000 *Nikkeijin* workers and their families had registered as residents in major manufacturing cities, such as Hamamatsu and Toyohashi in Tokai and Ota and Oizumi in Gunma Prefecture (Roth 2002; Tsuda 2003; Yamanaka 2000a, 2003b). Clearly this law offered a golden opportunity to ethnic Japanese from Latin America. However, it closed the door to other unskilled workers, mostly Asians without Japanese ancestry. But, even after the passage of the revised law, Asian workers continued to enter the country with non-employment visas as tourists, business personnel, company trainees, students, and entertainers, often overstaying when their visas expired. By 1993, immigration records suggested a population of 300,000 illegal visa-overstayers of diverse nationalities (Cornelius 1994: 384). This type of de facto immigration policy is elsewhere termed a "back door" policy (Yamanaka 1999).

Valuable Workers

Responses of employers to the 1990 immigration reform varied depending on available capital and labor pools. Threatened by criminal penalties, middle- to large-scale employers with more than thirty employees and a secure financial basis discharged unauthorized workers and replaced them with *Nikkeijin*. Mini- to small-scale employers (with less than thirty employees), however, could not afford the luxury of hiring *Nikkeijin* who, as documented immigrants, commanded higher wages than illegal workers. When these employers could not satisfy their labor needs with local workers, they turned to illegal visa-overstayers despite possible criminal charges. My Nepali research sample comprised one of many such illegal labor pools readily available for such employers in the Tokai Area. Once they had accepted illegal workers, they often discovered the high quality of the their labor. One employer told me why he had ignored the 1990 Revised Immigration Law when he hired Nepali employees:

> My Nepali workers are smart and dedicated to their jobs. They have learned everything very quickly. They arrive here early in the morning before anyone else and go home late in the evening after everyone has gone. They are much younger than my Japanese workers, who are in their fifties and sixties. Their good eyesight is very helpful in inspecting the machine parts. Even though the law says I should not hire illegals, I see no reason to replace them. Because our products do not carry my company name, I do not

have to worry about the company image. If I were caught by the police, the local newspaper would report it in only one line. Nothing more than that.

The employer's conjecture proved to be right. Shortly after the interview, three apartments near his factory were raided by immigration officials. Six unauthorized Nepali were arrested and deported, two of whom were his employees. But he was not cited, and following the arrests, the three remaining unauthorized Nepali continued in his employ. This example clearly suggests that labor-short small-scale employers lose little and gain much by hiring unauthorized workers. The criminal penalty for hiring unskilled foreigners has existed since June 1990, but it is rarely enforced. Cornelius (1994: 391) reports that in each of the years 1991 and 1992, only 350 Japanese employers were penalized for violations of the revised law. This suggests that although the law was implemented to stem an influx of undesirable foreigners, the government is reluctant to enforce it rigorously because employers need their labor. At the same time occasional, often publicized, incidents of enforcement are necessary to demonstrate to workers and employers alike that immigration officers have the situation under control.

Visible vs. Invisible Foreigners

In the meantime, the mass media have broadcast police reports of increasing violence and crimes committed by foreigners at both national and local levels. In Hamamatsu in 1994, eighty-eight foreigners were apprehended as suspects in 120 criminal cases according to Hamamatsu Police Headquarters (1994, 1995, 1996). In the following year, the figure rose to ninety-four foreigners apprehended in 505 cases. Most of these were for minor offences such as petty theft or shoplifting. According to Herbert (1992), Japanese police reports on the crime rate among foreign workers are inflated as a result of bias against them and serious flaws in data collection. For example, the "crimes" included those that could only be committed by foreigners, victimless crimes such as expired visas and undocumented employment. In Hamamatsu, during 1994, such crimes accounted for 44 percent of all crimes by foreigners. Yet these contributed to the reported increase in crime rates by foreigners and to their growing image as dangerous criminals threatening the safety of Japanese citizens.

Prior to the influx of *Nikkeijin*, Japanese citizens of Hamamatsu rarely saw "foreigners" with distinctive language, behavior, dress, and physical appearance. By the mid 1990s, as a result of the *Nikkeijin* influx, *Nikkeijin* Brazilians and their children were visible in many everyday settings, including supermarkets, shopping malls, public transportation, public housing developments, festival and entertainment sites, public parks, and schools. The sudden increase in "foreigners" (*Nikkeijin*), many with Japanese facial features but with distinctly foreign dress, demeanor, and language, spawned confusion, fear, and resentment among local citizens (Weisman 1991). Increasing media reports on crimes by foreigners, including *Nikkeijin* Brazilians, led Japanese citizens to direct their suspicion at Brazilians. The recent racial discrimination lawsuit brought by legal Brazilian resident Ana Bortz, journalist and non-*Nikkeijin* wife of a *Nikkeijin* immigrant in Hamamatsu, epitomized the process of racialization of Japanese Brazilians as cultural strangers and even criminals (Yamanaka 2003a).

In contrast to documented Brazilians, unauthorized Asians, many of whose phenotypes resemble that of Japanese, tend to remain invisible in public. For example, the Nepali who regularly congregate in certain meeting places on Sunday afternoons are mostly of Tibeto-Burman ("Mongol") appearance. As a result, most ordinary citizens are unaware of their presence on Hamamatsu streets, looking on with complete indifference when they encounter them. John Lie (2001: 21) describes a similar situation in downtown Tokyo: "In a bustling cosmopolitan city like Tokyo, civil indifference is the hegemonic mode of social interaction. In repeated observations in public places, I rarely spotted anyone showing interest in the Asian workers."

In short, an understanding of the passive acceptance of illegal workers by Japanese must be sought in the context of national ideology and stereotypes, laws, and institutions, all of which emphasize social homogeneity, on the one hand, and in the context of Japan's rapidly aging population and economic conditions that contribute to the prevailing labor shortage on the other. The closed national ideology led the government to implement a contradictory policy in 1990, which permitted only skilled foreigners to work in the country, while the labor shortage led it to leave a "back door" open for unskilled Asian foreigners to enter and fill jobs shunned by Japanese. This contradiction has resulted in widely inconsistent foreign labor policies, practices, and responses among a broad range of parties, including employers, the national government, municipal governments, media, and ordinary citizens.

Transnational Grassroots Coalitions

This examination of Nepali community activities highlights the emergence of transnational civil activism at the grass roots. Immigrants and Japanese volunteers have come together to seek humanitarian policies and practices for the rights of immigrant workers and noncitizen residents (Gurowitz 1999; Roberts 2000). A unique feature of this transnational coalition is that the Nepali are unauthorized workers whose ability to defend their rights on their own is extremely limited. Business establishments frequently exclude or discriminate against foreign customers by demanding official documents or proof of a Japanese citizens' guarantee in exchange for providing service (Yamanaka 2003a). Without Japanese NGOs and individual citizens' cooperation and assistance, it is unlikely that Nepalis would be able to arrange to hold an event in a public space or negotiate with abusive employers for unpaid wages.

Nepali Community Activists

The Nepali are well aware of these legal and social constraints on their residence, employment, and freedom. To reduce them, some of them have taken interethnic collective action aimed at promoting the interests of all Nepali nationals in the Tokai area. In 1995 in Toyohashi, those who wished to address common problems arising from their immigration status and cultural unfamiliarity launched a mutual-help organization, the NWSJ. Two years later, those who were concerned about the preservation of Nepali culture established the Himalayan Club. In the same year, those interested in sports organized the Mount Everest Club. In contrast, organizations such as the Gurung Association and the Magar Association are organized on the basis of ethnic membership, thus promoting the identity and culture specific to Nepali of particular ethnic communities throughout Japan. Leaders of these organizations make special efforts to cultivate rapport with Japanese NGOs and citizens sympathetic to their plight. They frequently call upon these Japanese for advice and help in times of crisis. Frequently they invite them to Nepali community events as honored guests, requesting public speeches, and thanking them with gifts and awards.

An active member of the NWSJ explained in 1998 why he and others are committed to organized activities:

> We lack freedom here because we don't have proper visas. We have many prob lems. For example, those who have just arrived are so afraid of being arrested that they stay in their apartments for weeks. Because Japan has been in recession for years by now, unemployment is rapidly increasing among us. Job hunting is difficult. Unpaid wages frequently occur. But we have nowhere to report abuse cases. Nepali are afraid of the Japanese authorities and therefore do not want to have anything to do with them. So they often put group pressure on someone who has been injured at work so that he will not bring the case to the Labor Bureau for the compensation he is entitled to. It is sad. We need to educate ourselves. We also need to be in touch with Japanese because we are unable to help ourselves.

Japanese Civil Activists

By the mid 1990s Hamamatsu witnessed the establishment of a number of grassroots organizations by citizens and noncitizens, including the Hamamatsu Overseas Laborers Solidarity (Herusu no Kai) formed by citizens to protect foreigner's labor rights; the Grupo Justiça e Paz (Group Justice and Peace) committed to increase foreigners' enrollment in the National Health Plan; and the Medical Aid for Foreigners in Hamamatsu (MAF) organized by citizens and noncitizens to provide uninsured foreigners with free annual checkups (Yamanaka 2005)

These NGOs and their volunteers believe that immigrants, especially unauthorized immigrants, are victims of extreme labor exploitation and human rights violation based on nationality, ethnicity, and legal status. They blame these injustices on the globalized labor market system operating within now defunct nation-state frameworks. Labor unionists fear that employment of foreign workers will undermine Japanese labor standards for which they and their predecessors have long fought. Medical professionals are concerned that general health conditions may deteriorate if immigrants do not receive medical check-ups and treatment equal to those of the Japanese. Religious workers are interested in reaching those foreigners who share their beliefs and rituals. Human rights activists are motivated to eliminate open hostility and discrimination against immigrants.

As Japan becomes a multiethnic society, members of Japanese civil society are becoming energized to seize the opportunity to act on their agenda and interests (Shipper 2002). In the view of concerned citizens, unauthorized foreigners are "the new untouchables" of the world—victims of the contradictory systems that produce and reproduce suffering among immigrants from the Third World (Harris 1995). They believe that the negligence of the state allows such injustice to go unattended despite the fact that corporations continue to demand inexpensive labor (Roberts 2000). The combination of increasing global immigration and growing civil society in Japan has thus spawned a significant, albeit small, alternative to global governance, in which immigrants and citizens both play a major role in defending migrants' rights, human rights, and cultural rights, thus enhancing their agency in Japan and in today's increasingly interactive world.

Conclusion

The example of Nepali visa-overstayers in Japan shows the importance of "transnationalism from below" in the analysis of immigrants' agency and governance under expanding global capitalism. The study findings highlight: Nepali transnationalism drawn from shared identity and social capital; contradictions in Japanese immigration policies and practices that attract illegal Asian workers; and Nepali-Japanese grassroots coalitions that bridge immigrants and citizens in efforts to redress global and local inequality.

By initiating community actions transcending borders and cultures, the unauthorized Nepali attempt to control their living environment—an environment that is predominantly defined by their illegal status and consequently weak market position (Yamanaka 2000b). Rather than forfeiting their right to self-determination, the Nepali have chosen to exercise their agency and creativity for local survival by mobilizing their transnational resources to generate empowering community actions.

The Nepali are attempting to reconstruct the kind of everyday life in which they might have participated in Nepal. Such activities include holiday celebrations, cultural performances, community association meetings, wedding receptions, and various types of sports and leisure. Thus, Nepali immigrants confirm with one another their Nepali identity and migrant solidarity while demonstrating their ability to be good citizens to the Japanese public. They are simultaneously sending a message to their homeland that, despite their long absence, they still belong to its people and soil. Transnational community activities by unauthorized Nepali in Japan thus exemplify agency, resistance, and the will of self-governance among one of the world's most vulnerable populations.

Notes

1. This is an expanded version of "Transnational Activities for Local Survival: A Community of Nepalese Visa-Overstayers in Japan," in *Behind Many Masks: Gerald Berreman and Berkeley Anthropology, 1959–2001*, ed. K. MacKinnon, a special issue of *Kroeber Anthropological Society Papers*, 2002: 146–167. I wish to thank Gerald Berreman, my husband, for introducing me to Nepal and offering his support throughout this research. I am deeply indebted to many Nepali friends in Japan and Nepal without whose cooperation this study would have been impossible, but whom must remain anonymous.
2. I estimate the proportion of women in the Tokai Nepali community at around 20 percent. Most are wives of Nepali migrants and are themselves working in manufacturing industries (Yamanaka 2000b: 82–83).
3. After a few years in Japan, some Nepalis develop friendships with Japanese while a few Nepali men marry Japanese women (e.g., Kaneko 1998). It is my observation that most Tokai Nepali men lack the opportunity to meet anyone outside of the Nepali community and their workplaces.
4. There is a small police station (*koban*, "police box") in the park directly across from the landscaped area where these Nepalis routinely congregate. Through the *kôban*'s large one-way window, the police can easily monitor their activities, but I have not heard of any police intervention.

References

Banskota, Purushottam. 1994. *The Gurkha Connection: A History of the Gurkha Recruitment in the British Indian Army.* Jaipur: Nirala Publications.

Berreman, Gerald D. 1963. "Peoples and Cultures of the Himalayas." *Asian Survey* 3 (6): 289–304.

Blaikie, Piers, John Cameron, and David Seddon. 1980. *Nepal in Crisis: Growth and Stagnation at the Periphery.* Delhi: Oxford University Press.

Brinton, Mary C. 1993. *Women and the Economic Miracle: Gender and Work in Postwar Japan.* Berkeley: University of California Press.

Brown, T. Louise. 1996. *The Challenge to Democracy in Nepal: A Political History.* London: Routledge.

Caplan, Lionel. 1970. *Land and Social Change in East Nepal.* Berkeley: University of California Press.

CIVICUS (World Alliance for Citizen Participation). 1994. *Citizens Strengthening Global Civil Society: World Assembly Edition.* Coordinated by M. D. de Oliveila and R. Tandon. New York: McNaughton and Gunn.

Constable, Nicole. 1997. *Maid to Order in Hong Kong: Stories of Filipina Workers.* Ithaca, NY: Cornell University Press.

Cornelius, Wayne A. 1994. "Japan: The Illusion of Immigration Control." In *Controlling Immigration: A Global Perspective,* ed. W.A. Cornelius, P. L. Martin, and J. F. Hollifield, 375–410. Stanford, CA: Stanford University Press.

Cross, J. P. 1985. "Introduction." In *Gurkhas,* ed. S. Tucci, 8–34. London: Hamish Hamilton.

Des Chene, M. 1991. *Relics of Empire: A Cultural History of the Gurkhas, 1815–1987.* Ph.D. diss., Stanford University.

Guarnizo, Luis E., and Michael P. Smith. 1998. *Transnationalism from Below.* New Brunswick, NJ: Transaction Publishers.

Gurowitz, Amy. 1999. "Mobilizing International Norms: Domestic Actors, Immigrants, and the Japanese State." *World Politics* 51 (3): 413–445.

Hamamatsu Police Headquarters. 1994. *Hamamatsu Chiku Hanzai Hakusho.* [White paper on crime in the Hamamatsu area].

———. 1995. *Hamamatsu Chiku Hanzai Hakusho.* [White paper on crime in the Hamamatsu area].

———. 1996. *Hamamatsu Chiku Hanzai Hakusho.* [White paper on crime in the Hamamatsu area].

Harris, Nigel. 1995. *The New Untouchables: Immigration and the New World Worker.* London: Penguin Books.

Herbert, Wolfgang. 1992. "Conjuring Up a Crime Wave: The 'Rapid Growth in the Crime Rate among Foreign Migrant Workers in Japan' Critically Examined." *Japan Forum* 4 (April): 109–119.

Hitchcock, John T. 1966. *A Mountain Village in Nepal.* New York: Holt, Rinehart and Winston.

Höfer, Andras. 1978. "A New Rural Elite in Central Nepal." In *Himalayan Anthropology,* ed. James F. Fisher, 179–186. The Hague: Mouton.

Hoftun, Martin, William Raeper, and John Welpton. 1999. *People, Politics & Ideology: Democracy and Social Change in Nepal.* Kathmandu: Mandala Book Point.

Janoski, Thomas. 1998. *Citizenship and Civil Society: A Framework of Rights & Obligations in Liberal, Traditional, and Social Democratic Regimes.* Cambridge: Cambridge University Press.

Kaneko, Anne. 1998. *Overstay* [73-minute video]. Los Angeles: Pacific Rim Center.

Lie, John. 2001. *Multiethnic Japan*. Cambridge, MA: Harvard University Press.

Mahler, Sarah. 1998. "Theoretical and Empirical Contributions toward a Research Agenda for Transnationalism." In *Transnationalism from Below*, ed. L. E. Guarnizo and M. P. Smith, 64–100. New Brunswick, NJ: Transaction Publishers.

Macfarlane, Alan. 1976. *Resources and Population: A Study of the Gurungs of Nepal*. Cambridge: Cambridge University Press.

Morita, Kiriro, and Saskia Sassen. 1994. "The New Illegal Immigration in Japan 1980–1992." *International Migration Review* 28 (1): 153–163.

Nepalese Central Bureau of Statistics. 1996. *Statistical Pocket Book*. Kathmandu: His Majesty's Government National Planning Commission Secretariat: Central Bureau of Statistics.

Pettigrew, Joyce. 2000. "'Gurkhas' in the Town: Migration, Language, and Healing," *European Bulletin of Himalayan Research* 19: 7–39.

Pignède, Bernard. 1966. *The Gurungs: A Himalayan Population of Nepal*. Kathmandu: Ratna Pustak Bhandar. First published in 1966 by Mouton & Co, The Hague and École des Hautes Études en Sciences Sociales, Paris.

Piper, N., and A. Uhlin. 2002. "Transnational Advocacy Networks, Female Labor Migration and Trafficking in East and Southeast Asia: A Gendered Analysis of Opportunities and Obstacles." *Asian and Pacific Migration Journal* 11 (2): 171–195.

Portes, Alejandro, L. E. Guarnizo, and P. Landolt. 1999. "Introduction, Pitfalls and Promise of an Emergent Research Field." *Ethnic and Racial Studies* 22 (2): 217–237.

Putnam, Robert. 1995. "Bowling Alone: America's Declining Social Capital." *Journal of Democracy* 6 (1): 65–78.

Roberts, Glenda S. 2000. "NGO Support for Migrant Labor in Japan." In *Japan and Global Migration: Foreign Workers and the Advent of a Multicultural Society*, ed. M. Douglass and G. S. Roberts, 275–300. London: Routledge.

Robinson, Mark. 1996. "Governance." In *The Social Science Encyclopedia*, ed. A. Kuper and J. Kuper, 347–348. London: Routledge.

Roth, J.H. 2002. *Brokered Homeland: Japanese Brazilian Migrants in Japan*. Ithaca: Cornell University Press.

Shipper, Appichai W. 2002. *Pragmatism in Activism: Organizing Support for Illegal Foreign Workers in Japan*. Civil Society in the Asia-Pacific Monogram Series. Cambridge, MA: Harvard University, Program on US-Japan Relations.

Subba, Pranay. 1996. "Unemployment: Time-Bomb Is Ticking." *Spotlight,* January 5: 16–20.

Stienstra, Deborah. 1999 "Of Roots, Leaves, and Trees: Gender, Social Movements, and Global Governance." In *Gender Politics in Global Governance,* ed. K. Meyer and E. Prügl, 260–272. Lanham, MD: Rowman & Littlefield Publisher.

Tsuda, Takeyuki. 2003. *Strangers in Their Ethnic Homeland: Japanese Brazilian Return Migration in Transnational Perspective.* New York: Columbia University Press.

Tsuda, Takeyuki, and W. A. Cornelius. 2004. "Japan: Government Policy and Immigrant Reality." In *Controlling Immigration: A Global Perspective,* 2nd ed., ed. W. A. Cornelius, T. Tsuda, P. L. Martin and J. F. Hollifield, 439–476. Stanford, CA: Stanford University Press.

Weiner, Myron, and Tadashi Hanami, eds. 1998. *Temporary Workers or Future Citizens? Japanese and U.S. Migration Policies.* New York: New York University Press.

Weisman, Steven R. 1991. "In Japan, Bias Is an Obstacle Even for the Ethnic Japanese." *New York Times, International Edition,* November 13.

Yamanaka, Keiko. 1993. "New Immigration Policy and Unskilled Foreign Workers in Japan." *Pacific Affairs* 66 (1): 72–90.

———. 1999. "Illegal Immigration in Asia: Regional Patterns and a Case Study of Nepalese Workers in Japan." In *Illegal Immigration in America: A Reference Handbook,* ed. D. W. Haines and K. E. Rosenblum, 471–499. Westport, CT: Greenwood Press.

———. 2000a. "'I Will Go Home, but When?' Labor Migration and Circular Diaspora Formation by Japanese Brazilians in Japan." In *Japan and Global Migration: Foreign Workers and the Advent of a Multicultural Society,* ed. M. Douglass and G. S. Roberts, 123–152. London: Routledge.

———. 2000b. "Nepalese Labor Migration to Japan: From Global Warriors to Global Workers." *Ethnic and Racial Studies* 23 (1): 62–93.

———. 2003a. "A Breakthrough for Ethnic Minority Rights in Japan: Ana Bortz's Courageous Challenge." In *Gender and Migration: Crossing Borders and Shifting Boundaries,* Vol. 1, International Women's University Series, ed. M. Morokvasic Mueller, U. Erel, and K. Shinozaki, 231–259. Oplanden: Verlag Leske + Budrich.

———. 2003b. "Feminization of Japanese Brazilian Labor Migration to Japan." In *Searching for Home Abroad: Japanese-Brazilians and the Transnational Moment,* ed. Jeffrey Lesser, 163–200. Durham, NC: Duke University Press.

———. 2005 "Migration, Differential Access to Health Services and Civil Society's Responses in Japan." In *Migration and Health in Asia,* ed. S. Jatrana, M. Toyota, and B. Yeoh. London: Routledge.

9

"Newcomers" in Public Education: Chinese and Vietnamese Children in a Buraku Community

Yuko Okubo

Introduction

IT IS OFTEN MENTIONED BY JAPANESE researchers that foreign children are "invisible" or "nonexistent" in Japanese schools (Ota 2000; Shimizu and Shimizu 2001). Some put the blame on the nature of the Japanese education system for being nationalistic and thus argue for educational reform to accept children with different cultural backgrounds (Ota 2000; Yoon 1996, 1997).

However, "newcomers,"[1] both Vietnamese and Chinese children in my field site, are quite "visible." There are signs written in Japanese, Vietnamese, and Chinese languages by the front door of the elementary school saying, "Please turn off your cell phones inside the school buildings, for there are students with heart problems using medical devices." Hanging in front of the teachers' office, there is a sign on which a school rule is written each week in Japanese, Vietnamese, and Chinese, such as "Do not run in the corridors." There are signs in three languages by the door of special classrooms such as the school infirmary (*hoken-shitsu*), the music room (*ongaku-shitsu*), the library (*tosho-shitsu*), and so on. From these signs, you will realize that the school regularly uses languages other than Japanese. There are also materials in school that suggest the presence of other cultures. If you look at the walls of the corridors, you see the Vietnamese children's drawings and writings about Vietnam and Vietnamese customs. On the windows of a classroom, you see colorful lanterns made with a thin stick whittled from a piece of bamboo and origami, lanterns slightly differ-

---

Endnotes for this chapter begin on page 183.

ent from rounder Japanese *chôchin*. You see the drawings of giant pandas and bamboo painted with black ink displayed on the windows. Whether these drawings and handicrafts are different from those of Japanese children is another issue that needs close examination, but you will notice the school's efforts to present itself as *tabunka kyôsei*, "multicultural."[2]

In this chapter, I argue that the abundant cultural and educational opportunities for the "newcomers" at school and in the community turn out to function as a different kind of "outcast" program for the children, who do not have the same history of being outcasts as the Burakumin and resident Koreans. This program forces students to use their ethnically distinctive names and learn their mother languages with the goal of "retaining and nurturing ethnic identity." The marginalization of "newcomers" in the school community goes together with the homogenization[3] of the "old minorities" at school and in the community, a process that makes them "invisible." There are several factors involved in this process, such as the tradition of minority education of the city, teachers' culture and school culture in Japan, and the attitude of the Japanese toward foreigners. These factors are related to each other, resulting in a unique environment for "newcomers" in a Buraku community.

The Demographic Context

From the 1970s onward, Japanese society went through a transition that resulted in an increase in the presence of foreigners who worked mainly as unskilled laborers. After normalizing diplomatic relations with China in 1972, the Japanese women and orphans in China who had been displaced by the Sino-Japanese and Second World Wars started returning to Japan with their children and grandchildren in the 1970s. Foreign women started coming to Japan on entertainer visas from the Philippines, Korea, Taiwan, and Thailand at the end of the 1970s. Refugees from Indochina started landing in the 1980s, followed by a sudden increase in migrant workers of Japanese descent (*Nikkei*) and their spouses of non-Japanese descent from Latin America in the 1990s (Sekine 2003). The percentage of registered foreigners in the whole population surpassed 1 percent for the first time in the nation's history in 1992 (Zengaikyô 1999: 9).[4] By 2003, the total number of registered foreigners in Japan was 1.91 million, excluding those who had naturalized through residence or through marriage (Hômushô Nyûkoku Kanrikyoku 2004).

As for the populations relevant to this chapter, the total number of Chinese in Japan was 253,000 in 2000, the second largest group of foreigners after the Korean nationals. The total number of Vietnamese in Japan was 14,800 in 1999 and 12,900 in 2000, much smaller than that of Chinese (Kawakami 2001: 117; Sômushô Tôkeikyoku 2004).[5] As many of the foreigners (including resident Koreans) are concentrated in Kansai and the urban areas, the proportion of registered populations there tends to be higher than the average. For example, the proportion of foreign nationals in the population was 2.36 percent in Osaka, 2.09 percent in Kyoto, and 2.22 percent in Tokyo, compared with the national average of 1.2 percent in the same year (1998) (Zengaikyô 1999: 10). Although the percentage of foreigners is still smaller than in some other highly industrialized countries, the changes have had quite a dramatic impact on Japan, highlighting the issue of foreign residents who had previously been hidden by Japan's representation as a "homogeneous" nation (Lie 2001; Oguma 1995; Weiner 1997).

Aoyama City (pseudonym), the city where I did my research, is located in southeastern Osaka Prefecture, where many small to middle-sized companies are operating. In 1998, the number of registered foreigners in the city was 7,900, adding up to 2.8 percent of the total resident population in the city, more than double the national average of 1.2 percent (Zengaikyô 1999: 10). Out of that number, the largest group was Korean nationals, totaling 6,000 and accounting for 76.5 percent of the whole foreign national population. The second largest group was the Chinese with about 900 residents, and the third largest was the Vietnamese with approximately 400 (Aoyama City, Osaka Prefecture).

There is another unique aspect to my field site. Miyako (pseudonym), the school and the community where I conducted research, contains one of the two Buraku communities in Aoyama City. The Burakumin, members of a former group of outcasts, are still said to be prone to social discrimination such as in employment and marriage (Davis 2000), similar to that experienced by resident Koreans (Ryang 2000).

The Field Site: The Demography of the School

My initial visit to Miyako Elementary School was in the summer of 1996, visiting the office of the Osaka Prefecture Resource Council for Education of Foreign Children in Japan (Ôsaka-fu Zainichi Gaikokujin Kyôiku Kenkyû Kyôgikai).[6] The council is for public schools and schoolteachers in Osaka concerned about and interested in educating foreign children. I asked the director, who had been teaching at the school before taking that position, whether he knew any school where I could do long-term fieldwork on "newcomers" and other minority groups. Through this introduction I entered my field site and began my fieldwork, which lasted for almost 16 months, from September 1998 to March 2000. Even though I realized that the school had a history of involvement with the Buraku liberation and civil rights movement and the Koreans' ethnic educational movement, the site for me was more interesting because of the "newcomers," the Chinese and Vietnamese, rather than the "oldcomers," the Burakumin and resident Koreans. Gradually, I came to realize that my ideas needed to be modified; I was doing research on "newcomers" in a Buraku community in Osaka. And the fact that a Buraku community was in the school district of Miyako Elementary School in Osaka was a decisive factor distinguishing it from other schools. Even though Miyako had various educational programs for "newcomers," for the majority of Japanese who know the name of the area it was a Buraku community. I therefore undertook my project in a Buraku community where ethnic Koreans resided, where Vietnamese and Chinese were entering as refugees and returnees since the 1980s, where there was a history of civil rights activism for the Burakumin and resident Koreans, and where there was a tradition of minority education for these groups.

Miyako Elementary School had an enrollment of 418 children from the first grade to sixth grade in 1998, which reflected the demographics of Aoyama City's foreign nationals. Of these, the number of "Buraku" children was 203, or 48.6 percent of the total. However, the number includes many non-Buraku who had moved into the community, leaving the actual number of Buraku children at 46 according to the community official. The student body included 19 Vietnamese (including one Japanese national), 12 Chinese (including one Japanese national), 59 ethnic Koreans (including 33 Japanese nationals), and 2 half-Japanese children (*daburu*), totaling 92 children with a family or cultural background other than Japanese. Because of this demographic profile, Miyako Elementary School was designated by the city as a school for promoting *Dôwa* Education, "education for solving problems caused by Buraku discrimination," and given additional teachers and special financial aid (Hirasawa et al. 1995: 2). The school also received additional teachers and financial aid for enrolling foreign children and children with disabilities. Moreover, in the academic years 1998 through 2001, Miyako Elementary School was designated the Center School (*Sentaakô*) of the Area for the Promotion of Educating and Receiving Foreign Children (*Gaikokujin Shijo Kyôiku Ukeire Suishin Chiiki*) by the Ministry of Education, Culture, Sports, Science, and Technology (hereafter the Ministry of Education), owing to the increase in the number of Vietnamese children in the area. This area consisted of two junior high school districts, in which there were three elementary schools and two junior high schools.

The Vietnamese started going to school in this area in the late 1980s. This was because Vietnamese workers moved into public apartment complexes originally built for former coal miners (*koyôsokushin jûtaku*) and all three complexes of this housing in the city were constructed in the area. As for my field site, there were two types of apartment complexes (*danchi*). The first consisted of eight buildings for workers, and the second, managed by the city, was a complex of fourteen apartment buildings in the Buraku community called *shiei jûtaku* (municipal dwellings). These were constructed as an outcome of the Burakumin civil rights movement. The *danchi* for workers was constructed in my field site, for it was easier to purchase land there than other places due to the *Dowa* improvement measures that signaled the Buraku community in the area in the mid 1960s.[7] The Chinese started moving in from the northern part of Aoyama City from the mid 1990s. Most of the resident Koreans in the area migrated from Osaka City where resident Koreans were concentrated after the war to look for employment opportunities.

Japanese Language Instruction and Ethnic Club Activities

As a number of children were in need of Japanese language instruction, a "Japanese as a second language classroom" (*Nihongo kyôshitsu*), was opened at schools in the area in 1993. In 1998, Miyako Elementary School had two Japanese language classrooms, one for Vietnamese children and another for Chinese children. They had one Japanese language classroom before 1998, but owing to a sudden increase of Chinese children returning from China, the grandchildren of war-displaced Japanese orphans or women, the school provided a Japanese language classroom especially for Chinese children after the arrival of a teacher who was fluent in Chinese. This division of the Japanese language classrooms made it difficult for a child who did not fit into either category to participate in a Japanese language classroom or ethnic club activity, for the classrooms started to be oriented toward Chinese and Vietnamese children.

Both classrooms had one teacher in charge of classroom activities, most of which took place after school. Because of the larger number of Vietnamese children, the Japanese language classroom for Vietnamese had an assistant teacher as well as the teacher in charge. Vietnamese and Chinese children were automatically registered in each Japanese language classroom after entering school, as well as being registered in a homeroom. Most children at school had only one homeroom and one homeroom teacher, but both Chinese and Vietnamese children had a homeroom teacher and a teacher in charge of the Japanese language classroom. The disabled children also had two teachers and two classrooms: a shelter classroom and a special education teacher in charge of the classroom activities. One first grade Chinese girl refused to go to the Japanese language classroom on the grounds that she would be regarded as "disabled," but the teachers saw this as just laziness. The teachers in charge of Japanese language classrooms were supposed to assist homeroom teachers in teaching these children; however, in reality, the whole school seemed to depend on the two second language teachers when dealing with the problems of the Chinese and Vietnamese children. When a child was absent or late for school, it was usually these teachers who telephoned the family to find out how the child was doing. If something happened to Chinese and Vietnamese children in their homerooms, their homeroom teachers usually consulted with their Japanese language classroom teachers. To other teachers and children, these language homeroom teachers were known as "the teacher in charge of Chinese" (*Chûgoku tantô, Chûgoku no sensei*) and "the teacher in charge of Vietnamese" (*Betonamu tantô, Betonamu no sensei*), respectively.

The Japanese language classroom teachers assisted the homeroom teachers who sometimes had more than thirty students to deal with by taking out those who did not know enough Japanese language to understand the class (*chûshutsu shidô*), or by sitting next to a child in the homeroom who needed assistance in understanding the class (*hairikomi shidô*). In the academic year 1998–1999, two Chinese fifth graders were assisted in the first of these ways, and both Vietnamese and Chinese first graders were assisted in the latter way. Other Vietnamese and Chinese children, who did not receive any special language instruction, met in each Japanese language classroom after school at least once a week to study the Japanese language and review lessons from their homeroom class under the instruction of the teacher in charge. In 1998, all twelve Chinese children had been born in China and nine had been in Japan for two to three years or longer. Three children had just returned from China and they had started learning the Japanese language after entering school in Japan. Of the nineteen Vietnamese children, fifteen were born in Japan. Of the four children born outside Japan, three had a functional command of conversational Japanese.[8] Two came to Japan as infants and one as a child. During my research, only one Vietnamese child, who arrived in Japan half a year before (in March 1998), was struggling to learn the language for the first time.

Japanese Language Instruction

Each teacher prepared the materials used in the Japanese language classrooms, and the contents of the lessons were left to their discretion. For the Chinese children, the focus was on mastering and reviewing the homeroom classroom work, as most of the children in need of special language instruction were in the first and second grades. They even reviewed the mathematics lessons in the Japanese language classroom. For the Chinese children, the Japanese language classroom was used for supplementary lessons, for most of them were behind their class in their homeroom lessons. While reviewing the homeroom lessons, the teacher corrected their mistakes in Japanese as well. On the other hand, the teacher in charge of the Vietnamese children was concerned about their inability to handle abstract thinking, so she focused more on teaching correct Japanese grammar and appropriate Japanese word usage, even for those who did not have much of a problem in communication. The teacher modified pages from a Japanese textbook designed for those who were learning Japanese as a second language.

The Japanese language classrooms had an assistant instructor from outside the school, hired by Aoyama City Board of Education, in addition to

the two teachers in charge of the classrooms. The Japanese language classroom for Vietnamese children had a Vietnamese college student who came
to Japan as a refugee when she was in elementary school, and a Japanese
teacher who visited several Japanese language classrooms in the city. The
Japanese teacher visited the classroom once a week and told the children
about cultural issues in Japan and in Vietnam, such as holidays in Japan,
Japanese customs, how to use a Japanese dictionary, and so on. She sometimes gave them an assignment, to write a composition about topics such
as their favorite food, their New Year's resolution, or reflections on the academic semester. The Vietnamese college student did not take any initiative
in teaching Japanese, but she was there to share her experience with the
children and act as a role model, as a Vietnamese elder (*senpai*) living in
Japan. She visited the classroom twice a week, once for the Japanese language classroom and once for the ethnic club activities. The Japanese language classroom for Chinese had a Chinese college student who was
studying at a graduate school in Osaka. She visited the classroom twice a
week as well, including the day scheduled for the ethnic club activities.

Another important task of the Japanese language classroom teachers
was to translate official letters (*oshirase*) from school to families in each language, for most of the parents had difficulty reading Japanese. Those letters included a monthly schedule of school events, a letter about family
visits (*katei hômon*), and health examination notices.

Ethnic Clubs

The ethnic club activities were offered in each Japanese language classroom once a week after school. The tradition of ethnic clubs goes back to
Korean ethnic clubs, which started in the community in 1974, and began
in Miyako Elementary School in the early 1980s. The Japanese teachers in-
structed the ethnic clubs for Vietnamese and Chinese children, with assistance from the Vietnamese and Chinese instructors hired by Aoyama City
Board of Education. As for the Vietnamese ethnic club, a resident Korean
instructor came from the Korean ethnic club in the local community, since
resident Koreans in the local community had experience in ethnic education. On the ethnic club activity day, another resident Korean instructor also
came from the local community to run the Korean ethnic club at school.

The purpose of ethnic clubs for the "newcomers" was to learn about
their cultures and languages, and according to a teacher, the goal of these
club activities was to "retain and nurture the ethnic identity" (*minzokuteki
aidentiti no hoji shinchô*) of the Vietnamese and Chinese children. I often
heard this phrase when I was in the field from 1998 to 2000, but its origin
remained a mystery to me for a while. Teachers said that the phrase was
"from the Ministry of Education" and that "it was all over their materials."
It was interesting to know that, in spite of the popularity of the phrase, not

many knew its origin. As the Ministry of Education has not shown an interest in foreign children other than those who need Japanese language instruction (Enoi 1997; Ota 2000: 26–28), and as they have not acknowledged the importance of special education for foreign children other than the language instruction (Enoi 1997), I assume that the teachers' interpretation of the phrase is more influenced by the local context: education for the *Dôwa* and the resident Koreans in the city.

The two ethnic clubs participated in ethnic cultural festivals sponsored by Aoyama City Teachers' Association for Education for Foreign Residents and the teachers' union, along with Korean ethnic clubs at school and in the community, and ethnic clubs at other schools in Aoyama City. The Vietnamese children from Miyako Elementary School sang a Vietnamese song about the moon festival and performed a play with two other ethnic clubs. Other than a few phrases like *"xin chào"* (hello) and *"cám ơn"* (thank you), all the lines were in Japanese. The play was based on the Vietnamese fable, "Luck Loan Quan and Au Ko," and it explained historically how the country was founded. Chinese children greeted the audience with *"ni men hao"* (how are you?) in Chinese and then introduced themselves in Japanese. The fifth and sixth graders recited a few Chinese poems, while the first and second graders showed the written script to the audience. Both groups of children wore ethnic dress, Vietnamese *aodai* and Chinese *chipao*. These festivals were in the fall, in October and November, and practice and preparation began in September, as soon as the second semester started. Besides preparing for the performances at the festivals, each club had its own activities. As their club activities, Vietnamese children played traditional games, learned about Vietnamese history (fifth and sixth graders), learned how to make Vietnamese noodles and pancakes and a Japanese lunch box for the field trip, and created a picture book of how their families came to Japan based on stories they heard from their parents. Chinese children played Chinese chess, sang a Chinese song, learned how to make pancakes (because it was thought that Chinese cooking was too difficult for children), and played a game translating Chinese words into *katakana* Japanese words. The two clubs organized joint activities for the Star Festival in July, a Christmas party in December, and a Tea ceremony in March to learn about Japanese culture.

In addition to teaching cultural issues, the teacher in charge of the Vietnamese children was enthusiastic about introducing Vietnamese language instruction for the Vietnamese children to maintain their native language. The Vietnamese college student was asked to read stories out loud in Vietnamese, pronounce the Vietnamese words, and speak to the children in Vietnamese. She was asked to share her experience at school with children, for the teacher thought it would be encouraging to learn how their *senpai* was managing "as a Vietnamese living in Japan." The Vietnamese language instruction was regarded as important for three reasons: so that children could maintain a Vietnamese language ability to communicate with their parents who did not speak much Japanese; to improve their Japanese; and to nurture children's identity as Vietnamese. In the classroom for Vietnamese there were both implicit and explicit messages for the children. "You should not speak only Japanese, you should speak both Japanese and Vietnamese." "Be proud of yourself as a Vietnamese in Japan." To a child who was using a Japanese name, the message was "You should use your real ethnically distinctive name." It was stated in a school report that a Vietnamese child decided to use her Vietnamese name for graduation after realizing its importance from talking with the Vietnamese college student (Aoyama-shi Miyako Chûgakkô Miyako Shôgakkô 1999: 9–10). But these messages were common at schools in the city where foreign children were enrolled, and the more these messages were heard, the more a school would be regarded by teachers as enthusiastic (*nesshin*), and as having a good educational program. These messages were generated from the teachers' understanding of the goal of ethnic clubs, that is,"retaining and nurturing ethnic identity." In this case, their understanding had meant nurturing self-awareness as a member of a minority group in society, based on the tradition of *Dôwa* education and the education of resident Koreans in the city.

No More *Dôwa* Education and Inactive Korean Ethnic Clubs

The high visibility of "newcomer" children at school is linked with the homogenization of the old minorities (the resident Koreans and Burakumin) at school and in the community. Since the mid 1990s, education for Buraku children has changed direction, from focusing just on the Buraku human rights issue to treating the Buraku issue as one among several minority groups issues. *Dôwa* education therefore has stopped stressing that Buraku children should be taught awareness of being members of the *Dowa* community, and has shifted its focus to other educational issues such as peace, development, the environment, and international understanding. Accordingly, the Buraku children where I studied lacked information about themselves as Burakumin, for neither the teachers at school nor the community center (which used to be for the Buraku children) taught them about the issue. According to teachers and local activists, the reason for this was the improvement of living conditions, so that the children and even some of their parents could no longer relate to being members of a disadvantaged group. Because of the decrease of population of actual Buraku families in the community, it had become difficult to teach children about the issue. In interviews, a few parents in the community showed their concern about the fact that these days neither schools nor after-school activity centers were teaching their children about the Buraku issue. They said they did not know how to take on that responsibility. As a result of the transition from *Dôwa* education to education based on a wider concept of "human rights," together with the introduction of participatory learning methods, "newcomer" children, who can provide the educators with "cultural" materials, have also been made part of the internationalization process at the grass roots. It is partly because human rights education that sends a message to children on the importance of "human rights" also functions as another slogan in school.

Unlike the Chinese and Vietnamese clubs, the two Korean clubs at Miyako Elementary School, one for first through third graders and the other for fourth through sixth graders, have been open since the mid 1980s to anyone interested in learning about Korean culture. It was not mandatory for the nearly sixty children with Korean backgrounds to participate, but some Japanese who were interested did participate in the club activities. They were able to learn how to play Korean musical instruments, dance a Korean dance, and cook Korean food. However, the two Korean ethnic clubs at the school also faced a critical moment to their survival in May 1999. The club for first through third graders had seventeen children who wanted to join, but no children in higher grades wanted to join. At a teachers' meeting, one teacher said they should take this situation seriously, for the school and the community had a history of Korean ethnic education, and that they would need to discuss how to improve the situation. The conclusion of the meeting was that the teachers had asked the students if they were interested in the club, but the students were more interested in sports lessons at the community center instead. The Korean children's loss of interest in the Korean ethnic clubs was often mentioned during my fieldwork. It was the same for the Korean ethnic club in the community, which decided to open up its participation to "newcomers" in the name of "international exchange" (*kokusai kôryû*) in 1994. The resident Korean instructors were enthusiastic about "newcomers'" participation in the club, for they said they could relate these children's experience with their own. With the assistance of the Teachers' Association for Education for Foreign Residents and the teachers' union in Aoyama City, they undertook a project for "international exchange." Because of the systematic engagement of educators with "newcomer" children in and out of school, events targeted especially for them were planned. In the 1998 academic year, a field trip for foreign children and their parents was planned in the spring, and a winter school involving cooking and listening to a *senpai* who was going to high school was planned for "newcomer" children in the area during the winter break. In 1999, some of the Chinese and Vietnamese children became involved in these "international exchange" activities on a weekly basis. Participation was not mandatory, but the opportunity to take advantage of these low-cost activities was only given to Vietnamese and Chinese children, and not to resident Koreans or Burakumin. Even after school and during the school break, these Vietnamese and Chinese children were busy participating in these "cultural" events created in the name of "international exchange" and "international understanding," but at the same time they were trapped in these categories of "newcomers," Vietnamese or Chinese. The system forced these children to see themselves as simply Vietnamese or Chinese, rather than as Vietnamese Japanese, as Vietnamese born in Japan, as Chinese Japanese, or as the grandchildren of Japanese orphaned in China. The differential treatment of minority groups, which results from homogenization of old minorities and the teachers' belief in "retaining and nurturing the ethnic identity" of "newcomer" children, is further complicated by the cultures of teachers and schools in Japan, and the attitude of the dominant Japanese toward foreigners.

First, Japanese teachers in general have a tendency to treat a child as an individual without considering his or her background. The same is true for dealing with a minority child; the child is not considered as being a member of the disadvantaged groups in society, in spite of the teachers' interest in minority groups as a social issue. They are reluctant to associate any problems with a child's social and cultural background (Shimizu and Shimizu 2001: 75). Even when discussing Chinese and Vietnamese children at school, teachers' attention is focused on their language ability, academic ability, and their behavior. Moreover, teachers these days prefer to distance themselves from children's families, respecting the families' right to privacy. During my fieldwork, I heard that teachers used to visit children's families more frequently but that they seldom did anymore except when a child caused a problem at school and during the annual family visiting (*katei hômon*) week. In a sense, they are becoming more conservative, and some emphasize their identity as public officials (*kômuin*). One politically active teacher told me that she was disappointed because another teacher criticized her for being involved in a local community project requesting an interpreter system for the Vietnamese in Aoyama City. "I am doing this, for I care about Vietnamese children in my school, but he criticized me saying that I should not be involved and told me not to forget that we were public officials. I nearly cried from feeling so frustrated."

Second, owing to a general lack of information, Japanese tend to create stereotypical images of foreigners based on their national cultures within the framework of "internationalization" and to overlook the diversity found within groups of foreigners. In the case of my fieldwork, teachers lumped together all the children from China as Chinese, and children whose parents were from Vietnam as Vietnamese, neglecting the diversity within the groups. As for Chinese children, at least two groups existed, those who might return to China and those who would stay in Japan permanently. Vietnamese children were more diverse, including divisions between those who were born in Vietnam, in Japan, and outside Japan; between the Chinese-Vietnamese and the Vietnamese; between those whose parents had stayed in Japan for shorter versus longer periods; between political refugees and economic refugees; between those whose parents were both refugees and those of whom only one parent was a refugee; between those who were permanent or temporary residents of Japan; and so on. Creating groups based on countries of origin may be an efficient way to deal with foreign children; however, being efficient does not necessarily mean being educationally acceptable, considering the actual diversity existing within each group.

Because of these characteristics of teachers' culture and the dominant Japanese attitude toward foreigners, teachers in general do not try to find out much about children's family backgrounds, which results in their relying on the resources created by Aoyama City teacher's association and the local tradition of minority education. This tends to strengthen teachers' belief in the importance of "retaining and nurturing ethnic identity." As teachers are reluctant to get involved in education for Buraku children or resident Koreans these days, "newcomer" children are becoming the focus of attention in the cultural enterprise of internationalization.[9] The "visibility" of these children increases as they are pushed into the cultural categories of Chinese and Vietnamese, derived from a Japanese stereotypical image.

According to a survey I conducted in 1999, twelve out of fourteen Chinese children said they regarded themselves as Chinese because they were born in China, while two said they regarded themselves as Chinese because their parents were Chinese. As for eighteen Vietnamese children, sixteen of them said they regarded themselves as Vietnamese, and fourteen of them said that it was because their parents were Vietnamese. Two gave their ability to speak the Vietnamese language as the reason they considered themselves Vietnamese. Two children, both first graders, said they regarded themselves as Japanese because they were born there. While filling out the questionnaire, one child said, "My father told me that I am Japanese, because I was born in Japan."

Talking with the Vietnamese adults, I sensed that they were caught in the dilemma between their eagerness to become like the Japanese and the resentment of being excluded from the society (*Nihonjin ni naritaikedo narenai*). Some say they want their children to become Japanese. Other parents eventually identified themselves strongly as Vietnamese; for example, Tuan, a 27-year-old male who came to Japan as a child and naturalized, rediscovered his Vietnamese identity after his stay in southern California. In another case, Nhat, a mother of three children who arrived in Japan in her early twenties and who was in her late thirties at the time of my interview, said, "A name is like a sign [*kigô no yô na mono*]." For her, Japanese citizenship and a Japanese name made her life more convenient in Japan. I met several other Vietnamese who had naturalized or who were saying that they would consider getting Japanese citizenship and using a Japanese name for convenience. But since using Japanese names is discouraged by the local ideology of minority education, especially by the education for resident Koreans, even Vietnamese who were born in Japan are encouraged to live as Vietnamese. It is because teachers are aware of the exclusive nature of Japanese society in relation to foreigners[10] and it is because they want these children to be strong enough to overcome discriminatory practices in the society. Everything they do is in good faith. But we should not forget that the issue of identity among the old minority groups, the Burakumin and resident Koreans, has become a personal choice left to each family and individual.

Conclusion

The degree of "visibility" of Vietnamese and Chinese children where I carried out my fieldwork is high, for they have become cultural beings through the local educational programs of "international exchange" and "international understanding." Their "visibility" is also enhanced by the homogenization of the earlier generation of minority groups in the educational setting, for there are no longer any attempts on the side of the educational authorities to educate Burakumin and resident Koreans as minority groups. However, the newcomer cultural categories of Vietnamese and Chinese are given new meanings by the ideology of local minority education, and "newcomer" children are transformed into "minority children" who are expected to live as members of minorities, and therefore to challenge the dominant Japanese society.

The internationalization of education has given these children their ethnic identity and native language to a certain extent, but they have been deprived of the option to live like other Japanese or to live "in between" Japanese and the Vietnamese or Chinese. They are treated and marked as foreigners, which has negative connotations in Japan, especially when they are from non-Western countries. As Morris-Suzuki argues, these new categories of ethnic minorities are placed alongside the "mainstream Japanese" culture without recognizing the differences existing within the category of "Japanese," producing "minorities" in relation to a "majority" (1998: 208–209). This strategy of placing ethnic minorities next to Japanese and keeping the "international" outside the boundary of Japanese citizens results in (ethnic) minorities being structurally excluded from the socio-judicial realm, all in the name of multiculturalism. This is an example of how ethnic "others" are created in the process of internationalization in the cultural realm.

Notes

1. "Newcomers" are broadly defined as foreigners who arrived in Japan for employment purposes as "foreign workers" since the latter half of the 1970s (Ota 2000: 5; Shimizu and Shimizu 2001: 3).

2. There are some works discussing education for ethnic minority children in public schools in Japan. See for example Ota (2000) for an ethnographic study of the school life of South American Japanese descendants in T City in the Tokai region; Shimizu and Shimizu (2001) on education for newcomers (Japanese Brazilians, refugees from Southeast Asia, and Korean immigrants) in the Metropolitan area and the Chubu region; Hester (2000) for *Minsokkyô*-style ethnic classes (*minzoku gakkyû*) for Koreans in an elementary school in Osaka City; Linger (2001) on a *Kokusai* classroom for Brazilians in a middle school in Toyota City, Aichi Prefecture; Tsuneyoshi (2001) for *Nikkeijin* in the international classroom of an elementary school in Ayase City, Kanagawa Prefecture; Nukaga (2003) for a "multicultural coexistence" education model in an elementary school where returnees and newcomers are enrolled, in Kawasaki City, Kanagawa Prefecture; and Takato (2004) for the experiences of *Nikkei* children from Latin America in an elementary school in an urban industrial and "multiethnic" context with a history of migration from Korea and Okinawa.

3. Here, I use the term "homogenization" to describe the educational activities of a school and a local community that identify the old minority groups as "culturally assimilated" but not necessarily "structurally assimilated." See Gordon (1964: 71) for the concepts of "cultural assimilation" and "structural assimilation." I would like to thank Meryl Siegal for suggesting this term to me after reading a paper I presented at the 2001 American Anthropological Association annual meeting.

4. However, Sômushô Tôkeikyoku (2004) put the total number of foreigners in 1995 at 1.31 million or 1.03 percent of the total population, the first time it had exceeded 1.0 percent since World War II.

5. In 1999, the Vietnamese entering Japan as trainees (*kenshûsei*) or students amounted to 4,480, almost 30 percent of the total number of Vietnamese (Kawakami 2001: 141).

6. The "Teachers' Association for Education for Foreign Residents" in Aoyama City is regarded as a unit of Osaka Prefecture Resource Council for Education of Foreign Children in Japan (Ôsaka-fu Zainichi Gaikokujin Kyôiku Kenkyû Kyôgikai), which was founded to promote education for foreign children in 1992. The aims of this council are to establish the direction of education for resident Koreans and newcomers, to exchange information on how to teach Japanese children about foreign cultures, to examine their teaching methods, and to pursue forms of education that transcend the principles of assimilation and exclusion in an internationalizing society (*kokusaika shakai*). It is partially funded by Osaka Prefecture Education Board as a supplementary organization (*hojo dantai*). See the inaugural issue of their association published in December 1992 for more details.

7. See Neary (1997) for the discussion of the implementation of the special measures legislation of Burakumin.

8. Of the three Vietnamese children born outside Japan, one was born in Vietnam and two were born in refugee camps in Malaysia and Indonesia. Two of them arrived in Japan when they were infants and one when the child was three years old.

9. I agree with John Clammer (2001: 28) that differences such as race, multiculturalism, and minorities, which would be read as political in other countries, are "removed from the realm of the political and placed squarely in the cultural" in Japan.

10. In describing the exclusivity of Japanese society, those who are engaged in Korean ethnic education use the term "assimilation" and say, "The pressure

on ethnic minorities to assimilate is strong in Japan [*Nihon wa dôka no atsuryoku ga tsuyoi*]."

References

Aoyama-shi Miyako Chûgakkô Miyako Shôgakkô. 1999. *Heisei 10.11-nendo Gaikokujin Shijo Kyôiku Ukeire Suishin Chiiki Shitei Jigyô Monbushô Shisatsu Shiryô* [Materials prepared for the visit of the Ministry of Education to the Area for the Promotion of Educating and Receiving the Foreign Children in 1998–1999].

Clammer, John. 2001. *Japan and Its Others: Globalization, Difference and the Critique of Modernity.* Melbourne: Trans Pacific Press.

Davis, John. 2000. "Blurring the Boundaries of the Buraku(min)." In *Globalization and Social Change in Contemporary Japan,* ed. J. S. Eades, Tom Gill, and Harumi Befu, 78–85. Melbourne: Trans Pacific Press.

Enoi, Yukari. 1997. "Gakkô deno Tabunka Kyôsei Kyôiku no Kanôsei ni tsuite" [On the possibility of multicultural education at school]. *Aoyama-shi Zainichi Gaikokujin Kyôiku Kenkyûkai Jigyô Hôkoku* 6.

Gordon, Milton. 1964. *Assimilation in American Life: The Role of Race, Religion and National Origins.* New York: Oxford University Press.

Hester, Jeffry. 2000. "Kids between Nations: Ethnic Classes in the Construction of Korean Identities in Japanese Public Schools." In *Koreans in Japan: Critical Voices from the Margin,* ed. Sonia Ryang, 175–196. New York: Routledge.

Hirasawa, Yasumasa, Yoshiro Nabeshima, and Minoru Mori. 1995. *Dôwa Education: Educational Challenge toward a Discrimination-Free Japan.* Buraku Kaihô Kenkyûsho [Buraku Liberation Research Institute].

Hômushô Nyûkoku Kanrikyoku. 2004. *Kôhô Shiryô. Heisei 15-nenmatsu Genzai ni okeru Gaikokujin Tôrokusha Tôkei ni tsuite* [Public information. On the statistics of foreign residents at the end of 2003]. Immigration Bureau, Ministry of Justice.

Kawakami, Ikuo. 2001. *Ekkyô Suru Kazoku: Zainichi Betonamukei Jûmin no Seikatsu Sekai* [Families crossing borders: the life-world of Vietnamese residents]. Tokyo: Akashi Shoten.

Lie, John. 2001. *Multiethnic Japan.* Cambridge, MA: Harvard University Press.

Linger, Daniel Touro. 2001. *No One Home: Brazilian Selves Remade in Japan.* Stanford, CA: Stanford University Press.

Morris-Suzuki, Tessa. 1998. *Re-inventing Japan: Time, Space, Nation.* Armonk, NY: M. E. Sharpe.

Neary, Ian. 1997. "Burakumin in Contemporary Japan." In *Japan's Minorities: Illusion of Homogeneity,* ed. Michael Weiner, 50–78. London: Routledge.

Nukaga, Misako. 2003. "Japanese Education in an Era of Internationalization: A Case Study of an Emerging Multicultural Coexistence Model." *International Journal of Japanese Sociology* 12 (1): 79–94.

Oguma, Eiji. 1995. *Tan'itsu Minzoku Shinwa no Kigen: 'Nihonjin' no Jigazô no Keifu* [The origin myth of ethnic homogeneity: A genealogy of Japanese self-images]. Tokyo: Shin'yosha.

Ôsaka-fu Zainichi Gaikokujin Kyôiku Kenkyû Kyôgikai. 1992. *Chigai wo Yutakasa ni: Ôsaka-fu Zainichi Gaikokujin Kyôiku Kenkyû Kyôgikai Kessei Kinen* [Make differences into richness: Inaugural issue of Osaka Prefecture Resource Council for Education of Foreign Children in Japan].

Ota, Haruo. 2000. *Nyûkamâ no Kodomo to Nihon no Gakkô* [Newcomer children in Japanese public schools]. Tokyo: Kokusaishoin.

Ryang, Sonia. 2000. "Introduction: Resident Koreans in Japan." In *Koreans in Japan: Critical Voices from the Margin*, ed. Sonia Ryang, 1–12. London: Routledge.

Sekine, Masami. 2003. "An Introductory Note on the Special Issue on Japanese Society and Ethnicity." *International Journal of Japanese Sociology* 12 (1): 2–6.

Shimizu, Kokichi, and Mutsumi Shimizu, eds. 2001. *Nyûkamâ to Kyôiku: Gakkô Bunka to Esunishiti no Kattô o Megutte* [Newcomer and education: On the conflict between school culture and ethnicity]. Tokyo: Akashi Shoten.

Sômushô Tôkeikyoku. 2004. *Heisei 12-nen Kokusei Chôsa Gaikokujin ni kansuru Tokubetsu Shûkei Kekka* [A national census for 2000. The special result of foreigners]. Statistics Bureau, Ministry of Internal Affairs and Communications.

Takato, Michiyo. 2004. "Imagining Ethnicity and Polyphony at Margins: Nikkei Migration, School, and Everyday Life in Japan." Ph.D. diss., Columbia University.

Tsuneyoshi, Ryoko. 2001. "Newcomers in the Japanese Classroom: Implications for Change." In *The Japanese Model of Schooling: Comparisons with the United States*, 119–142. New York: Routledge Falmer.

Weiner, Michael, ed. 1997. *Japan's Minorities: Illusion of Homogeneity*. London: Routledge.

Yoon, Keun-Cha. 1996. "Kokumin Keisei to Minzoku Sabetsu: Sengo Kyôiku Kenkyû no Otoshiana" [Nation formation and discrimination based on ethnicity: The trap of educational research after the war]. In *Kyôikugaku ga Wakaru* [Understanding Educational Research], ed. Asahi Shinbunsha, 139–143. Tokyo: Asahi Shinbunsha.

———. 1997. "Nihon Kokumin" to iu Otoshiana: Sengo Nihon no Shisô to Kyôiku ni kanren shite [The trap of "Japanese Nation": Regarding philosophy and education after the war]. In *Nihon Kokuminron:*

Kindai Nihon no Aidentitî [Japanese nation: Identity of modern Japan], 241–261. Tokyo: Chikuma Shobô.

Zengaikyô. 1999. *Zainichi Gaikokujin Kyôiku Q & A* [Q & A on the education for foreign residents]. Kyoto: Zenkoku Zainichi Gaikokujin Kyôiku Kenkyû Kyôgikai.

10

A CRITICAL REVIEW OF ACADEMIC PERSPECTIVES ON BLACKNESS IN JAPAN

Mitzi Carter

Aina Hunter

Corporate multiculture is giving the black body a makeover. We are witnessing a series of struggles over the meaning of that body, which intermittently emerges as a signifier of prestige, autonomy, transgression, and power in a supranational economy of signs that is not reducible to the old-style logics of white supremacism (Gilroy 2000: 270).

SCHOLARS HAVE ADDRESSED THE PROBLEMS black people can face in Japan, and these problems, which begin with stereotypical images imported from the States, have been fetishized in the media to the extent that American academics often leave unchallenged the view of rampant Japanese racism specifically targeting blacks. In addition, because most scholarship is primarily concerned with the triangular relationship between African American men and Japanese women and men, the experiences of black women are marginalized or neglected altogether. For these reasons, the authors focus on interpretations of their personal experiences and how they might diverge or stand outside the scope of the conventional wisdom.

In his 1996 essay on personal ethics and fieldwork, Walter Williams concludes: "My general approach to life is to accentuate the positive, [but] I find many academics so overwhelmingly pessimistic and critical that they unwittingly discourage others. I have presented my experiences not to glorify myself but in the hope that such knowledge may encourage others to accomplish better ethnography in the future" (Williams 1996: 84). It is in this spirit the authors of this chapter share their stories. Mitzi Carter is biracial, Okinawan and African American. She taught English in rural Japan and also spent time reconnecting with her mother's family in Okinawa. Aina Hunter, on the other hand, came to Japan as a complete foreigner and spent a year first as a student, then as a teacher. Because of the differences in their backgrounds and the significant differences between big-city and small-island life, their experiences were occasionally at variance. They are often congruent, however, and what can be taken away from the discrepancies is proof that racial essentialism is no longer a useful tool for understanding the lives of black people in Japan.

This chapter is more a critique of existing scholarship and theories than a fully developed proposal on how to proceed correcting them. It is rather a topic of great personal interest for both authors and a call for alternative perspectives on these matters.

Aina—On Arriving

I left for Japan in the spring of 2000. Although I had previously visited Haruko, my high school best friend, twice at her father's home in Yokohama, and then years later on her farm in Hokkaido, I worried about my reception at Meiji Gakuin University. When I told an instructor about the National Security Education Program grant that made it possible for me to study abroad, she remarked, "You're going to Japan? They hate blacks, you know!" I didn't know quite how to respond.

And then there was the interview I endured before being officially admitted to the Berkeley program. The professor from the International Studies Department asked how I planned to deal with racism if it became an issue. I told the interviewer I had no reason to expect any problems. She shook her head at my naiveté and said Japanese people have a reputation for being racist, and that one should be prepared for that.

After the "interview" I recalled a disturbing passage in Edwin O. Reischauer's *The Japanese Today* in which he stated definitively that Japanese people "tend to look upon blacks with wonderment and revulsion" (1988: 397). I began to doubt myelf, but I need not have worried. At the tail end of March I flew into Narita, took the trains into Shinjuku, and was immediately embraced by Emiko's family. Although it was only seven in the evening, Emiko's mother, father, aunt, and uncle insisted I take a bath and change clothes after my long flight. There was nothing to do but follow directions, so I bathed and reluctantly put on the square pajamas printed with *manga*. I sat at the table, self-conscious and humbled where the four of them sat, fully dressed, drinking beer and smoking. "Much better!" they exclaimed. You even look like Emiko now! Same-shaped head!" The sushi delivery arrived and, incredibly, I began to relax. Their warmth and concern made me feel that I was a member of the family; albeit the most junior, pajama-wearing member. After dinner Emiko's uncle surprised me with a spontaneous offer of employment. "My wife," he said, "has an English tutor. A white guy." He made a face. "I want you to be her new teacher!"

I would experience this drawing in many times over, later at Meiji Gakuin and still later when I started work teaching *eikaiwa* (English conversation classes). In contradiction to the predictions of my Berkeley instructors, I was embraced by my classmates and students alike. When one girl (who later became a good friend) confessed that she found her teacher, who was tall and blond, intimidating, I began to suspect that my brown skin gave me an advantage, as far as being allowed into certain intimate spaces.

I came to understand that some students at Meiji saw me as more approachable because of my non-whiteness, in part because they viewed me as occupying marginal space in the US power structure, which they quite openly expressed distaste for. At any rate, I was permitted access to the back-regions of their lives; their inner thoughts, fears and other intimacies, whereas my two white friends from Berkeley were unable to access these psychological spaces.

Mitzi—On Arriving

A year before I went to Japan, a "blackanese" friend of mine, a male in his late twenties, wrote me a letter and in a mixture of good humor and unabashed candor said, "I don't know how long this is gonna last, so you'd better get your butt out here before your blackness goes out of style." I laughed and thought for some time about this comment. What happens if I do go out of style? Was he implying that I just won't be given the extra "super star" attention many young white foreigners sometimes get when they go to Japan or does that mean he is assuming that prior to this "fad," blacks were treated poorly and will again be treated poorly after the fascination with things black has been quickly discarded into the secondhand graveyard along with Pokémon, Digimon, and ankle-breaking platform shoes. I wrestled with these feelings before leaving for Japan, vacillating between feeling uneasy at being the object of exotification and feeling that perhaps it would be better than being ignored or treated with outright disdain as I had heard about in stories of Japanese racism towards blacks from various people. Echoing Aina's experience, the news I got from most people before heading to Japan seemed dismal, "Those Japanese are racists, you know." Other reactions included, "Those Japanese are so used to living in a homogenous land that they don't know how to react to different people—it's cultural racism." Academic literature on black people in Japan has not veered too far from these statements. Pick up any article or book on black people in Japan and you will find within the first three paragraphs a statement on the racist comments made by Prime Minister Nakasone Yasuhiro and Minister of Justice Kajiyama Seiroku in the late 1980s and early 1990s. This is used repeatedly as the leveraging point for the idea that Japanese are racists. In his book *Multiethnic Japan,* John Lie argues against this kind of thinking and cautions that "Japanese racism is far from being an essential Japanese characteristic" (2001: 177). We still tend to think of blacks as having no agency in Japan. We position them through our discourse as being stuck, entrapped in the quicksand of nonbelonging or forever floating on the edges of *uchi/soto* margins. And by positioning Japanese as racists who accept blackness only through consumption, we also privilege the state and corporations and give secondary consideration to the everyday practices and the ways that blackness is negotiated outside of these institutions.

John G. Russell, an African American professor teaching at Gifu University, has probably written the most on issues of this nature in Japan. As an anthropologist, Russell is concerned with looking at the micropractices in the consumption of blackness, the interpretations and translations of blackness, and how these practices take shape discursively, textually, and aesthetically. Russell asserts that particularly American forms of blackness are rearticulated in Japan. Although he says of course there is room for improvising after the media has served the masses blackness, he pays little attention to this kind of "wiggle" room. I do not disagree with the power and role of American media abroad but the increasing movement of Japanese abroad and the movement of blacks throughout Japan, whether in the military or as teachers, has started to whittle at marketed images of blackness. He mentions briefly in his article, "Consuming Passions: Spectacle, Self-transformation, and the Commodification of Blackness in Japan" (Russell 1998: 161), that black men have become associated with the US military and may therefore serve as a convenient scapegoat for feelings of national humiliation by white men, but he never develops this theory fully. This would then incite a different model for rethinking blackness in Japan and what kinds of signifiers are enabled and what work they do.

Russell's work is profound and adds much to our understanding of imaginings of blackness in Japan in the past, and to some degree the present, but he is still using the strictly essentialist positions on blackness. Russell's most argued point, and one that is the most contentious for me, is his idea that Japanese use commodified blackness as a tool for escape. By constructing his argument around this essentialized version of blackness, he is positioning Japanese as static and passive if not overt racists. Blackness becomes the mask that is tried on by Japanese women to escape their subservient positions. To perform blackness, he argues carefully, is to domesticate and control it. "As glossed in the transnational marketplace," he says, "'blackness' is first and foremost an overpowering physical presence, an invitation to forbidden pleasures and sexual experimentation that offers the illusion of personal and racial transcendence" (Russell 1998: 127). We shouldn't assume "the Japanese" still think or have ever only thought of blackness as a mere site, as a place for touristic pleasures where Japanese women and rebellious youth can escape to some liminal destination and lose themselves or find a new, "unbound" self in this place of blackness where they can explore the Other only to reify their authentic Japanese identity once past this performance stage. It makes for an interesting and compelling argument but, if we are not careful, it may serve to harden stereotypes and benefit those who thrive on racist accounts of Japanese only to mystify their own xenophobia. It would be interesting to see a series of interviews done on this topic in different spaces—urban, rural, militarized zones, and transnational spaces in which certain actors might see themselves as more internationalized. It would also be useful to research how perceptions of blackness shift when black women are the primary subject. To argue that blackness is consumed as such with little emphasis on the consumption of whiteness, and other forms of racialized bodies, much is missed in teasing out issues of how these forms are negotiated and blackness therefore still remains a "thing" for "the Japanese" to manipulate.

In her essay, "Fetishized Blackness: Hip Hop and Racial Desire in Contemporary Japan," Nina Cornyetz offers a different reading of the signification of blackness in Japan. She suggests that the contemporary reproduction of blackness through style and consumption of hip-hop attire and skin darkening "signifies a potential transnational identity, supplementary to a previously interjected, Western imperialist black-white binary paradigm, revelatory of a desire and a propensity for racial identificatory slippage" (1994: 115). Like Russell, she says many images of African Americans and blackness and the seemingly enthusiastic celebration for this style, people, and look are imported via MTV and Hollywood movies and not internally generated in Japan. However, she argues that the widespread consumption of blackness as a style in Japan is reproduced and consumed differently than in a place like white suburban America where hip-hop has been marketed and consumed heavily. She notes, "In the Japanese reproduction, while many of the origins of hip hop are erased, they are erased differently; most notably, they are not 'whitened'" (1994: 119).

We are not dismissing all of what Russell and others with similar reasoning have to say. Just as the appropriation of urban forms of "blackness" adopted by many white, middle-class youth in rural spaces in the United States does not necessarily signal growing equality and acceptance of racialized people, the same can be applied in Japan. Russell asserts, "Both [the acceptance of black cultural forms and foreign loan words] function decoratively to bestow on the user a certain degree of prestige and fashionability, while insuring that the objects of imitation are excluded" (1999: 147). For Russell, blackness then becomes a neatly packaged *omiyage* (a gift which symbolizes the place of its origin)—the site of its origin is clearly understood and the quasi-tourists can easily find these tokens of blackness, try them on, perform them, and make love to them. Cornyetz also critiques anthropologist Karen Kelsky for a similar analysis because she "blurs the distinctions between the Japanese processing of whiteness and blackness and thus is not attentive to the role of power informing the logic of a black-white antipodal paradigm and the resultant production of Japanese hybridity" (1994: 131). Cornyetz's analysis allows for more theoretical movement by paying close attention to that which has been added to the older systems of racial Othering practices at work in Japan: "African Americans as signs are encoded with additional, new significations: the images of African Americans are not the same old thing but something *different*" (1994: 122); and she adds, "difference is affirmed through the surety that outfits and skin darkening do not erase their own Japaneseness" (1994: 132) and does not solely function to reaffirm "the Japanese self."

Although Russell's and Kelsky's analyses may be appealing for many scholars in the United States because they work well in talking about certain meanings of African Americans in North America, they may narrow the academic room for defining blackness in Japan and particularly blackness deriving from the United States. Black women do not completely fit into this kind of consumed blackness. Russell argues, "The Japanese imaginary regards black women as less alluring and refined than white women ... she is seldom depicted as an object of romance or sensual desire" (1999: 152). But it is interesting that many black women who have written about their travel and work experiences in Japan do not relate to this statement. And it tends to disregard what Cornyetz argues is only a recent practice, affixing the positive term *akogareta* (to yearn for, desire) to African Americans.

And who is to say we want to be depicted as these sensual objects of desire?

Aina—On Black Beauty

I do, I do!

When I walked into the *gaijin tarento* agency, a photographer immediately approached me and said that my face was perfect for a liquor ad. He explained that a beverage company wanted a black model's face rising from a moonlit pool of water. I was thrilled and immediately posed for headshots. A week later he told me that the company had chosen another model. He said they wanted a woman with "hard eyes." When I saw the model ultimately chosen, I decided that the client probably wanted someone more definitively "black." I could go further and think about John Russell's symbols of blackness, and reflect on the fact that black models are rarely seen on ads for English conversation schools or for "wholesome" products, but I don't really see the point in this kind of exercise. I just don't know how meaningful it is. For one thing, during my entire year in Tokyo I did not encounter a single demeaning image of an African or African American person. (There was, however, a fairly ubiquitous and not particularly attractive image of a black-skinned East Indian who serves as the mascot for a certain brand of curry.) I do not doubt that the absence I observed is due, in part, to efforts of writers like Russell who initiated critical discussion of stereotypical images in Japan ten years ago. Yet even before Russell there was an organization called the Japan African American Friendship Association (established in 1981), the predominately Japanese members of which discourage the proliferation of derogatory images.

Whoever deserves credit, in the summer of 2000, my attention was constantly drawn to the arresting images of black women in the billboard-style ads and the black mannequins in Shibuya boutiques. There was also an enormous and popular ad campaign in progress featuring Naomi Campbell, nicknamed *"buraku biyûti."* In the summer of 2000 it seemed I could hardly turn a corner in the Shinjuku train station without meeting the haughty gaze of the British model.

Russell would hold that the popularity of black models does not mean that life is great for all black women in Japan, but racial essentialism fails to account for the many different variations on what he would call "the black experience." Russell's conclusions err on the side of cynicism: who could argue that the experiences of a black British model in Shibuya, an illegal immigrant from Ghana, an American banking executive in Tokyo, an American GI stationed in Yokohama, and an English teacher in rural Japan could ever share a similar "black experience"?

Mitzi—On Being Blackanese

This is only a beginning, an opening for looking at how current discourse positions Japanese as having fixed notions of blackness. This is not to say that blacks have not been and are not treated badly in Japan. I learned about this side of Japan from my mother and from other friends who have experienced direct and oppressive forms of racism. While in Japan or in situations when around Japanese people, my Okinawan mother still tries to pull me in to being more *uchi*. I was never allowed to play outside until the sun went down or else she warned me, "I would become more like my father's color" and therefore less Japanese. Perhaps many of her fears came from the uneasy times she spent with my older sister living in Korea, Thailand, and Japan in the 1960s and 1970s. She was constantly the object of harassment for having a "Sambo baby" and was called the nastiest names for betraying the nation with her sex. She was immediately associated with military domination, with prostitution, with misplaced allegiances. My mother had told me many stories about why she refused to enroll my sister in a Japanese school and they all seemed to stem from the belief that it would be detrimental to her daughter's self-esteem. She would rather leave Japan than have my sister suffer from the kind of name-calling she received outside of school hours. My cousins who are half Okinawan and half white American had similar stories of buses passing them by and stories of bullying in school and how even later, signs on certain dance clubs in Koza City would not only say, "no Americans" or "no GIs" but also "no *hâfu*" allowed. The undercover Japanese have the potential to be the most threatening because our allegiances are hard to place. My friend Tatsu Yamato (whose father is Japanese and mother black) lived in Japan for years and was repeatedly frustrated that his name, which can be written in full *kanji*, was always changed to *katakana* so that he did not "trick" anyone into thinking he was "really" Japanese before meeting in person.

I am aware that being "*hâfu*" in Japan is different from being just "*gaijin*." In his documentary *Doubles* (1998), Regge Life interviewed "*hâfu*" living in and outside of Japan and from varying generations. Their experiences varied from painfully unpleasant to very positive. What struck me was the way in which those who were half black living in Japan had experiences that were not too wholly different from those who were half white living there. If we look critically at marginal, hybridity, or borderland theories, we may be able to flesh out how biracial Japanese move between the spaces of *uchi* (inside) and *soto* (outside), *omote* (front stage) and *ura* (back stage). These boundaries are more porous than we allow in academic literature. In his essay "On the Borderlines," James Valentine discusses these "third spaces" in reference to mixed race people in Japan: "An *ainoko* (child of mixed Japanese and foreign parentage) is more marginal, yet at the same time more rejected, than a 'pure' gaijin. Through such rejection s/he paradoxically becomes in some senses more outside than the complete outsider" (1990: 39). But this does not mean that *hâfu* are barred from having a foot inside either and are then more inside than the outsider, whether one parent is black or not. This brings to mind a personal experience of mine. When working in Sado Island, a fellow colleague from the United States who had been in Japan for much longer than I was a bit shocked when I told her that I was being asked to cut the persimmons and help serve tea in the mornings. She exclaimed, "I don't think I know any other *gaijin* teacher that's been asked to help out like that, regardless of how demeaning that may be as a woman and a newcomer. It means you're being pulled into a more *uchi* role and that the other teachers trust you." However, I had a feeling at times that I was on the border of disappointing everyone for not knowing better and on the edge of forgiveness because my blood has betrayed me from ever *really* becoming Japanese. However, never did the issue of me being half black ever come into those feelings of nonbelonging I may have felt, neither was that ever raised or insinuated in any context. I do not take my experiences to be universal but I think there is still a hole in academic literature in regards to this issue. The project still needing attention is that which addresses the racial meanings of blackness in terms of spatial differences in Japan—the militarized zones around Yokohama and Okinawa, urban spaces where alterity is highly celebrated, and rural villages where encounters with "live" African Americans is still rare. For examples of shifting identity and perspectives on race in a militarized zone, see Masamichi Inoue's (2007) discussion of a quickly formed alliance between African American soldiers in Koza City and Okinawan anti-base citizens in the 1960s. Although this may have been a temporary moment of solidarity where race and difference were highlighted, in a later historical modality of Okinawan identity, images of blackness, especially in relation to the rapists of a schoolgirl in 1995, were suppressed and erased in Okinawan media images of the US military to construct a monolithic, homogenous military system which to oppose. I believe there is a sharp distinction between the many Africans living in Japan and African Americans, but more ethnographic work needs to be done on how and why and what that means for meanings of blackness and its consumption. Doing so helps to create a rupture in the understandings that imaginings of blackness are wholly imported from the United States and that they still operate on a similar plane of racial ordering.

The important question for us then, is who benefits from these tacit understandings that Japanese are racist against blacks?

Aina–On Using "Japanese Racism" to Conceal White Racism

A black friend of ours applied for a job at an Australian-owned *eikaiwa* school in Japan. Based upon his resume, he was invited for an interview. Upon his arrival, he was told because the Japanese are such racists, they would prefer to hire a white teacher because, "the Japanese would be able to 'deal with it' better." But I know of many black English teachers who had very positive experiences, so who benefits by the perpetuation of this myth?

Black Americans live in a country with recent histories of hangings, cross-burning terrorism, and car draggings, so one should consider carefully before crying "racism" when speaking about well-publicized Japanese biases. Just as we now find it ill-considered to use the word "holocaust" for anything less than genocide, we shouldn't substitute the word "racism" for naivite or xenophobia. This leads to another quibble with Russell. In "Consuming Passions" (1998), he uses the word *kurombo*, insisting that the best translation is the notorious "N" word. He does not state how he arrived at this interpretation, but I am not convinced that that particular word could ever be directly translated into a culture that does not have the particularly hateful history of the United States towards African

Americans. I find his interpretation unnecessarily inflammatory. I fear that it reinforces the suspicions of black Americans who suspect that foreign countries are particularly unwelcoming and secondly it feeds into an Anglo American belief that bigotry is not an American problem, or even a white problem, but rather a cross-cultural difficulty that stems from some inherent quality of blackness.

Mitzi—On Critiquing Russell

Our focus and critique of Russell's work in particular is not to suggest we run gleefully into the pluralistic positions that can shelter power that exist in less defined forms, those nonessentialist positions that scholars like Paul Gilroy (2000) and Liz Bondi (1993) argue leaves constructions like "blackness" floating around, waiting to be signified at any given moment. There is no doubt the invisible geographies of power that Russell is very conscious of exist and to ignore those is precarious. On the other hand, to also not give credence to the changing images of blackness is just as dangerous. If we have for so long said blacks do not have the means to their representation in Japan, but then dismiss the growing collection of narratives of blacks who have had positive experiences either as tourists, temporary workers, or now living permanently in Japan, is to commit the same error that we accuse Japanese of doing—that is, dismissing any blacks as anomalies who or when they speak against the grain of the current models of blackness in Japan. Furthermore academics should pay more attention to the nonacademic work produced by African Americans about being black in Japan, which can offer valuable narratives until fuller ethnographic work is completed in this field. For instance, Regge Life (1993) produced a film that documents the experiences of several different African Americans living in Japan. Kathryn Leary (1991) wrote an essay in the popular-culture African American magazine *Essence* about her experiences in the early 1990s as an African American woman in Tokyo. Both Life's and Leary's work offer good examples of African Americans, and especially African American women, who understand that being interpreted as black in Japan is different from in the United States. Historical works that focus on racial relations between African Americans and Japanese, and ideas of blackness in Japan such as those from Yukiko Koshiro (2003), in conjunction with emerging work from academics involved in the Japan Black Studies Association and narratives from Japanese and blacks inside and outside of Japan can help open up discussion of Japanese perceptions of blackness, which have often been perceived as static by previous writers.

What academics need to further emphasize is that not all Japanese accept black people as appendages—chopped up, packaged, and ready to be consumed. To bring over to Japan these arguments that may rightly describe racialized bodies as targets of the actions of government in the United

States is a tenuous project and one which may produce more harm than good in attempting to analyze how to deal with the very real and lived social injustices and marginality that exist in other forms.

References

Bondi, Liz. 1993. "Locating Identity Politics." In *Place and Politics of Identity,* ed. M. Keith and S. Pile. 84–101. London: Routledge.

Cornyetz, Nina. 1994. "Fetishized Blackness: Hip Hop and Racial Desire in Contemporary Japan." *Social Text,* October: 113–139.

Field, Norma. 1991. *In the Realm of a Dying Emperor.* New York: Pantheon Books.

Gilroy, Paul. 2000. *Against Race: Imagining Political Culture beyond the Color Line.* Cambridge. MA: Belknap Press of Harvard University Press.

Inoue, Masamichi. 2007. *Okinawa and the US Military: Identity making in the Age of Globalization.* New York: Columbia University Press.

Koshiro, Yukiko. 2003 "Beyond an Alliance of Color: The African American Impact on Modern Japan." *positions: East Asia Cultures Critique* 11 (1): 183–215.

Leary, Kathryn D. 1991. "Taking On Tokyo: Afro-American Woman Visits Japan." *Essence Magazine,* October.

Lie, John. 1999. *Multiethnic Japan.* Cambridge: Harvard University Press.

Life, Regge. 1993. *Struggle and Success: The African American Experience in Japan* [video recording, 58 min.]. East Chatham, NY: Global Film Network.

———. 1998. *Doubles* [video recording, 58 min]. East Chatham, NY: Global Film Network.

Reischauer, Edwin O. 1988. *The Japanese Today.* Cambridge, MA: Harvard University Press.

Russell, John. 1998. "Consuming Passions: Spectacle, Self-Transformation, and the Commodification of Blackness in Japan." *positions: East Asia Cultures Critique* 6 (1): 113–157.

Valentine, James. 1990. "On the Borderline: The Significance of Marginality in Japanese Society." In *Unwrapping Japan: Society and Culture in Anthropological Perspective,* ed. Eyal Ben-Ari, 36–57. Manchester: Manchester University Press.

Williams, Walter. 1996. *Being Gay and Doing Fieldwork.* Chicago: University of Illinois Press.

11

Traversing Religious and Legal Boundaries in Postwar Nagasaki: An Interfaith Ritual for the Spirits of the Dead

John Nelson

AS JAPAN'S OFFICIAL WINDOW TO THE REST of the world between 1610 and 1868, the port city of Nagasaki developed a reputation as a place where the boundaries of a pervasive cultural logic were challenged, negotiated, and often reordered successfully. What is allowed inside or kept outside, what is up front and what is hidden, and especially what is domestic and what is foreign have all shaped the city's social dynamics from the early 1500s to the present day. Examples are numerous and emphasize the city as a base for late sixteenth-century Christian missionaries from four European religious orders, as a golden opportunity for Chinese and Korean merchants and refugees, as an outpost for administrators and military garrisons of the ruling Tokugawa Shogunate, or as a thriving international trading center for European, Japanese, and continental merchants for parts of the sixteenth, seventeenth, and then later nineteenth centuries.

Even when the allure and benefits of cultural exchange came to be considered politically subversive—evidenced by the sequestering in 1641 of all foreigners within the landfill island-compound of Dejima—like warm air rising, they still seeped into established social orders. Nagasaki's residents had little control over the ways their sociocultural boundaries were negotiated, manipulated, and transgressed politically, and so a local culture of cautious adaptation and tolerance developed to try and capitalize upon cultural difference rather than, as is so often the case in Japan, marginalize or subdue it.

Closer to our own time, Nagasaki remains a site where twentieth-century conceptual and political boundaries have been reordered because of the dropping of a plutonium atomic bomb. John Treat writes that if

Hiroshima initiated the nuclear age, Nagasaki confirmed it, turning a strategy into a tactic, one more easily applied to our own cities today wherever they are (Treat 1995: 302). The boundary in question here is the separation of military from civilian targets in a time of "war without mercy" (Dower 1993). From the Japanese invasion of Manchuria; to the Nazi blitzkrieg; to the U-2 rocket attacks on London; to the firebombing of Dresden, and of Tokyo (15 March 1945 in which 120,000 people died in a single night), and sixty other major Japanese cities, World War II initiated the practice of deploying devastating weapons on civilian populations to produce not only injury and death but terror as well.

As the last major attack of World War II, Nagasaki's place in history was sealed not so much because of its strategic military importance but simply because clouds obscured the original target at Kokura in northern Kyushu. Rather than lug the atomic bomb back to the base and risk running out of fuel, the Enola Gay crew followed orders to bomb Nagasaki. Clouds over Nagasaki caused the bomb to miss its target, the Mitsubishi factories and shipyards, by some two kilometers, with "Fat Boy" exploding above the city's northern neighborhoods and what was then the largest Catholic cathedral in East Asia. Due to mountainous terrain that shielded one half of the city from the bomb's lethal effects, *Life* magazine claimed shortly after the attack that while Hiroshima had been blown off the face of the earth, Nagasaki was merely disemboweled (cited in Treat 1995: 306). Over half of the city's population and its remarkable architectural blending of cultures and religions—including Christian chapels and Catholic churches, large Shinto shrines and Chinese-style Buddhist temples, Victorian houses built by the city's foreign community in the early 1880s—had survived. But 73,880 people did not, nor did 78,000 others escape severe injury. By 1950, based on reports from the Japanese Red Cross and a consortium of medical university researchers, the death toll from bomb-related injuries and radiation poisoning raised the figure to over 140,000 in Nagasaki alone (Treat 1995: 308).

Once the blanket of Occupation censorship on information related to the bombings was lifted in 1952 (see Rubin 1985), periodic services for the victims and survivors could now become more public events. Concerned initially with calming and soothing the spirits of the dead within a Buddhist context (called *kuyô*), these observances were soon supplemented by an increasingly political message.

Peace (*heiwa*) had become one of the "keywords" in postwar Japanese society. The Occupation-imposed constitution of 1946 was termed the "peace constitution" because of the second clause of Article 9 stating that Japan would never again wage war. Whether it came from politicians, student radicals, environmental groups, or the mass media, the concept of *heiwa* served "as [an] interpretive lens through which Japanese came to view their own culture and society" (Moeran 1990: 261; see also Kisala

1999). Through their repeated and overlapping use in a variety of performative contexts (such as atomic bomb commemorations, sports events, sessions of the Diet, in the classroom, and at Buddhist, Christian, and Shinto religious activities), keywords become "cultural productions of public identity" (Fox 1990: 3), which, with an ambiguity akin to symbols, can communicate a variety of context-dependent messages in ways both explicit and veiled.

Like Hiroshima, Nagasaki's city government allocated land in 1952 for two memorial parks near the center of the blast. The first marks the actual hypocenter above which the bomb exploded, while the second much larger park, the Peace Park, creates a public space to accommodate crowds, ceremonies, and monuments donated from the international community.

By 1955, the Peace Park had in it the giant statue called "the Peacekeeper" commissioned by well-known Nagasaki sculptor Kitamura Seibô. However, after the Summer Olympics of 1964 helped make the skeletal dome of Hiroshima known around the world, Nagasaki officials realized that the peacekeeper statue had failed to seize popular imagination. While symbolically meaningful, its presence did not effectively convey what had happened on 9 August 1945. Instead of becoming the predominant symbol of the city as originally intended, the statue and Peace Park were recontextualized in the early 1970s by city development and tourism officials. Messages of peace associated with the horrors of the atomic bombing would no longer be privileged among the city's rich urban landscape of cultural, historical, and leisure pursuits appealing to tourists (see Siegenthaler 2002; Yoneyama 1994 for the situation in Hiroshima). Only once a year would the city shine its promotional spotlight on the Peace Park commemorations, and invite leading politicians and civic leaders to participate in this event. But to the city's religious leaders, this new emphasis neglected the primary reason for the commemoration in the first place: to honor and console the spirits of the dead.

Shûkyô Konwa-kai: The (Nagasaki) Council of Religious Leaders

Nagasaki's religious leaders, who had begun collective memorial services for the dead in 1946, had lobbied various prefectural and city administrations for participation in the Peace Park's annual ceremony since its inception in 1955. They wanted to echo and reinforce through their own religious traditions the city's message of peace to an international audience. However, due in part to the Constitution and, more importantly, key Supreme Court rulings in the late 1960s and early 1970s regarding the problematic involvement of city governments with Shinto land-claiming rituals, they were told by city officials that the main ceremony could not accommodate any religious activity. "Without ever explaining in detail," one Shinto priest recalled while a Buddhist colleague listened, "we heard over and over about the Constitution forbidding state or local governments from sponsoring religious memorial rites."

A paraphrase of Article 20 of the postwar Constitution states that because freedom of religion is guaranteed to all, "no religious organization shall receive any privileges from the State nor exercise any political authority. The State and its representatives shall refrain from religious education or any other religious activity." Article 89 also notes that no public money or other property shall be appropriated or spent for the use, benefit, or maintenance of a religious institution or association (O'Brien 1996: 60). These clauses were implemented to prevent a revival of State Shinto in postwar society, but that's another story.

The Peace Park's nationally televised parade of city, prefectural, and Tokyo-based politicians (the current Prime Minister always attends), and of course its politically correct emphasis on "peace" and "nuclear disarmament," caused the city's religious leaders to grow increasingly concerned that the secular commemoration failed to provide proper ritual care and acknowledgment for the spirits of the dead. As one of the great and most long-lasting traditions of East Asia, the agency of departed spirits (commonly considered part of "ancestor worship") remains a powerful social, religious, and political force. This tradition combines Japanese as well as continental Korean and Chinese folk beliefs and practices, Daoist cosmologies, and Buddhist tantric demonology in ways syncretic, dynamic, and highly subjective (McMullin 1989: 292). Ancestral spirits can be helpful and benevolent to their descendants if proper rituals and commemorations are carried out. But if the spirits of the dead are neglected, as Nagasaki's religious leaders feared, they become vengeful and destructive, not only towards the immediate family but to the surrounding community and region as well.

The city's priests were advised to conduct their spirit-calming rituals within their respective temples, churches, and shrines, but they believed this fragmentation of memory and acknowledgment betrayed the enormity of the disaster. Something had to be done to regain and refocus attention upon the religious needs of the victims of the bomb, even if it meant challenging openly the myopic authority of city, prefectural, and national leaders. And so, the Nagasaki Council of Religious Leaders (Nagasaki Shûkyô-sha Konwa-kai) was formed in 1983. It included Buddhist, Catholic, Episcopalian, and Shinto leaders, as well as those of new religions such as Risshô Kôsei-kai and Ômoto-kyô, and even the city's Confucian/Daoist elders (due to its large Chinese-Japanese population). Their primary agenda was to implement the Hypocenter Park Memorial Service, specifically called an *irei-sai*, a ritual to comfort departed spirits. By doing so, they hoped first to console the spirits of the dead in a novel yet thematically traditional way. But they also wanted to steal some of the media spotlight away from politicians so as to illuminate the spiritual condition of the victims' souls. While messages of "peace" and "disarmament" were still part of the Council's overall agenda, these keywords were not emphasized. Instead, they seemed to serve only as public gateways into the rather unfamiliar terrain of an interfaith ritual service, one designed to remedy the religious neglect created by the politicians' ceremony in the Peace Park.

We see in the invented tradition of the Hypocenter Park ritual a number of conventional boundaries crossed, even subverted, in interesting ways. First, it is a commonly held stereotype that Shinto, Buddhism, Christianity, and Japan's new religions have always been separate institutions with diverse approaches to what each considers sacred. This view was reinforced in part by the separation of Shinto and Buddhism, and modernization strategies of the early Meiji government, as well as twentieth-century categories of religion that privileged belief over practice.

But the annual situation at hand on the evening of 8 August—soothing the spirits of the dead caused by a violent, cataclysmic event—was thought to require religious plurality and diversity in order to achieve the intended result. Religious differences are simultaneously emphasized and encouraged within a unity of purpose: each tradition provides an emphasis that contributes to the overall efficacy of the ritual. Like the various instruments in a chamber orchestra, the overall harmony of the performance takes precedence over individual differences.

The form of the event may be experimental and innovative, but the practice of priests joining forces in order to exert some control over a critical situation can be found throughout Japanese history as the norm rather than the exception. After all, what we today call "Shinto" and "Buddhist" were highly interactive for most of Japanese religious history. Whether petitioning the Buddhas and *kami* for successful rice planting or good harvests; for male children to head the household or take over the throne; for restoring the health of emperors, shoguns, and other officials; for warding off military, civil, atmospheric, or tectonic disasters—Japan's religious traditions have coexisted and cooperated for the good of the entire community more often than they have tried to advance their own traditions to the exclusion of others.

By 1983 when the Interfaith Council was formed, Japanese society was fairly saturated with an awareness of a new term, "internationalization" or *kokusaika*. From newspaper editorials to broadcast television to study groups and governmental think tanks, *kokusaika* was promoted as a policy that would help Japan's corporations and people compete more effectively within a global, highly diverse, and culturally complex marketplace. It was heralded for its openness to experience and readiness to learn from international norms and then incorporate what worked in the context of Japanese society and business. However, it soon became apparent that the government was not really interested in the actual practices, standards, or values of the international community. Instead, *kokusaika* worked to promote a flurry of initiatives and legislation—from defensive trade barriers to renewed governmental sponsorship for rituals honoring the military dead at Yasukuni shrine—that were more nationalistic than policies in the 1960s and 1970s.

The Interfaith Council's formation could not help but have been influenced to some degree by this sociocultural moment. The diversity of its charter members' political affiliations, wartime experiences, and personal backgrounds must have been a formidable hurdle to cross (one priest had even served as a *kamikaze* pilot at the end of the war), yet they exhibited an impressive ability to actually incorporate the spirit of a genuine internationalism. They overcame substantial differences to forge an alliance based on interreligious dialogue and pluralism before these terms became common in Western religious traditions. Unlike the national government, the Interfaith Council "internationalized" its message of peace and consolation to reach the broadest audience possible while also remaining focused on the immediate needs of the people of Nagasaki and the spirits of the dead.

The Ritual to Acknowledge and Calm the Spirits of the Dead

As the sun sets on the stifling hot evening of 8 August 1995, junior members of the lay Buddhist organization Risshô-kôsei kai process with lit candles through the hedge-lined pathways of the Hypocenter Park. They transfer their flames, symbolizing the light of salvation, to candles arranged at the black granite base of the central monument. Sparks are then conveyed to firewood in standing wire baskets (*takigi*) which, when set ablaze, are identical to those used at outdoor performances of Noh drama. Next, Pure Land (*Jôdô-shû*) Buddhist priests offer water and prayers to the spirits of the dead, just as they would in a memorial service (*kuyô*) at their temple for a deceased individual. These actions are followed by a long moment of silence (*mokutô*), which the entire assembly, many of them bomb survivors, dutifully and tearfully acknowledges. As if to lighten the burden of those painful memories, elegantly attired female attendants from Nagasaki's largest Shinto shrine then perform a slow, sacred dance called *kagura*. From an orthodox Shinto perspective, the spirits of the dead have been called forth and so must be offered food and drink, as well as entertainment and calming words of veneration. The shrine's chief priest provides these words (*norito*) spoken directly to the spirits. In 1995, this invocation touched upon the loss, injury, suffering, and destruction caused by the bombs, but it also referenced environmental issues, world poverty, nuclear proliferation, and a general anxiety about all these problems. A True Pure Land (*Jôdô-Shinshû*) Buddhist priest then formally concludes the spoken portion of the ritual, restating the desire for the invocation to have soothed the spirits of the dead.

As tables for flower offerings are positioned on each side of the central monument and priests form a single line before it, a choir from a local Catholic church, accompanied by an electric organ, breaks into a spirited rendition of "What a Friend We Have in Jesus." Once concluded, traditional court music (*gagaku*) filters over the public address system as pairs of priests approach the tables to offer white chrysanthemums before bowing in the style of their particular religious tradition. Although priests from the city's Catholic and Chinese religious traditions did not actively participate in the main ritual I observed, they joined in during these final prayers and offerings of flowers (Nelson 1996). Quoting one of the head organizers, a Nagasaki-born Buddhist priest now serving at Nara's Kôfukuji temple, "We want this ritual to acknowledge and calm the spirits of the dead. But we also hope the participation and cooperation of the city's religious leaders can serve as a model for other parts of the world where there is religious conflict and violence." Although it is unclear exactly which part of the world the priest had in mind, one might assume that his multicultural prescription for interfaith cooperation and peace would apply in any situation where religious ideologies are used to fuel political conflict.

A second area where conventional boundaries are challenged concerns the Interfaith Council's intent to reconfigure but not necessarily subvert the Peace Park's master narratives of remembrance, nonproliferation of nuclear weapons, and of course the message of peace. The victims of the atomic bombing are a constituency whose care is claimed by city and national leaders but the Interfaith Council asserts they are the proper custodians for these unhappy, tragic, and, if not appeased correctly, potentially vengeful spirits. The Hypocenter Park ritual wrests away from the Peace Park event its own territory and time of remembrance, based on religious rather than secular concerns. By holding this event on the evening of 8 August, one day before the Peace Park extravaganza, the ritual serves to shift attention to other interpretations before the main event asserts its own.

In this regard, the Interfaith Council has plenty of company. A number of organizations and individuals opposed to local and national Liberal Democratic party politics, or at odds with local elected officials and corporate interests, stage memorial services in rented auditoriums not far from the park. These take place at exactly the same time as the Peace Park event and are intended to challenge its hegemony of meaning. In 1987 and 1995, the two years I observed the commemorations on 8–9 August, participating organizations ranged from the Communist and Socialist parties, to the National Teachers' Union, to student political-action organizations from various universities, as well as Buddhist priests from various sects leading groups of parishioners from all over Japan. The monks and nuns of the Nichiren-Buddhist sect Nipponzan Myôhôji, banging hand-drums to break opposition to peace, positioned themselves at the Hypocenter Park, well within earshot of the main ceremony. In one way or another, all these groups believed the official Peace Park ceremony was compromised both by its messengers and sponsors.

According to Saitô Junichi, a Pure Land Buddhist priest from Nara prefecture:

> We're conducting our own separate meeting because we think it's a glaring contradiction to the message of "peace" that the city government allows individuals who had responsibility for the war effort and for weapons manufacturing to participate in or serve as sponsors of the so-called official ceremony. There are even sponsors who believe that Japan was not the aggressor in the war! We're not against honoring the victims of the atomic bomb of course, but it must be done in a way so as not to demean their tragic deaths.

Just as the Interfaith Council directs part of its ritual message to the international community, these countergatherings reference international as well as domestic concerns about war accountability and responsibility. Activists feel these tragic events are exploited by leading politicians to mouth messages of peace as a way to appeal to their constituencies and patrons. Yet, officials do next to nothing to turn fine-sounding slogans into economic or educational policies that might actually address the root causes of conflict and war. Many of these groups now have Web sites in English as well as Japanese that translate and disseminate their appeals to a global audience. Their activism and countermemorials on 8–9 August promote a kind of social memory informed by accurate history, instead of a carefully selected version that edits out key policy makers and culpable corporations such as Mitsubishi, Nagasaki's single largest employer.

Conclusion

In ways diverse yet complementary, the Interfaith Council's yearly ritual on 8 August and the countermemorials on 8–9 August reference and domesticate many international concerns about conflict, accountability, and responsibility. The resistance offered by all these groups in response to official narratives of 9 August helps to decenter and destabilize the ways in which the lessons of that dreadful day have been constructed and their boundaries maintained.

The Interfaith Council's Hypocenter ritual, through its subtle re-registering of emphasis and interpretation, can likewise contribute to a more profound understanding of both social and historical memory regarding exactly how the war ended and the policies responsible for such widespread devastation and human suffering. Its emotional agenda—aiming at calming the spirits of the atomic bomb victims while at the same time blurring cultural and religious boundaries to convey an authentic message of peace—speaks through the language of ritual in multivocal, transcultural ways. If this poignant event can gain increased visibility and participation, it can extend the range of what a single ritual can do to remember, acknowledge, and, perhaps most importantly, to heal.

References

Dower, John. 1993. *War Without Mercy: Race and Power in the Pacific War.* New York: Pantheon.

Fox, Richard. 1990. "Introduction." In *Nationalist Ideologies and the Production of National Cultures*, ed., R. Fox, 1–14. Washington DC: American Anthropological Association Monograph Series 2.

Kisala, Robert. 1999. *Prophets of Peace: Pacificism and Cultural Identity in Japan's New Religions.* Honolulu: University of Hawai'i Press.

McMullin, Neil. 1989. "On Placating the Gods and Pacifying the Populace: The Case of the Gion Goryô Cult." *History of Religions* 27 (3): 270–293.

Moeran, Brian. 1990. *Language and Popular Culture in Japan.* Honolulu: University of Hawaii Press.

Nelson, John. 1996. *Japan's Rituals of Remembrance: Fifty Years after the Pacific War* [video documentary]. Austin, TX: Center for Asian Studies.

O'Brien, David M. 1996. *To Dream of Dreams: Religious Freedom and Constitutional Politics in Postwar Japan.* Honolulu: University of Hawai'i Press.

Rubin, Jay. 1985. "From Wholesomeness to Decadence: The Censorship of Literature under the Allied Occupation." *Journal of Japanese Studies* 11 (1): 71–103.

Siegenthaler, Peter. 2002. "Packaging Experience for Nagasaki and Hiroshima Visitors, 1920–1997." *Annals of Tourism Research* 29 (4): 1111–1137.

Treat, John W. 1995. *Writing Ground Zero.* Chicago: University of Chicago Press.

Yoneyama, Lisa. 1994. "Taming the Memoryscape: Hiroshima's Urban Renewal." In *Remapping Memory: The Politics of TimeSpace*, ed. J. Boyarin, 99–135. Minneapolis: University of Minnesota Press.

12

OUTSIDE THE SUMO RING? FOREIGNERS AND A RETHINKING OF THE NATIONAL SPORT

R. Kenji Tierney

Introduction

ON 16 JULY 1972, ON THE LAST DAY of the Nagoya tournament, what had come to be seen as inevitable finally occurred. A foreigner had won the tournament in the national sport of sumo, prompting the following congratulatory telegram from President Nixon to be read on the sumo ring (*dohyō*):

> Dear Jesse:
>
> I was delighted to learn of your stirring victory in the Nagoya Sumo Tournament, and I want to express to you my personal congratulations and those of all Americans on your achievement.
>
> I understand that your sincere dedication to this sport has won you the respect of your Japanese hosts. Your performance has also won the admiration of your countrymen. Again, my congratulations, and best wishes for your continued success.
>
> Sincerely,
> Richard Nixon
> (Kuhaulua and Wheeler 1973: 19)

With the Emperor's Cup in hand, Jesse Kuhaulua stood at the center of all this attention. He was better known by his wrestling name, Takamiyama, and quickly became a celebrity with his quick smile, enormous body, and large sideburns. Nonetheless, his successes provoked the start of a nationwide debate on the national sport and the inclusion of foreigners. Upon

---

Endnotes for this chapter begin on page 216.

entering the top ranks (*sekitori*), Takamiyama was quickly identified as a threat to this age-old tradition. The media labeled him as the reincarnation of Commodore Perry's "Black Ships," this time knocking at the doors of sumo.

Seen as both a milestone in sumo, but also the end of sumo as a purely Japanese activity, Takamiyama's feat was largely interpreted as the breaking of a boundary. In general, crossing boundaries in sumo is not considered auspicious as crossing the boundary of the ring means that you lose. Still, what are the boundaries in sumo and who or what is crossing them? More to the point, who or what is grappling in the space of sumo and who defines these crossings? This chapter considers how sumo has come to be defined as something purely "native" and it is from this template that differing conceptions of "foreignness" are applied.

Defining the Native

Sumo needed to be defined as purely native in order for a crisis of the "foreign" to occur in sumo. As I have detailed elsewhere, although sumo was disparaged as a barbarian activity in the rush to Westernization in the thirty years after Perry's visit in 1853, by the first half of the twentieth century it was embraced by public intellectuals, government officials, and the like both as an activity and a national symbol. They, along with the wrestlers and elders of the various sumo associations, served to transform sumo from a popular form of entertainment into a symbol of Japanese culture, sport, and tradition—something explicitly Japanese and national (Tierney 2002, 2004).

Following Japan's victories in the Sino-Japanese and Russo-Japanese wars, one of the more significant changes occurred with the building of professional sumo's first permanent stadium in 1909. One of elders in sumo, inspired by the poet Emi Suiin's essay entitled "Sumo is the National Skill of Japan" (*Sumô wa Nippon no Kokugi nari*), argued that the new building should be called the "Kokugikan" (Hall of the National Skill).[1] His suggestion was accepted and sumo's new label as the "national sport/skill" gained increasing importance and prominence as the country became increasingly nationalistic. It was in the Kokugikan that professional sumo increasingly became a national organization with the various professional groups folding or joining the Tokyo group to become the Greater Japan Professional Sumo Association. Similarly, the crown prince donated a sum of money that was the basis for the Emperor's Cup.

On the organizational level, with the increased militarization of the 1920s, 1930s, and 1940s, the wrestlers and the Japan Sumo Association (hereafter referred to as the JSA) became closely aligned with the government and the military. In the 1920s and 1930s the wrestlers started to regularly hold matches and perform in front of the emperor, soldiers, colonists, and visiting dignitaries, among many others. Along with this, they conducted tours throughout the newly claimed territories under Japanese control, annually touring Manchuria, Taiwan, and Korea. On occasion, the professional wrestlers went as far as the South Pacific. At these various cities they performed for soldiers, settlers, and "native" elites such as the emperor of Manchuria while also consecrating sumo rings (dohyô) in schools and shrines.

Sumo's involvement with the government went beyond performances. The JSA actively maintained and expanded their ties with the military. In the 1930s, the JSA appointed two military officers as chairmen. In 1930, General Ono became chairman and, in 1936, Hirose Takeo, a Russo-Japanese war hero who later was enshrined as a war deity, took over. Meanwhile various public intellectuals published books and articles reinterpreting sumo through nativistic ideologies such as bushidô or the "way of the warrior." In the case of sumo, the wrestler was recast as a contemporary samurai, a native warrior following sumôdô or the "way of the wrestler." Along with other citizens, the wrestlers made numerous contributions to the national war efforts. The wrestlers whose bodies could still be shaped into soldiers were drafted and the JSA created a special column on the ranking sheet listing the names of all of the wrestlers who were serving. On the other hand, those mainly top wrestlers whose large size prevented active participation as soldiers performed symbolic military training in local parks. Photo opportunities featured the wrestlers practicing military training drills under the hot sun, sometimes wearing custom-made outfits, and sometimes only in their wrestling belts (mawashi).

This transformation into a militarized, national sport/tradition was not a simple and straightforward process. Throughout the first few decades of the twentieth century, there were numerous rebellions by wrestlers against the policies of the JSA, including strikes, the creation of competing sumo organizations, and the like. An underlying theme of these rebellions was resistance to the larger "traditionalization" of sumo. Nonetheless, by the 1940s, the JSA had a very tight relationship with the government and much of sumo's place as a reified and codified national tradition had been solidified.

This situation continued from the postwar period to the present. The JSA retains its position as a nonprofit group under the Ministry of Education. The JSA and its wrestlers now regularly engage in extensive travels in conjunction with various government ministries, featuring the wrestlers as cultural ambassadors to the world. They went first to Hawaii in 1964, and then to Moscow in the following year. Since then, they have visited China, London, Los Angeles, Vancouver, San Jose, Brazil, and so on, including semipolitical engagements such as visiting World War II memorials and the like. They have been designated "hadaka taishi" or "naked ambassadors," reflecting the politico-cultural conceptualization of them as quintessentially Japanese.

Finding the Foreign in the Native

Since the 1980s, sumo's place as the national sport seems to be threatened. Increasingly, sumo's problems have been interpreted as a "crisis of the foreign." Nonetheless, the nationalistic and nativistic narratives surrounding sumo in the prewar period can be reconsidered to shed light on contemporary Japanese discourses of the "foreign" Other.

As many scholars have pointed out, it is important not to project into the past contemporary notions of Japaneseness that often consciously or unconsciously conflate the notions of nation, race, ethnicity, and language. In the prewar period, native conceptualizations of the nation were configured in opposition both to the Japanese diaspora and the larger conceptualization of Japan as an empire. As such, certain wrestlers, by contemporary criteria, would have been considered foreign. Nonetheless, this chapter should not merely be read as a project in labeling certain wrestlers as foreign, but as considering ways in which sumo can be de-linked from nationalistic conceptions of Japan.

Two Examples of Prewar "Foreignness": The *Nikkeijin* and *Rikidôzan*

A look at the participation of Japanese Americans in professional sumo provides a way to reconsider the relationship between the nation and sumo. With the large-scale emigration at the end of the nineteenth century and the beginning of the twentieth century, tens of thousands of Japanese nationals emigrated throughout the world, establishing many large communities in Hawaii, the western parts of North America, and throughout Central and South America. As I have detailed elsewhere (Tierney 2002), sumo was transforming, yet remained popular both as a participatory sport and a part of other types of celebrations. That the emigrants brought sumo to their new homes is not a surprise; however, what is somewhat surprising is the strong ties that overseas sumo leagues created with the professional organization in Japan. (These ties were, of course, ruptured, if not severed, with the start of the Pacific war and resulting anti-Japanese activities.)

Thus, in the prewar period, numerous Japanese Americans ended up in Japan as professional sumo wrestlers. Sometimes sumo was seen as an opportunity in Japan and they went to join a stable (*heya*). At other times, they joined while they were visiting or living there. Wrestlers like Harley Ozaki or Toshio Koga went far up the ranks. Ozaki was wrestling in Japan when hostilities broke out. He wanted to go back to the United States but he ended up trapped in Japan. Bowing to pressure from his Japanese relatives and the JSA, he eventual gave in and took Japanese citizenship.

Not only were there individual wrestlers who went to Japan to wrestle, strong institutional ties existed between the amateur league in the western

United States and the amateur and professional organizations in Japan. Sumo was performed with all the accoutrements of the amateur groups in Japan, with elaborate ring-entering ceremonial aprons (keshō mawashi) and support groups (kôenkai). The JSA even sanctioned one of the referees (gyôji) in Southern California. Meanwhile, teams of Japanese amateurs traveled to the United States and Japanese American amateurs went on training tours in Japan. Also, the professional wrestlers made many trips to the United States. The most famous of these were the trips that Hita-chiyama made to the White House in 1907 and 1911, where he performed in front of President Theodore Roosevelt and presented him with a samu-rai sword. Others, such as Ônishiki, traveled to Hawaii and California, performing in front of thousands of immigrants.[2]

Thus, the extensive travels between the United States and Japan, non-Japanese citizens in the professional ranks, the international recruiting sys-tem, and global profit-making tours of the professional all suggest that sumo was not confined to Japan's national borders; it served to link peo-ple in Japan with its various colonies and immigrant communities throughout the world.

A second case also illustrates this point. One of the most famous wrestlers of the modern era, Rikidôzan, is less famous for his career as a sumo wrestler than for his post-sumo career as a Western-style profes-sional wrestler. He eventually became famous as a "Japanese" hero, bat-tling foreigners in the ring (Thompson 1986). Yet, his origins complicate the story further. He was born Kim Sin-Nak in present-day North Korea in 1924, and brought to Japan as a young man. He started his career in sumo in 1940 at the age of sixteen. While it is well known that numerous Korean athletes were recruited onto the Japanese national Olympic team, such as the marathon runner Sohn Kee-Chung (Kitei Son), in the case of Rikidô-zan, a Japanese birth story was fabricated. He was given the name Momota Mitsuhiro and a new identity as the third son of a Nagasaki farming fam-ily (Ushijima 1978). This fiction was maintained until Rikidôzan was "outed" as Korean much later in the postwar period.

Thus, while sumo has been largely constructed as the purest of Japanese traditions, I would like to point out that this process has not been as sim-ple nor as neat as a cursory glance would have it.

Back to the Postwar Period

As noted, the last thirty years have largely come to be characterized as the "crisis of the foreign" in sumo. Much media attention in Japan and through-out the world has portrayed this as a situation of foreign bodies invading the sacred space of sumo in Japan. Still, this conceptualization of "foreign-ness" is tied to an idea of "legibility."[3] There are numerous resident Korean wrestlers in sumo, such as a wrestler I knew well at the stable where I stayed for two years, but they are not identified as "foreign." While there have been a few exposés on the influence of Koreans in sumo, such as the magazine that "outed" some top wrestlers,[4] this is not couched in terms of foreignness.

Kelly (1998) discusses similar parallels in the case of Japanese professional baseball, where the postwar period saw numerous "liminal figures"—either Japanese Americans or the offspring of former colonial subjects. One does not have to look beyond the list of grand champions (*yokozuna*) to find the same in sumo. For example, Taihô Kôki, one of the most famous and dominant wrestlers of the postwar period, was born in the Russian Sakhalin Islands to a Russian father and a Japanese mother. Other "liminal" grand champions include Tamanoumi and Mienoumi, both of whom were of Korean ancestry.

By and large, the "foreign problem" is not one of Korean Japanese, but concerns those who are read as being non-Japanese. The first "open" foreigners in sumo started appearing at the end of the 1960s. As the Japanese economy and standard of living started to boom in the 1960s, Japan became an increasingly attractive place for foreigners, as many of the chapters in this book attest. The same is true of sumo. While the success or failure of these wrestlers can be attributed to individual circumstances, their presence in sumo results from the structural organization of the JSA and the changing realities of Japanese society.

At the root of the influx of foreign wrestlers lies the organization of the JSA. Previously, rules and conditions worked against the opening of numerous smaller *heya*. In the postwar period, for a variety of reasons that I will not discuss here, it has become easier and more lucrative for stablemasters to open up new stables rather than serve as assistants in existing ones. The resulting *heya* are on average much smaller, numbering around twenty wrestlers each, compared with the prewar ones that sometimes exceeded one hundred wrestlers. Presently, each stable receives a monthly stipend from the association for each wrestler (according to his rank) and given economies of scale, the expense of adding further wrestlers keeps going down for each one added. Thus, just as there are reasons to open new stables, there are also strong reasons for stablemasters to keep adding new wrestlers. As such, each stable is always actively searching for recruits and often employs "managers" whose sole task is to follow up leads for new potential.

This scramble for new recruits contrasts with the reality of contemporary Japanese society, where today's youths show decreasing interest in sumo. The average athletically inclined youth is far more likely to be attracted to baseball, soccer, or basketball. The few that do participate in sumo do so in the small but significant amateur leagues. Of course, there are highly sought-after recruits, and there are numerous rumors of bidding wars occurring for the top stars of the amateur leagues. Thus, to the average stablemaster who cannot afford to recruit the top college wrestlers, the prospect of strong, willing, hard-working foreign youths is quite appealing.

In fact, the college stars have radically changed sumo as they often are ranked much higher initially than the standard recruits and their quick success often upsets the traditional hierarchy based on a mixture of rank and seniority. As such, the average foreign recruit is much closer to the "traditional" native recruit. Although I often joked with the head of the *heya* where I did research that I would drop off some Oakland high school students at their doorstep, the "wish list" of desirable qualities in the wrestlers does mirror the characteristics of many foreign wrestlers. The ideal recruits in sumo were traditionally tough and raw country boys from the hinterland (*inaka*). The standard reasons corresponded: they want boys from poor circumstances, so that they are not used to luxury or being catered to. Being from the countryside, they cannot easily board a train and go back home, a major problem in sumo. Also, they are thought to have natural strength from a rural upbringing, which coincides with the beliefs of many professional coaches who look down on the weak youth of the city.

In the end, the foreign recruits are not as disrupting a presence as the college recruits, whose initial high rankings can disrupt traditional hierarchies based on seniority in the stable. Lastly, because of the intense nature of the training and the way in which the sumo lifestyle has become very different from surrounding society, retraining a new recruit in the most basic acts is not unusual in sumo. One native recruit that I knew well was struggling with re-learning how to sit down and how to walk. While recruits from Japan have an advantage over the foreign wrestler due to Japanese language ability, they are nonetheless retaught how to speak "properly." At the stable I was researching, the new Mongolian wrestler was in the process of learning the main duty of the lowest wrestlers—shopping. The top wrestlers joked with me that his first Japanese word was "tofu." Thus, while there have been famous scandals surrounding foreign wrestlers, the problems tend to be more about human relationships between wrestlers living together in the same room than any larger issues.

The crisis of the foreign in sumo, by and large, is not within sumo itself; it concerns sumo's position as the national sport. The first "crisis," discussed in the introduction, was caused by the Hawaiian wrestler, Jesse Takamiyama, who won the Nagoya Tournament in 1972. The sight of a foreigner with huge sideburns holding the Emperor's Cup and President Nixon's congratulatory note provoked an extensive media debate. While he never dominated sumo, his success and staying power prompted the JSA to pass a rule requiring Japanese citizenship for all stablemasters. Although he was already married to a Japanese woman, upon retiring, he took Japanese citizenship and became a stablemaster (*Azumazeki-oyakata*). He later opened a stable under the name of Azumazeki. Although he has now recruited numerous Japanese into his stable, foreign wrestlers dominated in the beginning.

Through the late 1980s and the early 1990s, Hawaiian wrestlers were extremely successful in sumo. While Takamiyama was a large wrestler, his recruits were even larger. The first was Konishiki (274 kilo and 183 cm), who joined the same stable as Takamiyama (*Takasago-beya*). He was very large from the beginning. At his official weighing in 1982, two scales were necessary. Within two years, he had reached the top ranks (*sekitori*), using his "bazooka-like" thrusts to knock out famous wrestlers (Konishiki 1998). His explosive presence was also described as a second "invasion" following that of Commodore Perry (*Kurobune Shūrai*) or, less eloquently, as a "meat bomb" (*nikutai bakudan*).

The ways in which Takamiyama, Konishiki, and others, including some South Americans, were different from the other wrestlers was that they were visibly "foreign" and numerous intellectuals and members of the media went on to criticize their presence. One famous article, entitled "The Essence of Sumo is Japanese," was written by well-known sumo critic Kojima Noboru. To Kojima, sumo is not just a sport, rather it is "a unique product of the nation, manifesting itself unchanged since ancient times and transcending social change, having been continuously defended by the Japanese people" (1992: 372–373). Much of the debate focused around the definition of a grand champion (*yokozuna*). Many argued that a *yokozuna* was more than a successful wrestler. Rather he embodied sumo and thus he was required to have nobility or grace (*hinkaku*), something that many nativists argued was peculiar to Japanese wrestlers.

Eventually the recruiting of foreign wrestlers was unofficially banned in the spring of 1993 when it was announced that there would be a "voluntary show of self-restraint in the recruiting of foreign wrestlers." Around this time, Akebono, a Hawaiian, became the first foreigner to be promoted to *yokozuna*. Nonetheless, the ban effectively ended the recruiting of foreigners until mid 1998 when many of the Hawaiians had left and the remaining ones, such as Konishiki and Akebono, were embraced as stars. The new policy was enacted, which initially encouraged foreigners who were not as visibly foreign—and the first new "foreign" recruit was a champion of Korean sumo. Later, numerous Mongolian wrestlers, including the one that ended up in my *heya*, started entering professional sumo, along with Koreans and Chinese.

Conclusion

While the new policies did have their intended effects for a while, many changes have occurred in sumo still more recently. Currently Asashôryû, a strong and talented Mongolian, dominates professional sumo, while below him are wrestlers from numerous countries including Russia, Bulgaria, and the Czech Republic. Meanwhile, professional sumo is suffering from low popularity. It is ultimately irresponsible and misguided to lay the blame for sumo's current low popularity at the feet of foreigners, though many do so. When the Hawaiians started appearing in sumo, their successes provoked much media hype and a certain amount of public consternation, but it was a boon to professional sumo. Their rise through the ranks did not translate into reduced popularity, but rather fans came to sumo in droves.

It is important to note that the Hawaiians, Akebono and to a lesser extent Musashimaru, were part of a larger rivalry. At the same time that the Hawaiians were rising through the ranks, the "Waka-Taka brothers" (Wakanohana III and Takanohana II), were matching them win for win, promotion for promotion. They were the "crown princes" of sumo, second-generation wrestlers whose father (Takanohana I) and uncle (Wakanohana II) had been immensely popular wrestlers and later stablemasters in their own right. Idolized by the Japanese public, the "Waka-Taka" brothers were a perfect combination of "traditional Japanese" and youth culture. Media attention only increased when the younger brother, Takanohana II, became engaged to a famous half-Dutch supermodel and actress, Miyazawa Rie.

Overall, this perfect narrative of "native-born sons" battling against the huge foreign invaders was irresistible to the media and the public. Sumo dominated the front pages of the sports newspapers and the JSA enjoyed an extremely profitable run. Popularity only began to drop when the Hawaiians quit and the "Waka-Taka" brothers were increasingly hobbled by injuries. When they retired a few years later, the popularity of the sport dropped immediately and precipitously. It is important to read sumo's current low popularity as involving far more than a single Mongolian who, while extremely talented and strong, cannot match the charisma and popularity of the Futagobeya-Hawaiian years. Professional sumo has always been dependent on a few wrestlers with star power to bring in the fans.

In conclusion, it seems as though the age of "multiculturalism" has arrived in sumo. Still, one must take considerable care when applying terms such as "native" and "foreign" to the case of sumo in order to not reify a conceptualization of "the Japanese" that continues to conflate ideas of citizen, race, language, customs, and nation. The case of sumo allows one to examine the long-term construction of and shift in the boundaries between the "native" Japanese and their "foreign" Others. As such, it is important to consider the agents who have been involved in the processes of construction and change, while continuing to examine the issues at stake when the categories of "native" and "foreign" continue to be pitted against each other.

Notes

1. Strictly translated it would be "national skill," but the spirit of the term has come to resemble "national sport/tradition."

2. While immigration officials mistook him and his fellow wrestlers for "picture brides," he misled other whites, saying that that all Japanese had grown as big as him.
3. Misa Oyama applies the concept of "racial legibility" to her analysis of depictions of race, specifically Asians and Asian Americans, in Hollywood silent period films. Her term is applicable in this situation as it provides a way to look beyond "race" as something essential, but to see it more as a sociocultural construction. In the case of Japan, as nationality and race are often conflated, "reading" someone as "foreign" is inherently racialized. For a more expanded discussion of "racial legibility," see Oyama (forthcoming) and Williams (2001: xviii).
4. See Lee (1998: 13–17).

References

Kelly, William. 1998. "Blood and Guts in Japanese Professional Baseball." In *The Culture of Japan as Seen through Its Leisure*, eds. S. Linhart and S. Fruhstuck, 95–111. Albany: State University of New York Press.

Kojima, Noboru. 1992. "'*Gaijin Yokozuna' wa Iranai*" [We don't need 'foreign yokozuna']. *Bungei Shunjû* 70 (4): 372–378.

Konishiki, Yasokichi. 1998. *Hadaka no Konishiki* [Konishiki revealed]. Tokyo: Yomiuri Shimbun-sha.

Kuhaulua, Jesse, and John Wheeler. 1973. *Takamiyama: The World of Sumo*. Tokyo: Kôdansha International.

Lee, Sun Il. 1998. "Mizukara no Kunô wo pawâ ni Kaeta Zainichi Korian 'Hîro Retsuden" [The Korean-Japanese who turned their pain into power: Biography of heroes]. *Sapio* 10 (209): 13–17.

Oyama, Misa. Forthcoming. *The Melodramatic Asian: Moral and Racial Legibility in Early 20th Century Fiction and Film*. Ph.D. diss., University of California, Berkeley.

Thompson, Lee. 1986. "Professional Wrestling in Japan: Media and Message." *International Review of Sport Sociology* 21 (1): 65–80.

Tierney, R. Kenji. 2002. *Wrestling with Tradition: Sumo, National Identity and Trans/National Popular-Culture*. Ph.D. diss., University of California, Berkeley.

———. 2004. "It's a 'Gottsan' World: The Role of the Patron in Sumo." In *Fanning the Flames: Fans and Consumer Culture in Contemporary Japan*, ed. W. Kelly, 107–125. Albany: State University of New York Press.

Ushijima, Hidehiko. 1978. *Mô Hitotsu no Shôwashi* [One more history of Showa]. Tokyo: Mainichi Shimbunsha.

Williams, Linda. 2001. *Playing the Race Card: Melodramas of Black and White from Uncle Tom to O. J. Simpson*. Princeton, NJ: Princeton University Press.

13

MULTICULTURALISM, MUSEUMS, AND TOURISM IN JAPAN

Nelson Graburn

Introduction: International and Domestic Tourism

THIS CHAPTER CONSIDERS JAPANESE DOMESTIC tourism in relation to sites of foreignness within Japan. It examines the relationship between *kokusaika* (internationalization) and *tabunka kyôsei* (multiculturalism). It is not my contention that overseas travel causes approval of multiculturalism at home, but the experience of other lifeways, other languages, and so on might create less fear or even greater acceptance of and interest in cultural difference.

By the 1960s Japan had risen from the political and industrial ashes of World War II to become an international success in the economic sphere as a world-renowned competitor in manufacturing and trade. After 1964 the numbers of Japanese touring overseas increased, paralleling their commercial might. Several institutions presenting "foreignness" at home were established to help Japanese feel more comfortable about cultural differences when traveling for business or pleasure. These institutions (see below) were among the first forms of *kokunai kokusaika* (internal or domestic internationalization). However by the 1980s, flows of foreign personnel as tourists and immigrant laborers brought less institutionalized forms of foreignness into people's lives. This led to the conceptualization of *tabunka kyôsei*, "many cultures living together," and the ideological step of moral obligation going beyond mere comfort and familiarity with "internationalism." One of the major original institutions of *kokusaika*, the National Museum of Ethnology, is presented in this chapter as a forceful example of this moral and cultural change.

Endnotes for this chapter begin on page 235.

Japanese Cultural Policies and National Museums

The dramatic "success" of Japanese industrial competition policy was followed by two other cultural policies. The first, a concomitant cultural internationalization under Prime Minister Nakasone in the 1980s, went along with Japan's ever-expanding commercial presence all over the world (Mannari and Befu 1993). Stung by anecdotes about the "ugly Japanese" (replacing the stereotype of the "ugly American" of the 1960s and 1970s) and their lack of cultural self-confidence, visible in their hesitation in speaking foreign languages and their "clannishness" in sticking together as groups, whether on business or as tourists, the government proposed a large number of programs intended to help Japanese learn foreign languages (overwhelmingly English) better and to give them opportunities to personally interact with foreigners. These included, for example, the Japan Exchange and Teaching (JET) program, which spends over $500 million a year placing English-speaking teaching assistants in nearly all Japanese high schools (McConnell 2000; see also Ertl, chapter 4), the proliferation of more than six hundred sister-city links in nearly fifty countries, and the surge of official and private programs for "homestays" and study abroad. In addition, the government has encouraged both governmental and nongovernmental efforts at building "foreign" institutions in Japan to accustom Japanese of all ages, but particularly the young, to "exposures" inoculating them against "fear of the foreign" (Hook and Weiner 1992). That is going to be a large part of the subject matter of this chapter.

By the 1980s, trade friction increased with accusations that Japan was a nation of workaholics competing unfairly against the rest of the world's workers and companies by cutting down on everything else in life, a kind of "Japan bashing" that the Japanese call *gaiatsu*, "foreign pressure." Partly in response to private outcries, the Ministry of Labor formulated policies calling for a decrease in Japan's working hours, by making weekends a one and a half or two days rather than a one-day break, and by increasing the number of paid holidays a year and the length of the annual vacations. In spite of surveys showing that many Japanese, especially the younger generations, were placing more importance on leisure activities (*Japan Times* 2002), at first these efforts were often unsuccessful in getting men to take off all the days that they were granted—whether because they didn't want to "let the team down" or appear to be slackers, or (in my opinion) because men enjoy the camaraderie of their work environments. Such policies became both more possible and more important after the economic "bubble" burst in 1990–1991 and businesses needed excuses to keep people away from work. These policies were successful in increasing Japanese desire to have more recreation time and tourism opportunities, and decreasing their guilt about not going to work (Harada 1998).

The National Museum of Ethnology

An early phase of the government's drive to familiarize the Japanese population with "foreignness" came with efforts to build two large-scale "national" anthropology museums. Both Minpaku (short for Minzokugaku Hakubutsukan), the National Museum of Ethnology in Suita, a northern suburb of Osaka; and the Little World Museum (Ritoru Wârudo), in the countryside about an hour north of Nagoya, came about at the behest of the Tokyo government in the 1960s, an early form of the initiative that was later officially known as *kokusaika*.[1] The two key people involved as advisors to the Prime Minister's Office were Kyoto-based anthropologist Umesao Tadao (now retired, former Director of Minpaku) and Tokyo-based Izumi Seiichi (who died in 1970).

Minpaku occupies the site of the Osaka World Fair, known as Expo '70, which was an earlier effort to internationalize the Japanese people and to open Japan to foreign tourists. It was built in a large park carved out of mainly rural land just outside the town of Suita. Expo '70 was the second major effort at internationalization following the Olympic Games held in Tokyo in 1964. Though the Olympics, Expo '70, and the construction of the *shinkansen* (bullet train) that joined these two venues were primarily efforts to open the successfully reconstructed Japan to the world gaze though the media and tourism, they were also in a sense the biggest opportunities for Japanese people to experience foreigners in their country since the Occupation.

Minpaku got off the ground with a lot of the material from the Expo '70 pavilions, but it was actually designed around collections from the Imperial Household and the University of Tokyo made prior to World War II, and materials gathered during World War II for the wartime Minzokukenkyûsho museum (Yamashita Shinji, personal communication, 2002). In addition, many artifacts (such as houses and boats on a reduced scale) were commissioned specially for the museum displays (see, for instance, Graburn and Ishimori 1979). Minpaku is an enormous anthropology museum whose public face consists of an "geographical-evolutionary" walk through the world's cultures, ending up with a magnificent Japan hall, stressing Japan's traditional (and now "exotic," see Ivy 1995) culture, supplemented by two comparative exhibition areas devoted to language and to music.[2] It also features a hall for temporary exhibitions, and some innovative "entertainment" features such as a "videotheque" where visitors can view short ethnographic films; a Dutch automatic organ played three times a day; as well as bookstores and cafeterias. Although it exposes tens of thousands of schoolchildren and other visitors to a wide array of cultural artifacts, the emphasis is uneven: it deals with the historical aspects of "advanced" cultures, then circles around the world, eventually arriving at East Asia, then Northeast Asia, then the Ainu, before finally landing in the glory of Japan.

When Minpaku first opened in the mid 1970s, Ainu spokesmen protested the display of their material culture, much of which they said had been obtained pre-WWII under the harshest of colonial conditions. Indeed, it was rumored that their radical allies, the Red Guards (the ones who delayed the opening of Narita Airport), had threatened to blow up Minpaku if the Ainu were not consulted about the conditions of display. When I first worked at Minpaku in 1979, I met the remarkable Ainu leader Kayano Shigeru (Kayano 1978), later a member of parliament, who was negotiating with the senior research staff member Sofue Takao about conditions of display. This was eventually settled by Ohtsuka Kazuyoshi and Director Umesao Tadao with the Ainu having rights to be consulted and to attend their Minpaku display and perform annual rites of renewal.

Multiculturalism at Minpaku

Minpaku has from its origins been associated with Japan's national policy of internationalization. It took a new direction with its major exhibition *Taminzoku Nihon* (Shoji 2004), which put it at the forefront of Japanese statements promoting *tabunka kyôsei*, the doctrine of "many cultures living together," or multiculturalism.[3]

Important changes to the main exhibitions have emerged in the past decade. For instance, the addition of English to the Japanese label text and a portable digital guide in Japanese, English, and Chinese implies an incipient multiculturalism or at least an accommodation of foreigners' needs. More up-to-date and engaging features have been added, including the exhibition of contemporary Canadian Inuit commercial arts and a section on Australian Aborigine land claims and antiracist demonstrations. This addition was suggested by the Australians but the Minpaku acceded to the insertion of these highly political pieces. Yet there is no real dissolution of the portrayal of Japan's uniqueness and the centrality of tradition. Staff members admit that attendance has been falling for at least two decades. Perhaps the museum's initial task of "internationalizing" Japanese people by exposing them to foreign cultures is less necessary because it has accomplished the task; because it has been superseded by other institutions such as *gaikoku mura* ("simulated foreign villages/environments," see below); as a result of the influx of foreign residents as well as foreign foods and fashions; and since Japan's entry into the world of the foreign through ever-expanding overseas tourism to over 15 million people a year since the 1990s.

Perhaps in response to the reduced attendance at the main exhibitions, an equally grand but separate hall for temporary exhibitions was opened in 1989. It has housed a series of splendid exhibitions, each lasting two to six months, accompanied by informative and well-produced catalogues. The topics of these exhibitions have gone far beyond the portrayal of exotic overseas cultures or Japanese traditional culture. Prominent subjects have included Japanese domestic minorities and foreign explorers of Japan. There have been two exhibitions on the Ainu and one on Okinawa, and there have been exhibitions devoted to the work of the foreigners Edward Morse (in 1990), Englebert Kampfer (1991), and Phillip von Seibold (1997–1998), who traveled in early Japan and helped interpret Japan for the outside world.

The exhibition on multiculturalism, open from 25 March through 15 June 2004, differed in some ways from all the preceding exhibitions. Called *"Taminzoku Nihon Zainichi Gaikokujin no Kurashi"* in Japanese and "Multiethnic Japan—Life and History of Immigrants" in English (not an exact translation), it focused on "ethnic" immigrant cultures and communities, people of other nationalities migrating to and settling in Japan. It was an entirely local effort, put on with local resources and with the help of local ethnic communities, without financial or intellectual support from its funding parent organization in Tokyo, Monbukagakusho (the Ministry of Education, Culture, Sports, Science, and Technology). In April 2004, a new national university corporation system was started and the national universities, which includes the teaching arm of Minpaku, became independent legal entities. From this point of view, Taminzoku Nihon was Minpaku's first *tokuten* (special spring or fall short term) exhibition after this system began.

This new exhibition did not even represent the interests of the majority of the anthropologists at Minpaku. The leader of the *Taminzoku* team who conceived of and put on the exhibition was Professor Shoji Hiroshi, trained in Helsinki and Osaka, an expert in Finno-Ugric languages, especially the survival of northern Eurasian minority languages (Shoji and Janhunen 1997).[4] Professor Shoji created this striking and original exhibition using methods new to Japan and rare elsewhere. In 1999 he organized a research group concerned with multilingualism, itself a form of multiculturalism. That year he worked with Professor Nakamaki Hirochika who curated the exhibition "Ethnic Cultures Crossing Borders: People Moving, Cultures Mixing," which ran from September 1999 to January 2000. This exhibit was about the movement and survival of ethnic minorities in the era of globalization. It stressed the appeal of ethnic arts and the power of ethnicity in plural societies. The brochure even described the "number of foreigners living in Japan who come from many different cultural backgrounds" and that all over the world "people from different cultures and ethnic backgrounds will live with each other in a multicultural and multilingual society." In 2000 Professor Shoji organized a study of groups in conflict in what came to be known as "Trans-border Anthropology." That year he talked with the Transborder group about the possibility of organizing an exhibition on immigrants and multiculturalism and he got in touch with other Japanese scholars, mainly sociologists, who were engaged in studies of these communities. Later Professor Nakamaki was responsible for the exhibition at JICA's (Japan International Cooperation Agency) Japanese Overseas Migration Museum, which opened in 2002 in Yokohama.

Nevertheless, when Shoji submitted his proposal to the Minpaku Exhibition Committee it was delayed by suggestions to rewrite or make substantial changes (which he did not do) many times in a row. He suggests that most Japanese anthropologists are still "other orientated" and want to study people outside their own country, and do not want to study Japanese or other people within Japan.[5] Asked how he managed to get it accepted, Professor Shoji said that he gained many important allies among the more engaged social scientists outside of Minpaku and that some of his friends at Minpaku, such as Professor Nakamaki, agreed to vote for the project but were not active in its implementation. While some Japanese anthropologists are especially interested and even active supporters of the Ainu and Ryukyuans (Okinawans), these indigenous struggles and minority issues are not being connected to a multiculturalism associated with ethnic immigrants. Many Minpaku anthropologists feared political problems with the right-wing activists who demonstrate against cultural or racial hybridity in Japan.[6] Professor Shoji was told that he alone would have to bear the responsibility for any disruptions or attacks that might result. In fact there were none, although there were a few letters of protest.

The team that organized the exhibition was built around those activist supporters outside of Minpaku who already had good contacts in the immigrant communities of the area. At Minpaku, the only faculty member involved was Professor Chen Tienshi, who was hired after the exhibit was accepted. Some graduate students at Minpaku and other universities were involved too; Kotani Sachiko (2004) for instance worked with the Chinese team, especially with Shirota Chika, to construct the Chinese immigrant children's "ethnic" school classroom, and later on other children's sections. Initially Shoji thought there might be problems filling the huge temporary exhibition hall. This had been classified as a "minor" exhibition by Minpaku and hence was given less than three months of exhibit time and lower financial support.

The immigrant communities were enthusiastic in participating because they were well connected to the twenty or more social scientists with whom Shoji was in contact. They presented no problems with "being exhibited" with the exception that the exhibit could not accommodate all the things they wanted to be shown. In many ways it was "their" exhibition: they participated in everything from suggesting themes to lending personal objects. Over 98 percent of the materials exhibited went back to the communities after the exhibit. The objects were intentionally exhibited as belonging to specific people in real communities. After the opening these communities were involved in bringing other community members including school children to the exhibition, and "performing" at the museum (by staging "ethnic classes" in the mock-up classroom and broadcasting on local ethnic community nonprofit radio stations). As the Minpaku brochure states, "members of the foreign communities in Japan … cooperated with the Museum in preparing for the exhibition, from planning and collecting articles to exhibit to displaying the articles."

The exhibition and the superb accompanying catalogue[7] both opened by emphasizing that this exhibition is about immigrants, that is, resident (*Zainichi*) foreigners or those who have "roots" (they use the Japanese pronunciation "*rûtsu*") in foreign countries. Thus, though the topic is "multiculturalism," the exhibition omitted the problematic questions of the indigenous cultures of the Ainu and the Ryukyuans (Okinawans), each of which had been the subject of previous temporary exhibitions at Minpaku, as well as the formerly culturally downtrodden group, the Burakumin (see Okubo, chapter 9). Concerning the inclusion of Euro-American immigrants, Shoji said that the organizers (including the minority communities) felt that they had been "pampered" in Japan up until now and there was no need to exhibit their history or life style (Shôji and Kim 2006: 27).[8]

The exhibition project brings Japanese museology well up to the forefront of international practice (Tai 2005). For a decade or more there have been discussions and struggles about the authority of curators to exhibit versus the rights of those often minority or marginal peoples to control how they are exhibited (Karp and Lavine 1991). As mentioned above, Minpaku itself originally faced opposition from radical Ainu groups before negotiating the conditions of display of its Ainu materials in the late 1970s.

At the welcoming corridor entrance, the visitor was greeted by a collage of faces and the title "Multiethnic Japan—Life and History of Immigrants" written in many languages. The first segment showed the increasing historical engagement of the Japanese with foreigners since the opening of Japan in 1853 and the Meiji restoration in 1868. This emphasized that the engagement has been two-way: there has been a diaspora of Japanese emigrants to many parts of the world, to North and South America and Hawaii, and through military expansion to China, Taiwan, Korea, Manchuria, and Micronesia, as well as more recent immigration of foreigners, some of who are the descendants of the former emigrants. The exhibition pointed out that until 1945 Japan was a de facto "multi-ethnic Empire" and that only after 1945 was the "myth of homogeneity" imposed, stripping resident foreigners of their visibility and distinctive status (see Lie 2001; Oguma 2002).

The historical graphs and narratives in the exhibition pointed to key events, such as the end of the war in 1945, when all resident Koreans who had been "Japanese" to that point were stripped of their nationality and declared to be foreigners, and when Japan signed the United Nations Declaration of Human Rights in 1995. The rapid increase of resident foreigners to nearly 2 percent of the total population is particularly striking after 1990. The exhibit pointed out that these immigrants are not evenly spread, but many are concentrated in certain manufacturing cities, particularly around Tokyo. The case studies showed that there are many types of minority communities: though there are some "ghettos," other immigrants are well integrated or even invisible in Japanese communities.

The lower hall dealt with major aspects of life common to the immigrant experience. Prominent were the immigrants' struggle to adapt to living in Japan, entering public schools; legal registration and the law; dealing with local governments; getting work; housing and health care; and overcoming discrimination. There was a section with books and pamphlets produced by national and local governments offering advice to immigrants, unofficial services by NPOs (non-profit organizations, which are not tax-exempt in Japan), and above all immigrant self-help (see Yamanaka, chapter 8). Grassroots organizations, including churches, many with help from sympathetic Japanese and other immigrants, provide services and assistance. The exhibit highlighted the media in the form of posters and pamphlets, ethnic newspapers and journals, and radio stations. More than twenty FM stations were featured with their broadcast schedules, and the Kobe FM station "FM Wai Wai" had a small studio in the exhibit from which programs in Tagalog, Portuguese, English, and Japanese were broadcast live.

Other less daunting features of immigrant life were also represented on the ground floor. The center area was given over to pictures and paraphernalia of ethnic festivals, from Brazilian *carnivale* to Chinese dragon dances. There were also colorful displays of ethnic stores and shopping, from a strictly Muslim (Pakistani) grocery to a walk-in Brazilian truck making the rounds of *Nikkei*-Brazilian (Brazilians of Japanese descent) neighborhoods. There was also a schoolroom illustrating the kind of *esu-nikku kurabu* (after-school "class" in which children learn about or play at being members of a specific non-Japanese ethnic group) that might be provided as part of Osaka's ethnically oriented education for recent immigrants from China (Kotani 2004; Shirota 2004; also see Okubo, chapter 9). It contained a map, Chinese masks, a video of pandas, and other things that visiting schoolchildren of Japanese and other ethnic backgrounds could try out to experience the immigrant classroom (Shirota 2006). There was an abundance of immigrant children's drawings showing how they saw their world and themselves. Professor Shoji said that although the immigrant groups had often suffered extensively in their forced or voluntary coming to Japan, he did not want to overemphasize the suffering and make them out to be nothing but victims appealing for sympathy. Shoji said he was reminded by a Brazilian colleague that though immigrants put up with hardships, they enjoy life, play when they can, and try to look on the bright side. Shoji was pleased that the exhibit could show a happy side of the immigrant experience even if it was difficult for the people themselves to show it. And he was happy when this was recognized: for instance the journal *Musée* (July 2004) stated "The manifold settings surrounding Taminzoku were *karatto* [literally "sun brightly"] shown." Even the gift store, always a large feature of Japanese public institutions, was transformed into an "ethnic store" offering goods such as Korean *yuzu* tea, and things seen in the shopping exhibits, especially toys aimed at child visitors (compulsory school trips brought in over 25 percent of the visitors).

The upper floor contained five distinct ethnic displays—Chinese, Filipino, Vietnamese, Korean, and Brazilian.[9] Each of these exhibited household possessions, such as photographs, clothing, and furniture, as well as festive items including music, costumes, masks, and so on that would be found mainly in these Kansai communities (the area around Osaka and Kyoto). The depth of the exhibits and the control exercised by the people themselves often revealed hidden meanings and categories—for example, subdivisions within the ethnic communities that might not otherwise have been known to the museum employees. In some cases special historical sections or events enlarged on community life: such as the Pilipino wedding, including clothes and photographs, and the illustrated section on Korean immigrants' history, emphasizing how they had been cruelly consigned to hard work and dangerous occupations prior to and during World War II. The Korean section also highlighted the many successful achievements of Koreans within Japanese life, especially in the entertainment and sports fields. But it is also true that many of these stars achieved their success only by hiding their Korean background (see Hester, chapter 7; Tierney, chapter 12); many only revealed their backgrounds after they were publicly revered.[10]

What was most remarkable about this exhibition was the degree of cooperation with the local ethnic communities, to a degree rarely found in museums outside ethnic communities themselves in North America. People were proud of their part in decision making and self-representation, as well as the exhibition of their personal items; they continued to bring new items and change the exhibits all during the exhibition period. The immigrant communities themselves insisted that there should be community programs and performances at the museum, and took on the responsibility for organizing them. This they thought would take things out of the realm of "politics" and make the exhibit more "educational." The museum board entirely agreed. The museum welcomed these people and the many performance events that accompanied the exhibition. There were well-publicized events by Brazilians and other Latinos, Arab-Muslims, Filipinos, and Chinese.

The organizing team made great efforts to invite attendance and involve participation by all the area's immigrant communities; for instance they sent out thirty thousand Korean fliers. They distributed some through teachers in schools with partly ethnic communities, and at educational, immigrant, and Kokusai Kôryû Kyôkai (International Exchange Association) religious and secular festivals. The members of these communities, many of whom were not from the more educated affluent classes of Osaka and had never been to Minpaku before, came to see their own communities in the exhibition, bringing other community members and friends. The communities themselves organized bus tours, coming from as far out of town as Tenri (in the Nara Valley). In addition, the museum organized trips from Osaka to some immigrant communities in other parts of Japan such as the heavily Latino town of Tsurumi in Yokohama, Kanagawa Prefecture. The exhibition got increasing publicity and became more popular some time after opening, rather than the visitors dropping off. In the end the exhibit attracted over thirty-seven thousand visitors.

This was the first time that such an exhibition had been put on by anyone at Minpaku. Shôji wished the exhibition had not been classified as "minor," so that it could have run for one hundred and not seventy-two days and had a larger budget. He also wishes he had done more advertising to the general public. Nevertheless, he and his research group, which still meets regularly, think that it was a success. All the press and media were invited and came. Shôji was interviewed on two NHK radio programs. Nearly all the two thousand copies of the catalog copies produced have sold, and it is used as a textbook by some high schools and universities. The exhibition sparked an NHK program director in Osaka to produce a year-long television series with monthly programs on the Asian communities in the Kansai region in consultation with Shoji. Other ongoing projects include further outreach in the schools, modeled on a teacher-initiated project that used the exhibition as the basis for a school curriculum segment on multiculturalism. In addition, the active members of the museum implementation project are preparing reflexive accounts of their experiences for inclusion in a further innovative volume (Shôji and Kim 2006). The significance of this exhibition to museum anthropology has already attracted international attention (Tai 2005).

This unprecedented exhibition was a triumph from the point of view of the advocates of immigrant rights and multiculturalism. As an exhibition it resembled the "immigration museums" of Ellis Island, New York, and Angel Island in San Francisco Bay, showing immigrant hardships and the lives of real, named people. It was not a professional permanent exhibit and it was open for less than three months, but it reveled in change and community involvement and became very much a part of the communities it depicted. Thus it linked with grassroots movements in Japan where marginal peoples have joined with sympathetic Japanese to get their voices across. They feel that they have more control over their own lives and their place within the Japanese mosaic, and stronger links with professional scholars such as Komai Hiroshi and other activists (see the introduction of this book) in promoting multiculturalism at the highest levels.

Little World

Little World is a completely different kind of enterprise, conforming more to the "foreign theme parks" (*gaikoku mura*) that I am proposing as important to the internationalization of (younger) Japanese people. After the success of Expo '70 in Osaka, it was decided to have as major *kokusaika* educational enterprises two "national" anthropology museums, Minpaku in Osaka and "Little World." Little World was to be different—with a superb indoor museum, arranged thematically by subsistence, economics, family, and transportation, and an innovative outdoor "museum" that consists of more than twenty-five "authentic" foreign villages, compounds, and hacienda separated from each other by hundreds of yards along a 2.5-km long road winding through the rolling countryside (Takada 1995: 119). Little World was opened in 1983 under the directorship of the famous archaeologist Egami Namio.[11]

Little World's focus on assemblages of housing, one of Izumi Seiichi's main interests, may be seen as an extension of the focus of Meiji Mura, another "museum" in the same complex, which opened in 1965 and displays real buildings from the Meiji era (1868–1912) that marked Japan's assimilation to the outside world (Takada 1995: 119). Both museums, together with the equally educational Primate World, were undertaken by the Meitetsu (Nagoya Railway) Company, which formed a foundation to run these three enterprises as an alternative "national" museum as part of the same central initiative (personal communication, Kobayashi Shigeki, chief curator, 1989). Little World has a small research department but it is consistently losing money. Meitetsu might gladly close it (together with Primate World) and just keep Meiji Mura, which with over a million visitors a year is not such a money loser. Recently, Showa Mura, based on Japan during the reign of Emperor Hirohito (1926–1989), has been opened nearby but not under Meitetsu sponsorship.

Little World has gone to great lengths to ensure the "authenticity" of materials, soils, animals, and guest performers. A number of the "villages" are "inhabited" (during opening hours) by people from the appropriate countries, lending a convincing "truth" to their "co-evalness" (coexistence in the present age; see Fabian 1983) even if, like Minpaku, there is an emphasis on rural and traditional ways of life. For instance, at the French farm complex, there are usually French female students (there for six-month stints from the Université d'Alsace) dressed in "peasant" clothes to help entertain the visitors by dressing Japanese (children) in those clothes and posing together for photographs. This exhibit, cows and all, caused my French anthropologist friend to exclaim that it really was like the village where he was brought up. The Balinese nobleman's compound (built of course by Balinese with materials from Bali) is only inhabited in the summer (by a full *gamelan* orchestra plus extras) because the Balinese found winter in Japan to be too cold. The Tibetan Monastery and living quarters were built by Tibetan priests and properly consecrated as one of the limited number of such monasteries in the world. The Peruvian hacienda, imported lock, stock, and barrel (including furniture previously imported from France to Peru), is not "inhabited" nor is its chapel consecrated, yet Catholic priests consider it so authentic that they have regularly conducted Catholic marriages there. There's a joke amongst the staff that when members of the diplomatic corps in Tokyo get homesick, they can get on a train and in 2.5 hours they can be at Little World enjoying a refreshing home atmosphere!

This also works to its disadvantage. Little World is sometimes judged "too authentic" by the visiting public. There are also the problems of the distance between villages (some of the shuttle "buses" are Filipino "Jeepneys"), the smells (Japanese are not used to seeing or living near cows and other farm animals in the open), and the awkwardness of some exhibits (many houses retain their original dimensions with small doors and rooms, so only a few people can enter). As a "commercial" enterprise there is now an abundance of foreign gift shops and restaurants incorporated into many of the attractions and we should note that these may be even more educational "internationally" for Japanese as potential overseas tourists than the imported houses themselves. Recent major acquisitions, including the Bavarian Village, with a beer hall, wine shop, and touristic dancing,[12] and a southern Italian restaurant (imported stone by stone from Apulia) complete with mini opera stage, seem aimed at popularity rather than authenticity. But nevertheless they are generating good revenue from visitors.

Gaikoku Mura: *Foreign Villages*

Japan is replete with all kinds of theme parks (Takada 1995: 114–122). Dominant among them is the immensely successful and "Japanized" Tokyo Disneyland (Raz 1999), also opened in 1983 and which continues to attract about 16 million Japanese tourists a year (nearly equal to the number who go abroad); in 2001 it was joined by the equally ambitious DisneySea Park. More than fifteen of these attractions are called *gaikoku mura*, or foreign country villages (Hendry 2000). Unlike Disneyland, which is specifically not seen as representing "America" or any other real country, these villages are representations of foreign places such that Japanese tourists would recognize the "real thing" abroad after visiting the imitation. Perhaps Little World was the original exemplar; most opened in the late 1980s or the 1990s and pay considerable attention to authentic detail, often bringing in foreign workman and materials, but like Disneyland, they are specifically commercial and were designed and operated to try to attract plenty of paying visitors. Here is not the place to examine them in detail (see Hamilton-Oerhl 1998; Hendry 2000; Hubler 1993; Talmadge 1996), but we should note some major features.

Most of the *gaikoku mura* represent countries that Japanese admire and might visit as tourists, and the more "popular" were built earliest and largest, including Glücks Königreich ("Lucky Kingdom," Germany, 1989, now closed); Oranda Mura (Holland Village, 1983), which developed into Huis ten Bosch ("House in the Woods," 1988–1992, bankrupt but still operating); Spain-mura (Parque Espana, 1988); and Canadian World in Hokkaido (1990). Apart from Disneyland (1983), which "represents" a fantasy culture of the United States, other theme parks "represent" (parts of) Turkey, Russia, Denmark, Britain, Spain, Scotland, Mongolia, Italy, and Switzerland. Finally, the French conglomerate Vivendi aimed at attracting at least 8 million Japanese a year in competition with Tokyo Disneyland by creating a more "genuine American experience" at its Osaka version of "Universal Studios" (Taniwaka 2001), which opened in spring 2001 at a cost of US $1.16 billion.

There are also theme parks that cover more than one country, such as REOMA World, which represents much of Southeast Asia; "Virtual Europe" Theme Park; and Tobu World Square, Nikko, built by Toho Eizo Bijutsu of *Godzilla* movies fame, where you can see 1/25-scale models of over a hundred of the world's most famous buildings all at once. "But for those who want to get the thrill of danger ... There among all the tiny plastic New Yorkers is a replica of Manhattan, a bank robbery is in progress" (Talmadge 1996). And just north of Miyazaki city, right next to a beautiful, unspoiled, sandy surfing beach is the "Sea Gaia Ocean Dome" wave pool (300 meters long), the world's largest indoor surfing beach with wave generator. Like some of the others, including Huis ten Bosch, it went bankrupt and Sheraton has since bought it.

Hendry is correct in stating, "Most share common features ... an extraordinary degree of attention to detail and an internal idea of authenticity.... The parks try to create a space that will induce the visitors to feel that they have actually entered the foreign country featured" (2001: 20). Nearly all of them have buildings that, like Little World, are faithful reproductions of foreign originals, and some are even built abroad or from imported materials by foreign workmen. Some represent famous landmarks such as the Royal Palace in Amsterdam (Huis Ten Bosch), the Domtoren (Utrecht), cottages from Stratford on Avon (Shakespeare County Park), Suzdai Cathedral (Russian Village), and Buckeberg Castle (Glücks Königreich). Also like Little World, nearly all of the European ones have churches or chapels. Often these are rented by Japanese couples who often prefer to get married "in white" in a church in Japan or abroad (for fashionability rather than Christianity), so the churches lend authenticity and are another source of income.

Again, like Little World, nearly all of them have foreigners from their "original" countries in various roles such as performers or interpreters, and many of them attract foreign tourists from those countries who happen to be in Japan. Many of these "entertainers" play the characteristic music, classical and folk, of their countries. Most of them are dressed in what the Japanese consider to be typical for the people of that country, and some guests were disappointed at the Canadian Village to have to be told "Canadians wear T-shirts at home" (Urashima 1996). Above all, the visitors like to interact with the foreigners in a situation where, unlike abroad, they are in the majority and their attempts at the language will not be out of place or mocked, and they love to be photographed with the suitably dressed attendants. This follows the Japanese tradition of *kinen shashin* (Graburn 1983) whereby Japanese tourists and pilgrims get someone to take a photograph of themselves at the place or with the personnel as a kind of proof that they were there.

Further enhancing the "foreign" experience are the many chances to eat and drink the cuisine of the country, sometimes with menus in the foreign language, and with all the authentic table settings. Yet, a number of accounts show that the food is somewhat modified to Japanese tastes. The beer halls at Glücks Königreich and in the Bavarian Village at Little World, and the pub at British Hills, are similarly opportunities to learn drinking styles or are substitutes for going abroad. Similarly, the opportunity to shop for characteristic goods, such as wines and pâtés at the French Village, beers and cuckoo clocks at the German, porcelain at the Danish parks, and rugs at the Turkish teaches the visitors what the *meibutsu* (famous things) are that they would be expected to buy as *omiyage* (souvenirs) as overseas tourists.

As most of these parks are for Japanese who have not already been abroad, their attraction depends on their appearing to be authentic to the visitor, and all judgments of authenticity by neophytes are mediated, that is, have to be judged against media-driven images. Japanese are exposed to representations of foreign countries throughout their education, in *manga* (comic books, mainly for adults), books, television, films, and videos, as well as from hearsay and friends' experiences and photos—and through *omiyage* received from those who have already gone abroad. Japanese culture tends to stereotype the icons of place (domestic or foreign) as *meibutsu*, which can be condensed into and purchased as *omiyage*. It is therefore not surprising that most of the *gaikoku mura* feature world-famous writers or their fictional characters as well as "brand names" known to Japanese who have had even the smallest exposure to literature or the media. Thus Denmark is indicated by Hans Christian Andersen (a statue at Nixe Danish castle), Britain by Shakespeare (Sakurai 1997), and Spain by Don Quixote at Parque España. Both were outdone by Glücks Königreich, which reproduced parts of Bavaria's Marchen Strasse devoted to the brothers Grimm, whose characters and dwellings were reproduced or named throughout. Even more focused is Canadian World, which takes advantage of the open spaces and the climate of Hokkaido to reproduce the fictional landscape and houses associated with *Anne of Green Gables* of the province of Prince Edward Island in Eastern Canada. Indeed, like the original locale, the topographical contextualization of the fictional character, known to all Japanese women as *Akage no An* (Red-Haired Anne) is symbolized by that of the author herself, Lucy Maude Montgomery, and many Japanese travel to Prince Edward Island, Canada to see the "originals" (Fawcett 1998; Rea 2000). The Canadian Park is not only filled with buildings and recreated environments that appear in the books about Anne, but Canadians dressed up as the fictional characters mingle with the guests.

In addition to the commercial and representational aspects of these parks, many of them express strong moral values, sometimes the vision of their founders, or flowery versions of general values such as "peace" and "understanding." Huis Ten Bosch grew from the founder's travel experience in Europe and his admiration for the "ecologically benign" way in which the Dutch have reclaimed land from the sea. It is designed for "coexistence of ecology and economy" by recycling water and all waste products, co-generating power, and providing efficient housing for the thousands of Japanese who live on the site, all with the aid of the latest in Japanese technology, at a cost of over US $2.5 billion (Appelgren 2004; Huis Ten Bosch 2000). In addition, Huis Ten Bosch, situated near Nagasaki, symbolizes Japan's "special relationship" with the Dutch, who would visit the restricted island of Deshima near Nagasaki for trade purposes when other foreigners were kept out of Japan during the Tokugawa era (1603–1868).[13] Other symbols of the relationship are found in the Dutch windmill surrounded by fields of tulips to be found at Sakura-shi, near Narita. Parque Espana's establishment was partly stimulated by a 1986 meeting of the Associacion Japonesa de Hispanistas that resulted in the founding of an Academic Friendship Association, CANELA. This is now associated with Nanzan University and holds an annual *Congresos* at Parque Espana, where its members get preferential rates in the hotel, according to its Spanish-language Web site. Somewhat similar, though more commercial, is British Hills outside of Tokyo, which provides a manor house, guest houses, and a pub representing the "medieval British lifestyle" where 140 paying guests can stay together to mingle with the foreign staff and learn English and cross-cultural communication skills.

On the other hand, straightforward commercial enterprises may be owners, partners, promoters, and beneficiaries of these theme parks. For instance, Canadian Village and the popularity of "Red-Haired Anne" inspired a consortium of thirty-six builders in Canada's employment-hungry Maritime Provinces to export three models of prefabricated "Green Gables-style" houses, which could be erected in Japanese suburbs for about US $300,000 (Whyte 1998).

Many other forms of parks and entertainment also contribute to familiarization with the foreign. Mentioned above is Meiji Mura, a popular park for the display of the Meiji Era (1868–1912) named after the first "modern" emperor. This era was notable for Japan's rapid incorporation of Western social and political forms (military, law, parliament, public education, Christianity) and equally notable Western technologies, such as trains, brick buildings, modern architecture, powered factories, roads and bridges, cars, electricity, and telecommunications. This wonderful park is the repository of all these once advanced technological forms, which are now looked back on with nostalgia (Graburn 1995); models here, like at Little World, are "the real thing": churches, railway stations, cafes, prisons, and barracks, mostly in working order, and most ironically a large segment of Frank Lloyd Wright's Imperial Hotel, one of the few large buildings to withstand the 1923 Kantô earthquake. This has been lovingly taken apart, transported and rebuilt for visiting and use (as a restaurant) outside Nagoya. Comparable as a repository of the early importation and experience with Westernness, though not officially a park, is Kitanochô (North ward) of the City of Kobe. There, especially on Ijinkan-dôri (Foreigner house street) are well-preserved Victorian and Edwardian buildings, many now open to tourists. These originally housed the consulates and living quarters of European and American institutions that were rapidly set up after Kobe was declared a "treaty port" after the opening of Japan. Kobe itself was, and to some extent still presents itself as, "exotic and foreign," and was known as *"hai kora"* (high collar, or sophisticated) because of the foreign presence. Nowadays Kitanochô is occupied by Japanese (as a prestigious area to live, in the hills with fine views) and has many fine foreign restaurants (Indian and Mexican as well as "Western") for the rich locals, the curious foreign tourists, and the many Japanese young people who go there hoping to see an "authentic foreignness" of the kind that they would, could, or will experience abroad (Uchiyama Hachirô, personal communication, 2001). Many large Japanese cities have similar sections of preserved Western living, such as Nagasaki's Glover (Grover) Park, but none as large and famous as Kobe's.

Conclusions

This chapter has focused on Japanese experiences of what I call "constructed foreignness" within Japan, select versions of foreign or "international" cultures introduced for educational and leisure experiences by governmental and profit-making institutions. Though, as I pointed out, such familiar sampling of the unfamiliar might engender a tolerance or even excitement about the foreign, visits to view the objects and to attend the events described here are voluntary. Although it is true that schoolchildren have to visit museums occasionally, most of the audiences of these institutions visit by choice, select what they want to buy or consume, and can ignore or laugh at things they don't like. Furthermore they are not ashamed at their judgmental behavior. This is very different from residing in multicultural neighborhoods that might house illegal or undesirable immigrants, and being subjected to noise levels, entertainment habits, or cooking smells that one does not like.

Thus these museum and theme park experiences are willingly undertaken and belong to the worlds of entertainment or voluntary education, much like the international tourism experiences they mimic. I had always thought that these domestic excursions were "practice" for overseas tourism for those Japanese lacking cultural self-confidence (Graburn 1983), places where they could sample cuisines, restaurant styles, clothing, and shopping in safe, linguistically unthreatening settings. Perhaps this is true for most visitors, but it has also been suggested that this is as far as some tourists want to venture: "Many of today's Japanese tourists don't want to be bothered by the horror, not to mention expense and trouble, of the real thing. They want a Berlin with no neo-Nazis; a New York they can visit for the weekend; and a London where everyone speaks Japanese. They want a sanitized, Japanized version of the rest of the world, a virtual vacation" (*Japan Times,* 13 April 1994). Or, as expressed by a visitor to the Russian Park, Niigata, "As a woman, safety is definitely something you take into account when deciding whether to go overseas. That isn't a concern here" (Talmadge 1996).

It should be apparent to the reader by now that Japanese young people and adults are awash with symbols and material content of *kokusaika,* internationalization, and though some (mainly older people) complain about it having "rammed down their throats," it has rubbed off. The continuing fascination and familiarity of the foreign make it commonplace for people to chose to go abroad, and some people may have done so multiple times, choosing their destinations for nuanced specializations, rather than simply becoming "cosmopolitan" (Appelgren 2007). Obviously many of the theme parks and other domestic tourist attractions are in competition with, or serve as practice for, the overseas "prototypes" of which they are simulacra.

So we cannot equate international tourism with multiculturalism. The original meaning of *kokusaika* was more about conditioning Japanese to travel, do business and be accepted abroad, rather than accepting foreigners, that is international tourists or immigrants in Japan. There is a danger that unreflexive foreign travel leads to "boutique" multiculturalism, that is the superficial importation and acceptance of foreign foods and chefs, arts and artists, clothing and couturiers, and even foreign words (*gairaigo*) and intellectual fashions. But that is not what this volume is about. Tsuda has suggested that the acceptance of middle-class, usually white people in no way signals Japanese acceptance of non-European working-class immigrants, legal or illegal (personal communication). We saw the converse of this in Shoji's exhibition where the "ethnic" minority immigrants wanted to have *their* show and not have to share with Euro-American "white" people whose cultures are more automatically admired and available for consumption and emulation.

I suggest therefore that we have to look back at these anthropological museums and *gaikoku* theme parks to see what exactly is presented and consumed. For the most part we see cultural simulacra and commercial offerings from such admired countries—mainly European, such as Germany, Holland, England, Spain, Scotland, and Italy—plus the Americas, the United States, and Canada. The two national museums of course display worldwide cultural samples, including those from "tribal" and "lesser developed" areas—one can try snake meat in the African area or dress up in saris at the Indian pavilion at Little World; but this is a very much a kind of "boutique" accommodation. Presentations from countries about which Japanese may be quite ambivalent, such as China, Russia, or Turkey, are available but less popular as destinations. Relations with Korea have changed to the positive because of the *hanr'yu* (Korean wave) of media and popular culture. But where are the Pilipino, Bangladeshi, Iranian, Congolese, or Sri Lankan villages? We have to suggest that multiculturalism, the acceptance of the foreign nearby or within, is still very much a racialized or class-bound cultural hierarchy, expressed in residential proximities, intermarriages, cultural emulation, and common schooling, as well as in domestic and international tourism.

Notes

1. I wish to thank Professor Shinji Yamashita (University of Tokyo) for information here. He asserts that the National Museum in Osaka was an academic and cultural symbol of Japan's successful recovery from World War II, reinforced by its placement on the site of Expo '70, Osaka. He also suggests a historical continuity with the *Minzokukenkyusho* (National Institute of Ethnic Studies), started in 1942 to help with policies towards peoples colonized overseas, noting that Umesao Tadao was involved in both projects. I wish to thank Director Umesao Tadao and Professor Ishimori Shûzô who hosted me at Minpaku in 1979 and in 1989 to 1990.
2. Minpaku functions as (a) the main center for anthropological research in Japan with a full-time research staff of about sixty, plus major journals, monograph series, and so on in English and in other European languages in addition to Japanese; (b) an important center for postgraduate training in Japan; and (c) the largest anthropology library in Japan and one of the major hubs of the interlibrary loan system.
3. John Ertl and I attended the opening of the exhibition and later reviewed it in detail in March 2004. We are extremely grateful to Professor Shoji and graduate student Kotani Sachiko who worked on the exhibition, for their time and expertise in explaining so much about the exhibition, its preparation and its aftermath when we revisited in February 2005 and for looking over a draft of this chapter in 2006.

4. Professor Shôji has continued his interest in multiethnic nations. In May 2004 he attended the symposium, "Diversity: The Effects of Immigration on Culture" in Osaka and in December he spoke about the increase in foreign language use in Japan at a conference on "Multilingualism and the Linguistic Landscape," in Tokyo. The Transborder Anthropology group organized its third symposium at Minpaku in March 2004 just days before the opening on the *Taminzoku* exhibition.

5. Japanese "anthropology" has bifurcated into two branches, each pronounced *"minzokugaku"* but with different characters. The original form, sometimes called nativist anthropology or ethnology in the old European sense, aimed at studying the origins and ethnos of the Japanese and it became identified with the militarist nationalism of the 1930s and 1940s. Now it has become a less academically central form of "folklore." (For a recent discussion of the status of these two forms of anthropology, see Yamashita et al., 2004). The dominant branch now resembles Western sociocultural anthropology with its world scope. Sekimoto (1995) suggested that this foreign focus since World War II was chosen specifically to avoid identification with the now disgraced branch (see also Shimizu and van Bremen 2003).

6. Apparently there was an exhibit at the Osaka Human Rights Museum (known as "Liberty Osaka") concerning human rights, Burakumin, and other such issues. The *uyoku* (extreme right-wing groups known by their loudspeaker-bearing black trucks) organized a loud public protest and discouraged visitors. Minpaku personnel feared similar actions but it was pointed out that the museum stands in the middle of the large Expo Park and only pedestrians can get within a few hundred yards of it. It is true that Minpaku symposia have tackled controversial subjects, for instance wartime anthropology in Japan (Shimizu and van Bremen 2003), but these events are not open to the general public.

7. Provocatively they wrote the title phase *ta-* (many) in kanji, *minzoku-* (tribal or ethnic peoples) in hiragana, and *Nihon* (Japan) in katakana, a style of writing usually reserved for foreign words, perhaps indicating that it is Japan itself that is foreign. Professor Shoji adds that use of kana deprives both Minzoku and Nihon of all their established exclusive militant associations. Hiragana (the more curvilinear syllabary) makes the word *minzoku* ambiguous, with the possible meaning of "ethnic." The use of *kana* ensures that the word for Japan is pronounced *Nihon* and prevents the more nationalistic pronunciation of *Nippon*, which is associated with its kanji characters. An exact English translation of the title would be *Multiethnic Japan: The Life of Immigrants* but the actual cover bears the Japanese title and its translation as "Life and History of Immigrants" in English, together with translations into Tagalog, Korean, Brazilian Portuguese, Vietnamese, and Chinese, repeated in variably focused overlays.

8. Their exclusion here reinforces, of course, their special status. Most "white people" (*hakujin*) have been persons of privilege and of positive cultural capital since the opening of Japan in the 1850s. Exceptions include the recent influx of Russians; they often arrive without visas and are involved, as are other poor Asian groups, in "entertainment," marriages of convenience, and prostitution (Akaha and Vassilieva, 2003).

9. The exhibition and catalogue consistently label this group *Brazileiros,* which correctly denotes that they come from Brazil and are seen as carriers of Brazilian culture. But this is a special group, descendants of Japanese emigrants, usually known as *Nikkeijin,* whose easy immigrant entry into Japan was facilitated by the law of 1990, which permitted them "free return" to Japan in the guise of visiting their ancestral country. This flow of *Nikkeijin* was engendered pre-

cisely to supplant the flow of immigrants of less desirable "races," with the idea that Brazilian Japanese would be much more compatible and acceptable to the majority of Japanese. However, as Tsuda shows (chapter 6), this was not exactly the case, and the Museum's use of the Brazileiro term confirms the finding that these *Nikkeijin* are not *Nihonjin* ("real Japanese"). The two musical performers at the opening ceremony were *Brazileiros* but not of *Nikkei* descent.

10. This strikingly parallels the professional successes and social mobility of many blacks in the United States. However, unlike the Koreans and Burakumin minorities in Japan, they could rarely disguise their origins.

11. Hendry (2000: 157–164) emphasizes the role of Ohnuki Yoshio, Izumi's former student, who originally worked on the development of Little World and who after working for a time at the University of Tokyo returned to become its director. I visited Little World a number of times in 1989 and 1990 and I thank then chief curator Professor Kobayashi Shigeki for his welcome. I visited again in 1991, and in 2004 with UC Berkeley graduate student Kensuke Sumii.

12. "Showing off" in front of the local Japanese, I asked the ice cream salesman in German where he came from. He replied that he was not from Germany but was Turkish. I have noticed in recent visits that the "staff" personnel are less likely to be from the actual country than they used to be, such as Romanian fiddlers in a Huis Ten Bosch restaurant and a Russian young woman in Little World's Alsace village but, like the Turkish ice cream salesman in the Bavarian village, these "exceptions" may accurately represent European realities!

13. Although limited trade was the object of this concession, Japanese also thirsted for European knowledge of medicine, geography, military techniques, and engineering, subjects that were previously censored and then taught as "Dutch studies" in a few private schools in Japanese cities.

References

Akaha, Tsuneo and Anna Vassilieva. 2003. "Russian Migrants in Niigata and Hokkaido." In *Human Flows Across National Borders in Northeast Asia*, ed. Tsuneo Akaha, 95–119. Monterey: Center for East Asian Studies.

Appelgren, Staffan. 2004. "Cultural Consumption in Japan: The Case of Huis ten Bosch." Paper presented at Gôteberg University, September.

———. 2007. "Huis ten Bosch: Mimesis and Simulatiuon in a Japanese Dutch Town." Ph.D. dissertation, Göteborg, Sweden:

Fabian, Johannes. 1983. *Time and the Other: How Anthropology Makes Its Object*. New York: Columbia University Press.

Fawcett, Clare. 1998. "The Influence of L. M. Montgomery on Japan's view of Canada." Manuscript, St. Francis Xavier University, Antigonish, NS, Canada.

Graburn, Nelson H. H., and Shûzô Ishimori. 1979. "The National Museum of Ethnology, Osaka, Japan: Research and Oceanic Collections." *Pacific Arts Newsletter* 9 (June): 14–18.

———. 1983. *To Pray, Pay and Play: The Cultural Structure of Japanese Domestic Tourism*. Aix-en-Provence: Centre des Hautes Etudes Touristiques.

————. 1995. "The Past in the Present in Japan: Nostalgia and Neo-traditionalism in Contemporary Japanese Domestic Tourism." In *Changes in Tourism: People, Places, Processes,* ed. Richard W. Butler and Douglas G. Pearce, 47–70. London: Routledge.

Hamilton-Oerhl, Angelika. 1998. "Leisure Parks in Japan." In *The Culture of Japan as Seen through Its Leisure,* ed. Sepp Linhart and Sabine Fruehstueck, 237–250. New York: SUNY Press.

Harada, M. 1998. "Changing Relationships between Work and Leisure after the 'Bubble Economy' in Japan." *Loisir et Société* 21 (1): 195–212.

Hendry, Joy. 2000. *The Orient Strikes Back: A Global View of Cultural Display.* Oxford: Berg.

Hook, Glenn D., and Michael A. Weiner, eds. 1992. *The Internationalization of Japan.* London: Routledge.

Hubler, Eric. 1993. "The Many Worlds of Fun in Japan." *New York Times,* July 4.

Huis Ten Bosch. 2000. "New Amsterdam in Nagasaki, Japan: Huis Ten Bosch Resort and Theme Park." http://www.HuistenBosch.co.jp Accessed 14 February 2002.

Ivy, Marilyn. 1995. *Discourses of the Vanishing: Modernity, Phantasm, Japan.* Chicago: University of Chicago Press.

Japan Times. 2002. "Japan's Workaholics Take Leisurely Cure." 20 February.

Karp, Ivan, and Steven D. Lavine, eds. 1991. *Exhibiting Cultures: The Poetics and Politics of Museum Display.* Washington, DC: Smithsonian Institution.

Kayano, Shigeru. 1978. *Ainu no Mingu.* Tokyo: Suzusawa Shoten.

Lie, John. 2001. *Multiethnic Japan.* Cambridge, MA: Harvard University Press.

Mannari, Hiroshi, and Harumi Befu, eds. 1993. *The Challenge of Japan's Internationalization.* Tokyo: Kôdansha.

McConnell, David L. 2000. *Importing Diversity: Inside Japan's JET Program.* Berkeley: University of California Press.

Oguma, Eiji. 2002. *A Genealogy of 'Japanese' Self-Images.* Melbourne: Trans Pacific Press.

Raz, Aviad. 1999. *Riding the Black Ship: Japan and Tokyo Disneyland.* Cambridge, MA: Harvard University Press.

Rea, Michael. 2000. "A Furusato Away from Home." *Annals of Tourism Research* 27 (3): 638–660.

Sakurai, Joji. 1997. "Japan Has Become Bard's Home Away from Home." *San Francisco Chronicle,* 23 December.

Sekimoto, Teruo. 1995. "Nihon no jinruigaku to Nihon shigaku" [Anthropology of Japan and Japanese historiography]. In *Iwanami kôza Nihon tsûshi*, Bekkan 1, ed. Asao Naohiro et al., 123–147. Tokyo: Iwanami Shoten.

Shimizu, Akitoshi, and Jan van Bremen. 2003. *Wartime Japanese Anthropology in Asia and the Pacific.* Senri Ethnological Studies, no. 65. Osaka: National Museum of Ethnology.

Shirota, Chika. 2004. "Panda Kyôshitsu–Chûgoku Kikoku Jidôtachi no Manabuba" [The panda classroom—the place to learn for the children of Chinese returnees]. *Taminzoku Nihon—Zainichi Gaikokujin no Kurashi* [Multiethnic Japan: Life and History of Immigrants]. ed. Shôji Hiroshi, 90–91. Suita: National Museum of Ethnology.

———. 2006. "Panda no Shippo ha Shiro ka Kuro ka: Chûgoku Kikoku/ Tonichi Jidô tachi no Tenjijyô kara Miru 'Chûgokujin,' 'Nihonjin,' 'Taminzoku.' ["Is panda's tail white or black: 'Chinese,' 'Japanese,' 'multi-ethnic.' Seen from the site of exhibition on the children of Chinese returnees]. *Taminzoku Nihon no Misekata: Tokubetsuten "Taminzoku Nihon" wo Megutte* [Presenting 'Multiethnic Japan,' a Special Exhibition]. eds. Shôji Hiroshi and Kim Miseon, 55–81. Senri Ethnological Report 64. Osaka: National Museum of Ethnology.

Shôji, Hiroshi, ed. 2004. *Taminzoku Nihon-Zainichi Gaikokujin no Kurashi* [Multiethnic Japan: Life and history of immigrants]. Suita: National Museum of Ethnology.

Shôji, Hiroshi and Juha Janhunen. eds. 1997. *Northern Minority Languages: Problems of Survival.* Senri Ethnological Studies, no. 44. Osaka: National Musuem of Ethnology.

Shôji, Hiroshi and Kim Miseon eds. 2006. *Taminzoku Nihon no Misekata: Tokubetsuten "Taminzoku Nihon" wo megutte* [Presenting 'Multiethnic Japan,' a Special Exhibition]. Senri Ethnological Report 64. Osaka: National Museum of Ethnology.

Tai, Eika. 2005. "Redefining Japan as Multiethnic: An Exhibition at the National Museum of Ethnology." *Museum Anthropology* 27 (2): 43–62.

Takada, Masatoshi. 1995. "The City and Its Model: A Civilization's Mechanism for Self-Expression as the Object of Tourism." In *Japanese Civilization and the Modern World*, ed. Tadao Umesao, Harumi Befu, and Shuzo Ishimori, 105–124. Senri Ethnological Studies no. 38. Osaka: National Museum of Ethnology.

Talmadge, Eric. 1996. "Travel Theme Parks Are Hot New Trend." *Japan Times*, 26 December.

Taniwaka, Miki. 2001. "Japanese Theme Parks Facing Rough Times." *Associated Press*, 2 March.

Urashima, Hisashi. n.d. "What Is the Theme of Hokkaido Theme Parks?" http://www.zmag.org/content/showarticle.cfm?SectionID=69&ItemID=7325. Accessed February 1996.

Whyte, Murray. 1998. "Japan's Obsession with *Anne of Green Gables* Takes Architectural Form in a Line of Emeryville Victorian 'Farmhouses'." *About Metropolis Online*, July.

Yamashita, Shinji, Joseph Bosco, and J. S. Eades, eds. 2004. *The Making of Anthropology in East and Southeast Asia.* New York: Berghahn.

CONTRIBUTORS

Mitzi Carter is a graduate student in the department of anthropology at the University of California, Berkeley. She graduated with a degree in anthropology from Duke University and spent a year in the Japan Exchange and Teaching (JET) program on Sado Island. Her research interests include U.S. military bases in Vieques and Okinawa and the construction and deconstruction of landscapes of sacrifice, memory, and activism, and race and governmentality. She has published "The Evolution of a Blackanese Contortionist" (1996) and "Being Blackanese" (1998).

John Ertl is a graduate student at the University of California, Berkeley. He worked as part of the JET program in Tochigi Prefecture for two years. His master's thesis, "The Making of Nishikata: Municipal-Level Community Building and the Invention of Tradition in Rural Japan" (2001), is based his experiences working in the JET program and further research conducted in 2000. He was a visiting scholar at the University of Tokyo in 2003–2004 and spent the year 2004–2005 conducting his dissertation research in a village in the Noto Peninsula. His research interests include social reproduction and change, traditionalism, place making, urban planning, and local government in Japan. Recently he was a visiting researcher at Kanazawa Gakuin University investigating intercultural exchange in Ishikawa Prefecture.

Nelson Graburn is a professor of anthropology, a curator of North American ethnology at the Hearst Museum, and co-chair of Canadian studies at U.C. Berkeley. Educated at Cambridge, McGill, and the University of Chicago, he has conducted field research among the Canadian Inuit since 1959. Since his first stay in Japan in 1974, he has been a visiting professor the National Museum of Ethnology, Osaka in 1979 and 1989–1990 and at the Research Center for Korean Studies, Kyushu National University, Fukuoka in 2005. He has interests in art, material culture, identity, museums, and tourism. Among his publications are *Ethnic and Tourist Arts* (1976); *To Pray, Pay and Play: The Cultural Structure of Japanese Domestic Tourism* (1983); *Anthropology of Tourism* (1983); *Tourism Social Sciences* (1991); *Catalogue Raisonné of the Alaska Commercial Company Collection, Hearst Museum* (1996); and *Relocating the Tourist* (2001). His recent research has focused on sites of foreignness in Japanese domestic tourism.

Tomoko Hamada is professor and former chair of anthropology at the College of William and Mary. She completed her B.A. in American studies at Vassar College, her M.A. in sociology at Keio University, and her Ph.D. in anthropology at the University of California, Berkeley (1980). She has taught at Damlin College and the University of Witwatersrand, Johannesburg, South America; was director of Asian studies at the Rose-Hulman Institute of Technology; and since 1988 has been a member of the faculty at William and Mary. Her publications include *American Enterprise in Japan* (1991), *Anthropological Dimension of Global Change, Anthropological Perspectives on Organizational Culture* (1994), and *Cross-cultural Management and Organizational Culture* (1990). She is the editor of *Studies in Third World Societies*, and is the author of numerous articles, the primary focus of which is the culture of complex organizations.

Jeffry T. Hester is associate professor of sociocultural anthropology in the Asian studies program of Kansai Gaidai University in Osaka, and completed his Ph.D. in anthropology at the University of California, Berkeley. His research focuses on place and identity, ethnicity and national identity, and cultural performance. Among his more recent publications is "Kids between Nations: Ethnic Classes in the Construction of Korean Identities in Japanese Public Schools" (2000). He has also contributed an article entitled "Repackaging Difference: The Korean Theming of an Osaka Shopping Street," to an edited volume, as well as an article on Koreans in Japan for the Macmillan *Encyclopedia of Culture* supplement.

Aina Hunter is a reporter for the *Village Voice* in New York. At the time of the conference she was a graduating senior studying Asian studies at the University of California, Berkeley. She went on to Columbia University where she was awarded her M.A. in journalism. Previously, she attended Meiji Gakuin University in Yokohama on a grant from the National Security Education Program in Washington, DC. Among her activities, she has published travel writing and literary fiction in various print venues as well as on the internet and, for a while she published an online magazine for women of color overseas.

John Nelson is an associate professor in the Department of Theology and Religious Studies at the University of San Francisco. He was awarded his Ph.D. in anthropology at the University of California, Berkeley. His research interests include the interface between politics and religion, Japanese religions, Zen Buddhism, and Japanese culture and society. He has published the following books: *Enduring Identities: The Guise of Shinto in Contemporary Japan* (2000) and *A Year in the Life of a Shinto Shrine* (1996). His most recent published articles include "Tempest in a Textbook: A Report on the New Middle-School History Textbook in Japan" (2002), "From Battlefield to Atomic Bomb to the Pure Land of Paradise: Employing the Bodhisattva of Compassion to Calm Japan's Spirits of the Dead" (2002), and "Shifting Paradigms of Religion and the State: Implications of the 1997 Supreme Court Decision for Social, Religious, and Political Change" (1999). He has also produced a documentary film entitled *Japan's Rituals of Remembrance: Fifty Years after the Pacific War* (1996).

Yuko Okubo completed her dissertation on minority education in Japan in the department of anthropology at the University of California, Berkeley. Her research interests include minority education, ethnicity, and nationalism, and the anthropology of Japan. Her publications include: "The Development of Educational Anthropology in the U.S." (2000, in Japanese), "Japan: 'Internationalization' of Education" (2000), "A Study of Various Facets of Multicultural Education in Oakland, CA" (2001, in Japanese), and "John Ogbu and Minority Education in Japan," *Intercultural Education* 17(2): 147–162.

Yasuko Takezawa is an associate professor at the Institute for Research in Humanities at Kyoto University. Her research concerns the construction of ethnicity in Japan and the United States. She is currently working on ethnic community relations in Kansai. She has published *Breaking the Silence: Ethnicity and Redress among Japanese Americans* (1995) and *Nikkei Amerikajin no Ethnicity* [Transformation of Japanese American ethnicity: the effects of internment and redress] (1994) along with nearly fifty academic articles including "Nikkeijin and 'Multicultural Coexistence' in Japan: Kobe after the Great Earthquake" (2000), "Racial Boundaries and Stereotypes: An Analysis of American Advertising" (1999), "'Race': From an Biological Concept to an Exclusive Worldview" (1999, in Japanese). Her most recent book is *Jinshu gainen no fuhensei o tou; Seiyoteki paradaimu o koete* [Is race a universal idea? Transcending the Western paradigm], published in Kyoto by Jinbun Shoin (2005).

R. Kenji Tierney is visiting professor of anthropology at Union College, New York. At the time of the conference he was a graduate student completing his dissertation on sumo wrestling in anthropology at the University of California, Berkeley. He has since held postdoctoral positions as a Reischauer Fellow at Harvard University, and in the EXEAS (EXpanding East Asian Studies) Program at Columbia University. His interests include historical anthropology, constructions and representations of "tradition," trans/nationalism, gift exchange and consumption. His publications include "It's a *Gottsan* World: The Role of the Patron in Sumô" (2004); and forthcoming: *"Bakuchi* (Gambling) and *Okome* (Rice/Money): The Construction of Value in Sumo" and "From Performance to National Sport (*Kokugi*): The 'Nationalization' of Sumô."

Takeyuki "Gaku" Tsuda is associate professor of anthropology at Arizona State University, Tempe. He completed his Ph.D. in anthropology at the University of California, Berkeley, and served as the Associate Director for the Center for Comparative Immigration Studies at University of California, San Diego. His research interests include international migration, ethnicity, identity and self, globalization, psychological anthropology, and Japan and Brazil. He holds degrees in anthropology from the University of Chicago and the University of California, Berkeley. His doctoral dissertation *Strangers in Their Ethnic Homeland: Minority Status and Migrant Nationalism in Transnational Context* was published by Columbia University Press (2003). His publications include: "When Identities Become Modern: Japanese Immigrants in Brazil and the Global Contextualization of Identity," in *Ethnic and Racial Studies* (2001); "Acting Brazilian in Japan: Performative Rituals as Ethnic Resistance among Japanese-Brazilian Return Migrants," in *Ethnology* (2000); "The Permanence of 'Temporary' Migration: The 'Structural Embeddedness' of Japanese-Brazilian Migrant Workers in Japan," in the *Journal of Asian Studies* (1999).

Keiko Yamanaka lectures in the Department of Ethnic Studies and in international and area studies at the University of California, Berkeley. Since 1994 she has studied international labor migration in Asia, focusing on four fields: Brazilian immigrant workers of Japanese descent in Japan; migration experiences of undocumented Nepali workers in Japan; feminized migration and resultant civil activism in East and Southeast Asia; and social transformation of East Asian societies as a consequence of global migration. On these topics she has published journal articles, book chapters, and newsletter essays, and has edited a volume of *Asian and Pacific Migration Journal*.

Shinji Yamashita is professor of cultural anthropology at the University of Tokyo. His research focuses on the dynamics of culture in the process of globalization, especially with reference to international tourism and transnational migration. His regional concern is with Southeast Asia, particularly Indonesia and Malaysia, and Japan. His books include *Globalization in Southeast Asia: Local, National, and Transnational Perspectives* (coedited with J. S. Eades, Berghahn Books, 2003), *Bali and Beyond: Explorations in the Anthropology of Tourism* (translated by J. S. Eades, Berghahn Books, 2003), and *The Making of Anthropology in East and Southeast Asia* (coedited with Joseph Bosco and J. S. Eades, Berghahn Books, 2004).

INDEX

Activism
  grassroots (civic), 1, 3, 9, 10, 16, 85,
    143, 152, 153, 160, 165, 166, 174,
    225, 227
  in Kobe, 32, 34, 36
  religious, 201–2, 206
  transnational civil, 152–4, 164, 167
African Americans, vii, 6, 20, 188, 192,
  193–4, 196, 197
Agency, exercise of, 13, 15, 64, 69–71,
  76, 152, 166–7
Ainu, minority, 22, 57, 58, 85, 119, 220,
  221, 222, 223, 224
Akogare (desire), 105, 110, 193
Alien Registration Law, 141, 142
Alienation, 14, 18, 120, 122
American automakers, 46, 47, 48, 50,
  54, 56
Appadurai, Arjun, 33, 108, 130
"Asia Town" (Kobe), 12, 36–38
Assimilation, 4, 16, 22, 23, 76, 96, 126,
  130–1, 133, 141, 143, 144, 147, 148,
  184n3, 184n6, 184n10, 228
Atomic bomb, 199–200, 201, 205, 206
  ritual services for victims of, 200,
  202–7
Authenticity, 228–9, 230, 231, 233

Bali, 18, 19, 101, 102, 103–4, 110–1,
  113n7, 113n9, 228
Balinese men, 14, 19, 103, 104–5, 110–1
Basic Plan for Immigration Control,
  11–12, 14
Befu, Harumi, 3, 5
Benedict, Ruth, 4, 93
Bicultural: *see* multiculturalism
Blackness, in Japan, 16–17, 188–97
  academic literature on, 188, 190, 193,
  195–6, 197

consumption of, 17, 191, 192–3, 196,
  197
gender, 16, 188, 191–4, 197
racism, 16, 188, 189, 190–1, 194, 196
stereotypes about, 188, 192, 194
Brazilians, 57, 95, 226, 236n9
  of Japanese descent, 14–15, 17, 22, 23,
    32, 33, 40, 42n2, 90, 113n12, 118–33,
    134n3–4, 135n7, 135n11–, 12, 154,
    156, 162, 163–4, 184n2, 225,
    236–7n9; see also *nikkeijin*
Buraku Liberation Movement, 6, 83,
  173
Buraku, -min, 4, 6, 16, 19, 119, 172,
  173–5, 179, 180, 182, 183, 224,
  236n6, 237n10
Burgess, Chris, 9, 13, 19, 20, 22, 23,
  63–87, 109

California, 19, 89, 101, 105, 111
Capitalism, 13, 44, 57, 59n1, 153, 166
Carter, Mitzi, viii, 16–17, 188–198
Caucasians: *see* Whites
Chihô-bunken, (decentralization), 13, 83,
  85, 86
China, 2, 10, 11, 24n6, 46, 63, 69, 87,
  88–89, 90, 102–3, 105, 108, 109,
  113n4, 125, 172, 175, 175, 181, 182,
  210, 224, 235
Chinese minority, 3, 4, 6, 10–11, 20, 22,
  57, 113n12, 172, 202, 223, 225–6
  in Kobe, 8, 12, 33, 37, 38, 39, 40,
    42n1–2
  in Osaka, 16, 20, 171, 173–8, 180–3
  wives, 68, 69, 74, 108, 110
Christianity, 17–18, 199, 201, 203, 230,
  233
Church, 10–11, 12, 17, 121, 123, 200,
  202, 205, 225, 230